An
ANATOMY
Of PROSE

THE MACMILLAN COMPANY
NEW YORK • CHICAGO
DALLAS • ATLANTA • SAN FRANCISCO
LONDON • MANILA

IN CANADA
BRETT-MACMILLAN LTD.
GALT, ONTARIO

An ANATOMY Of PROSE

CHARLES CHILD WALCUTT
Professor of English
Queens College

MACMILLAN COMPANY
NEW YORK

© Charles Child Walcutt 1962

Third Printing, 1963

Library of Congress catalog card number: 62–7514

The Macmillan Company, New York
Brett-Macmillan Ltd., Galt, Ontario

Printed in the United States of America

TO MY BROTHER LOWELL

WITH AFFECTION AND GRATITUDE

Table of Contents

PART I

PART II

PART III

A Letter to the Teacher

Instructors in the humanities have been known to lament that teaching in their fields suffers because they lack the organizing discipline of a specific body of work to be done, such as one finds in medicine, law, and the exact sciences. There the student has to master a body of knowledge and a set of skills that control his instructors just as surely as they control him. The common task sets its own standards, and this condition makes the teacher-student relation a cooperative one that is highly satisfactory.

The teacher of literature and the teacher of writing work with an undefined body of material. It is too extensive to be mastered in one course, or many; there are a frightening number of ways to approach it; and where the subject itself is indefinite, it is hard to establish standards, and therefore hard to set up and maintain a professional body and mode of work.

This book attempts to meet the problem by suggesting a program that can be pursued in a professional, objective, disciplined manner. It involves the assumption that writing is a skill that can be developed only by continual practice, that good writing is essentially the mastery of the sentence and the paragraph, and, most of all, that writing must be disciplined by specific assignments: the student must learn how to write so that he can communicate particular, specific information, rather than just spin ideas and associations out of his own wool.

The questions after each selection can provide this discipline, for they make definite demands; the passage must be read correctly; the question must be read correctly; the answer must be worked out; and the answer must be written clearly and accurately, so that it communicates unmistakably. Each step here is a considerable one. Every question presents a new problem. If some questions are assigned daily for written answers in the student's notebook, orderly, disciplined work habits can be established. Reading these answers aloud and discussing them can then be the main classroom activity. The advantages of discussing carefully prepared written answers are very great. The practice eliminates tedious gesticulation, second-guessing from the teacher's expression, and circling around a subject until something coherent works itself out. (As one student put it, "How do I know what I think till I hear what I say?") And it has the further value of keeping class attention on writing rather than on talking.

An unusual aspect of this text has evolved as a result of investigations into methods of teaching reading in our schools, and the discovery that the methods most in vogue during the past thirty or forty years have caused an alarming spread of retardation and near-illiteracy. We now have four kinds of reading: guessing, stumbling, skipping, and skimming. The guessers look at the picture in the margin of their primer to unlock the new word on the page. Later they guess from context, and they are praised if they see the word "pot" and say "bowl," for this is considered admirable as "bringing meaning to the printed page." The stumblers comprise the lower fifty or sixty per cent of our public-school population. For them, guessing does not, unfortunately, lead to confidence, let alone mastery of the printed page. Often they cannot read words that are familiar to them by ear; they get no more than a general notion of what goes on in literary prose; they are helpless before difficult writing.

The skippers are the people who have come to terms with their own stumbling and learned to get the gist of prose that they cannot read precisely. It is not always a reliable gist, however. The skimmers, finally, come from the top ten or twenty per cent of high-school graduates; they have learned to read, and they can, furthermore, often read with dazzling speed and comprehension. As college students, they will race through a 500-page novel over a weekend and come to class on Monday with an accurate knowledge of everything in it except, perhaps, certain questions of tone and effect that depend upon the subtlest turns of phrase.

How does such reading affect the writing of these students? It has become a commonplace today that people learn by doing. We all know that people talk the way they hear others talk—that a most effective way to learn to speak a foreign language is the way we learned to speak English, by ear. We also know that good writing, like good speech, is far more a matter of ear than of rules. Just as the child of cultivated parents speaks as they do, so the reader of cultivated sentences naturally writes the sort of sentences he is used to reading. Or does he? And if he does not, why does he not? Why do the facts seem to give the lie to these generalizations about the rôle of the ear in writing? Why, when they certainly know how to speak and to read, do so many students write sentences that have neither form nor coherence? An obvious answer is that they have not read enough good prose to train their ears. A less obvious but perhaps more accurate answer is that they have not heard the prose they have read. For here is where the types of reading just described let us down. No one of them is the sort of reading that trains the ear in the cadences of the classic patterns of the English sentence; and unless these patterns are heard they will not be known well enough to be used naturally and easily. Thinking that the obvious way to make students hear and feel the shape of the English sentence was to have them read aloud properly, I undertook with a composition class a systematic experiment in controlled reading aloud. The members of this class made greater progress toward writing good sentences than any group I can recall having taught in terms of formal grammar, syntax, and rhetoric.

This success was most impressive with the students whose writing had been virtually formless—composed of elements disconnected by dashes, fragments, and the sort of loose phrasings for the correction of which there are no usable rules because nothing is there that can be made literate and effective by any simple change; there is no real skeleton of syntax to mend. These students, coached in reading good sentences aloud, began to feel their shapes and presently to use them. By the end of the term they were writing surprisingly good sentences, and were generally able to hear the flaws in imperfect ones.

Because of this experiment, confirmed by further trial, I have, in the Study Questions, continually stressed the importance of reading aloud. The watchful instructor will find that he can tell exactly where a student does not understand, where he does not grasp the relation of parts, where he does not recognize subordination, and so on. Punctuation, which indicates the intention of sentence structure, is mastered as the good sentence is properly heard.

Accordingly, the choice of selections here has been guided first of all by a standard of style, and usually one or two of the study questions direct attention to qualities that can be identified and emphasized through oral reading. That most essential and most tormented mark of punctuation, the comma, can be mastered through discussion of sentences carefully read aloud: once the rhythms of Macaulay and Gibbon have been absorbed and appropriately discussed, no one will place a comma between subject and predicate, founder on the restrictive modifier, or commit the most ubiquitous of current errors: placing a comma at one end of a parenthesis, or interjection, or qualification, and not at the other.

Organization is perhaps the most difficult aspect of writing. For organization is thinking. It involves classification, ordering, and analysis. It involves taking a subject apart, identifying the elements of it that are important, and seeing how they may be related to each other significantly. The problem of "having something to say," which plagues every student and every teacher of composition, is closely related to this matter of organization. Form cannot really be separated from substance: one can write mature and vigorous prose only about an important subject penetrated to a significant depth. If this does not demand creative insights, it does demand knowledge—mastery of a subject to the point where the writer is analyzing and organizing for himself.

It is not difficult to teach the theoretical elements of organization, such as Controlling Purpose; Introduction, Body, and

Conclusion; Topic Sentence and Proof, or Illustration, or Ex-
emplification. The difficulty is to provide the substance that can
put flesh on these skeletal forms. The typical college freshman
can learn to impose these forms on a simple topic like Our Visit
to a Lumber Camp, but when we ask him to perform on Segrega-
tion, or Free Will, we usually find that he cannot rise above his
sources. He cannot, simply, know enough about such subjects to
achieve conclusions that are his own. And when the conclusions
and the ordering of the information are not his own, the language
also will not be his own; for the selection of the right word is an
aspect of original thinking, which in turn involves mastery of a
subject.

The step from writing simple sentences that are grammatically
correct to writing sentences that are original in thought and
language is a tremendous one, far too great for most college
freshmen. For the original management of language involves the
growth of the total intellect. This is a slow process. It is a word-
by-word process, sustained by devoted attention to language,
rather than by ambitious attempts to apply abstract principles of
rhetoric and construction to large bodies of fact or theory. If,
for example, a student is to write about the ideas in an essay by
Walter Lippmann, he must be able to think with the concepts that
are in the language of Walter Lippmann, and this is a very large
order indeed; for Lippmann's prose results from a lifetime of
thinking about words and of thinking with them.

If these generalizations are true, it follows that learning to
write is best achieved not by the application of theoretical rules
of style and structure to large and difficult bodies of knowledge,
but by a close attention to language, to good solid words in good
dense prose. That is the enterprise of this book. It seeks to provide a sound vocabulary growth, constant attention to the forms
and rhythms of superior sentences, and, for the analysis of these,
an abundant supply of problems within the scope of the student's
capacity.

The Study Questions are meant not only to elucidate and
analyze the texts, but also to provide the student with problems
of comprehension, analysis, organization, and writing. They call
not merely for answers, but for correct answers, formulated in

sentences that communicate their meanings clearly and unmistakably. And here the student will begin to emulate the quality that distinguishes the prose in these selections. He will begin to write sentences that say some*thing* well. From these utilitarian beginnings, style and elegance may grow fruitfully because the writing is disciplined by objective necessity. Less specific writing assignments are likely not to have this essential element of discipline. Where the student is asked to write from "his own experience," often he has been assigned only half a task. The disciplining limits of subject and space are missing. Here—among the Study Questions—the tasks are smaller but more exacting. Students required to write careful, precise answers in their notebooks to one or two questions for every class meeting get regular, disciplined practice in writing. When occasionally they are asked to read their answers aloud in class, they can tell, from the ensuing discussion, whether they have really communicated their answer, and whether it satisfies their colleagues.

Many of the single questions require enough study to constitute a fairly severe day's assignment; class discussion of all the questions on a selection could fill a week. One way to deal with a selection is to distribute the demanding questions to various individuals for prepared, comprehensive reports to the class. It is suggested that such reports be written out, preferably in the bound notebooks in which students write their daily answers, in the most careful sentences.

If Rome was not built in a day, neither can all the terms of grammar and syntax be taught in a semester. Some instructors will wish to review, some to teach, and some only to refer to the standard terms. For this reason, the questions touching these terms are unusually flexible. The instructor can dwell on them as much or as little as he chooses. Many college freshmen today have had no formal grammar at all. This fact makes it hard to discuss the structure of a sentence with them but does not necessarily mean that they are poor writers. Yet the terminology should be familiar to every college student. Because it can be absorbed incidentally to the discussion of questions on meaning and language, it has been mixed in with these more important matters.

The organization of the selections reflects the goals suggested in this Letter; the passages in Part I were chosen for the specific purpose of illustrating the form and cadences of the sentence in classic English prose of the eighteenth and nineteenth centuries, and in formal modern prose. Special attention is given, in the Questions, to what may be learned by reading these sentences aloud and learning to hear them well enough to imitate them naturally. One moves easiest who has learned to dance, and dancing is motion rather that theory. So here the oral reading, properly supervised and criticized by the instructor, will begin to make the student feel the rhythms of good sentences. It will also, in the process, teach him how to use the comma naturally and correctly.

The selections in Part II deal with people, places, and things. Here the stress is on concreteness of diction, first of all, although there are many questions on the other aspects of writing. Part III contains selections going somewhat further into the realm of ideas. They deal with the idea of America abroad, with manners and morals, with theories of history, with language, with the literary image of America, and so on. In Parts II and III there will be evident a progression in complexity and difficulty, as well as enough grouping of subjects so that the instructor may, if he chooses, take up two or three essays with contrasting approaches to a single topic.

I make grateful acknowledgment of the contribution of my assistant, Laura Jehn; it was not only editorial but also, in many respects, a collaboration.

Charles Child Walcutt
Douglaston, N.Y.
8 June 1961

＊＊＊＊＊＊＊＊＊＊＊＊＊＊

I

＊＊＊＊＊＊＊＊＊＊＊＊＊＊

The American

1. On a brilliant day
in May, of the year 1868, a gentleman was reclining at his ease
on the great circular divan which at that period occupied the
centre of the Salon Carré, in the Museum of the Louvre. This
commodious ottoman has since been removed, to the extreme 5
regret of all weak-kneed lovers of the fine arts; but our visitor
had taken serene possession of its softest spot, and, with his head
thrown back and his legs outstretched, was staring at Murillo's
beautiful moon-borne Madonna in deep enjoyment of his posture. He had removed his hat and flung down beside him a little 10
red guide-book and an opera-glass. The day was warm; he was
heated with walking, and he repeatedly, with vague weariness,
passed his handkerchief over his forehead. And yet he was evidently not a man to whom fatigue was familiar; long, lean, and
muscular, he suggested an intensity of unconscious resistance. 15
His exertions on this particular day, however, had been of an
unwonted sort, and he had often performed great physical feats
that left him less jaded than his quiet stroll through the Louvre.
He had looked out all the pictures to which an asterisk was
affixed in those formidable pages of fine print in his Bädeker; his 20
attention had been strained and his eyes dazzled; he had sat
down with an aesthetic headache. He had looked, moreover, not
only at all the pictures, but at all the copies that were going
forward around them in the hands of those innumerable young
women in long aprons, on high stools, who devote themselves, in 25
France, to the reproduction of masterpieces; and, if the truth
must be told, he had often admired the copy much more than
the original. His physiognomy would have sufficiently indicated

From *The American*.

3

that he was a shrewd and capable person, and in truth he had
30 often sat up all night over a bristling bundle of accounts and
heard the cock crow without a yawn. But Raphael and Titian and
Rubens were a new kind of arithmetic, and they made him for
the first time in his life wonder at his vaguenesses.

2. An observer with anything of an eye for local types would
35 have had no difficulty in referring this candid connoisseur to the
scene of his origin, and indeed such an observer might have made
an ironic point of the almost ideal completeness with which he
filled out the mould of race. The gentleman on the divan was the
superlative American; to which affirmation of character he was
40 partly helped by the general easy magnificence of his manhood.
He appeared to possess that kind of health and strength which,
when found in perfection, are the most impressive—the physical
tone which the owner does nothing to "keep up." If he was a
muscular Christian it was quite without doctrine. If it was neces-
45 sary to walk to a remote spot he walked, but he had never known
himself to "exercise." He had no theory with regard to cold bath-
ing or the use of Indian clubs; he was neither an oarsman, a
rifleman nor a fencer—he had never had time for these amusements—and he was quite unaware that the saddle is recom-
50 mended for certain forms of indigestion. He was by inclination
a temperate man; but he had supped the night before his visit
to the Louvre at the Café Anglais—some one had told him it was
an experience not to be omitted—and he had slept none the less
the sleep of the just. His usual attitude and carriage had a liberal
55 looseness, but when, under a special inspiration, he straightened
himself he looked a grenadier on parade. He had never tasted
tobacco. He had been assured—such things are said—that cigars
are excellent for the health, and he was quite capable of believing
it; but he would no more have thought of "taking" one than of
60 taking a dose of medicine. His complexion was brown and the
arch of his nose bold and well-marked. His eye was of a clear,
cold grey, and save for the abundant droop of his moustache he
spoke, as to cheek and chin, of the joy of the matutinal steel. He
had the flat jaw and the firm, dry neck which are frequent in the
65 American type; but the betrayal of native conditions is a matter
of expression even more than of feature, and it was in this respect

that our traveller's countenance was supremely eloquent. The observer we have been supposing might, however, perfectly have measured its expressiveness and yet have been at a loss for names and terms to fit it. It had that paucity of detail which is yet not emptiness, that blankness which is not simplicity, that look of being committed to nothing in particular, of standing in a posture of general hospitality to the chances of life, of being very much at one's own disposal, characteristic of American faces of the clear strain. It was the eye, in this case, that chiefly told the story; an eye in which the unacquainted and the expert were singularly blended. It was full of contradictory suggestions; and though it was by no means the glowing orb of a hero of romance you could find in it almost anything you looked for. Frigid and yet friendly, frank yet cautious, shrewd yet credulous, positive yet sceptical, confident yet shy, extremely intelligent and extremely good-humoured, there was something vaguely defiant in its concessions and something profoundly reassuring in its reserve. The wide yet partly folded wings of this gentleman's moustache, with the two premature wrinkles in the cheek above it, and the fashion of his garments, in which an exposed shirt-front and a blue satin necktie of too light a shade played perhaps an obtrusive part, completed the elements of his identity. We have approached him perhaps at a not especially favourable moment; he is by no means sitting for his portrait. But listless as he lounges there, rather baffled on the aesthetic question and guilty of the damning fault (as we have lately discovered it to be) of confounding the aspect of the artist with that of his work (for he admires the squinting Madonna of the young lady with the hair that somehow also advertises "art," because he thinks the young lady herself uncommonly taking), he is a sufficiently promising acquaintance. Decision, salubrity, jocosity, prosperity, seem to hover within his call; he is evidently a man of business, but the term appears to confess, for his particular benefit, to undefined and mysterious boundaries which invite the imagination to bestir itself.

※※※※※※※※※※

In these opening pages of a famous novel the writer undertakes to define the central character in a special situation. In a good novel the characters are not simply defined and then set in motion; rather they are portrayed in an action through which they develop, discover, and reveal themselves. The whole point of this passage is that the character finds himself in a situation that is completely new and different to him; and therefore James deems it fit and proper to indulge himself and his readers with several pages of discussion about his character and the strangeness of his situation—in what is skillfully rendered as a pause in the action before the action proceeds.

A James novel is a complicated transaction between the novelist and his reader. This is another way of saying that the element of *tone* is of first importance. What do we mean by tone? Tone is the writer's attitude toward his subject and toward his reader. When he speaks to the reader he has to speak about something, but his attitude toward his reader may be very different from his attitude toward his subject, yet the two sets of attitudes affect each other. You cannot maintain the highest formality in speaking of the most degraded subject. If you have humorous reservations toward your subject, some of these will enter into your relation with your reader.

The following questions will lead you to understand various aspects of tone in this selection. Observe James's attitudes toward reader, subject, and self, as well as the closely related matter of what objective information he gives us about his character. After the first 16 questions on the language, we move on to the intensive study of punctuation that is our central concern in the first seven selections. The relation of punctuation to tone is not obvious, but ultimately you will be able to see that a writer's punctuation participates in his tone as surely as does his choice of words. First, however, you must learn the mechanics of punctuation.

1.   Read the whole selection through twice, carefully, either aloud or pronouncing the words to the inner ear.

2.   Look up in the dictionary, *commodious* (line 5), *unwonted* (17), *jaded* (18), *aesthetic* (22), *physiognomy* (28), *candid* (35), *connoisseur* (35, and note the pronunciation), *ironic* (37), *mould* (38), *Indian clubs* (47), *grenadier* (56), *matutinal* (63), *paucity* (70), *credulous* (80), *sceptical* (80), *obtrusive* (87),

listless (90), *salubrity, jocosity* (97), and any other words that you are not perfectly sure of. Enter them in the back of your notebook, with the definition and a statement of the *etymology,* which will help you to understand and remember the word. For example, if taken literally *listless* means what *careless* means, that is, not heeding or minding.

3. What do these key words tell you about the gentleman or James's attitude toward him?—*flung* (10), *vague* (12), *formidable* (20), *must* (27), *new kind of arithmetic* (32).

4. Under what circumstances (would you guess) do the *vaguenesses* (34) appear which are now "for the first time" wondered at by the gentleman? What other highly suggestive or meaningful words can you point out and explain?

5. Is James's attitude toward his reader formal or casual? Consider the words in Questions 2–4. Note where the tone changes somewhat:
   (a) What does *weak-kneed* (6) tell you about James himself?
   (b) What impression do you get from the way that James conveys his confidence that you share his knowledge and appreciation of "Murillo's Madonna"?
   (c) Does James or the gentleman find the guidebook *formidable* (20)?

6. If there is an element of *irony* in the use of *connoisseur* (35), exactly what does it convey?

7. *Ideal* (37) is a word with a long, weighty history. You will learn something of it by reading the discussion of Plato's doctrine of Ideas in the *Encyclopaedia Britannica* (or another). The popular use of *ideal* to mean perfect does not give the full sense here.

8. What is the force of "none the less" (53)? Is it a tribute to the gentleman's temperance or to his physical condition? Hint: What does *but* (51) imply? What do the preceding four sentences deal with?

9. *Liberal* originally meant licentious or unrestrained. Does it retain any of this sense in line 54?

10. The quotation marks around "taking" (60) illustrate a proper

way to use them. But here there may be an ambiguity. Explain
the purpose of the marks and why they raise a question here,
namely whether it is the gentleman or James who disdains this
use of the word?

11.   *Matutinal steel* flashes an intrusion of James's later manner-
ism. What tone does the phrase bring to the paragraph? Since it
reflects something of the character of the author, what can be
said about what it tells of his hero? Suggest some homelier substitutes. Consider the sentence rewritten into about 14 words:
"He had clear, cold, grey eyes and was, except for his moustache,
clean shaven." What is gained and lost in the process of reducing
31 words to 14? If you are asked to write your answer to this
question be quite specific.

12.   *Flat* and *dry* (64) present some difficulty for the modern
reader. What meanings can you deduce from your own observation of national types?

13.   Lines 65–100 develop, with considerable restraint, the peculiar mixture of characteristics that makes this gentleman distinctive. James has set up his problem by establishing two very
general qualities—one of intelligent competence, the other of an
emptiness of mind that grows from the life of aggressive industry
and decision-making, where the occasions for thought arise only
from the situation. Now that the gentleman (his name is Chris-
topher Newman) has no serious business to conduct, he reveals
this emptiness. List in two columns the words that elaborate
each side of the man.

14.   Note that the pairs of words in lines 70–71 seem to make
one of the terms more specific. This is a useful device for defining
one's terms. Which word, in each case, is modified, which is the
modifier? The contradictions of lines 76–83 serve a different purpose. Define it.

15.   Now, try to explain how the paired qualities in lines 76–83
relate to the general pattern described in Question 11. Can all
the pairs be listed under the two large headings?

16.   After a generalized account of our hero, James comes, in
lines 83–88, to concrete details that perplex the modern reader.
We do not know how to *place* the moustache, as to taste or social
position; but some items in the sentence give us a hint to judge

by. What are they? Try to gauge the effect they should have on the reader's evaluation.

A short theme may be based on one of the questions above; on the manner in which James's man is presented; or on a gentleman whom you could describe from the same rigorously controlled point of view as that which James uses.

PUNCTUATION:

The comma and the semicolon are the important marks of punctuation. They are the ones that do most of the work of giving the sentence its form and meaning, and they are the ones that cause most of the problems and trouble for writers. If the outline or plan of a passage is like the steel frame of a building upon which the architect hangs his edifice of meaning, marks of punctuation are the rivets that hold it together. They must be placed right or they will do more harm than good. With a mastery of comma and semicolon one can write a good sentence—and everything else about writing that can be taught *as* writing follows easily. The larger substance of good writing—information, ideas, and thought—cannot be taught by any rules of composition, although it will be talked about continually in any writing course, and it will be developed through the study of language, which is inseparable from a concern with writing.

A painless, and possibly interesting, way of mastering the comma and the semicolon is to observe how their uses have changed over the past two centuries. These changes generally follow a shift of concern from *sound* to *syntax:* in the eighteenth century comma and semicolon indicated pauses in oral reading and divided a sentence into units of sound, whereas in the twentieth century they tend more exclusively to indicate the structure (or syntax) of the sentence, with much less attention to its sound. These generalizations may be tested or illustrated in our first seven selections, which have been chosen and arranged for this purpose.

We shall move back and forth between formal modern and formal early prose, in order to identify the function of the contemporary comma and semicolon. Only when you know the formal techniques can you know how to experiment and improvise with punctuation.

Henry James writes a formal prose that is just short of contemporary in its punctuation. It is also elegant, subtle, expert, and mannered. This selection is early James, written at a time when his punctuation, like his style, was less mannered than it later became.

17. James's punctuation is, as we have said, largely structural and, in this respect, modern. Where it guides the voice, as it does at one spot in line 7, it reflects the older tradition. How? Look at line 7: Generally, today, the comma does not separate pairs of grammatically parallel elements (not clauses) that are connected by *and* or *but*. The gramatically parallel elements of the clause are "visitor *had taken* . . . and *was staring.*" Two such parallel verb forms, having the same single subject, linked by *and,* are not today generally separated by a comma. Today's reader coming upon the comma after *spot,* expects a new subject-verb, rather than a second verb for the subject, *visitor.* The semicolon in line 6 serves this purpose exactly, introducing a new subject-verb sequence (i.e., a new *clause*). James has used the semicolon instead of a comma because he wants to indicate a major division between two parts of the sentence which contain numerous commas.

The comma after *and* in line 7 illustrates a second major use: that of setting off a modifying element. The important rule for this use is that there must be *two* commas or *none!* That is, if the comma after *and* is omitted, what subsequent comma must also be omitted?

A third major use can be identified in these first two sentences —and here sound and structure are both involved. The *which* clause in line 3, modifying *divan,* is not set off by a comma, because it is *essential* or *restrictive.* This fact is clearly indicated when one reads the sentence aloud with no pause after *divan* and the voice rising to a cadence-peak at *that period.* In short, *great circular* does not fully identify the divan; it is the divan-which-at-*that-period* (voice rising to the last word). If the divan were thoroughly identified by *great circular* and the *which* clause were *non-essential* information, how would the sentence be read? Try it aloud. In this event, would the divan still be there, at the time of the writing? Yes, probably it would. Certainly it would be somewhere in the Louvre or people would not recognize it from the label *great circular.* This reading-aloud test is amost infallible for this rule.

Now, suppose the *with* phrase beginning in line 7 were also *essential* and therefore not set off by commas! How would it be read aloud?—and what would it mean (granting that the meaning is absurd)? If you can master these three uses of the comma, you will have mastered 95% of all comma problems.

18. The third sentence (10–11) illustrates what use (or nonuse) of the comma described above? Identify two other situations that answer to the same rule.

19. The fourth sentence (11–13) embodies a subtlety of punctuation. Most writers would have a comma in place of the semicolon; this would make of the sentence a *series* of clauses (each with new subject and verb), each properly set off with a comma. Yet James has a reason for introducing that semicolon, a reason that reflects his meaning. What is it?

20. When writers use a series of parallel elements, they may give special care to the *length* and *sound* of these elements in order to make patterns that will impress and delight the reader. Count the words in each clause of the sentence in lines 19–22. Read it aloud. Is the pattern of "syllabic decrease" pleasing only as a pattern, or has it a significant relation to the factual content of the sentence? Write a short paragraph answering this question; you will have to choose your words very carefully to make your point.

Now consider lines 79–83:

> Frigid and yet friendly, frank yet cautious, shrewd yet credulous, positive yet sceptical, confident yet shy, extremely intelligent and extremely good-humoured, there was something vaguely defiant in its concessions and something profoundly reassuring in its reserve.

Underline in red the balanced elements. Note that the balancing words make a pattern of correspondence and variation: *frigid . . . friendly* are of equal length. *Shrewd . . . credulous* go from one syllable up to three; *positive . . . sceptical* are three-three; then *confident . . . shy* complete the pattern by going back down from three to one. With this turn completed, James gives two long *extremely* phrases and then comes to his main clause, which he wraps up with two elements that balance almost down to the last syllable.

The most difficult word in this beautiful sentence is *concessions*. What exactly does it mean here?

The Puritans

THOMAS BABINGTON MACAULAY

1. We would speak
first of the Puritans, the most remarkable body of men, perhaps,
which the world has ever produced. The odious and ridiculous
parts of their character lie on the surface. He that runs may read
5 them; nor have there been wanting attentive and malicious observers to point them out. For many years after the Restoration
they were the theme of unmeasured invective and derision. They
were exposed to the utmost licentiousness of the press and of the
stage, at the time when the press and the stage were most licen-
10 tious. They were not men of letters; they were, as a body, unpopular; they could not defend themselves; and the public would not
take them under its protection. They were therefore abandoned,
without reserve, to the tender mercies of the satirists and drama-
tists. The ostentatious simplicity of their dress, their sour aspect,
15 their nasal twang, their stiff posture, their long graces, their
Hebrew names, the Scriptural phrases which they introduced on
every occasion, their contempt of human learning, their detesta-
tion of polite amusements, were indeed fair game for the laughers.
But it is not from the laughers alone that the philosophy of history
20 is to be learnt. And he who approaches this subject should carefully guard against the influence of that potent ridicule which has
already misled so many excellent writers.

2. Those who roused the people to resistance, who directed
their measures through a long series of eventful years, who
25 formed, out of the most unpromising materials, the finest army
that Europe had ever seen, who trampled down King, Church,
and Aristocracy, who, in the short intervals of domestic sedition

From *The Public Character of Milton.*

12

and rebellion, made the name of England terrible to every nation on the face of the earth, were no vulgar fanatics. Most of their absurdities were mere external badges, like the signs of free- 30 masonry, or the dresses of friars. We regret that those badges were not more attractive. We regret that a body to whose courage and talents mankind has owed inestimable obligations had not the lofty elegance which distinguished some of the adherents of Charles the First, or the easy good-breeding for which the 35 court of Charles the Second was celebrated. But, if we must make our choice, we shall, like Bassanio in the play, turn from the specious caskets which contain only the Death's head and the Fool's head, and fix on the plain leaden chest which conceals the treasure. 40

3. The Puritans were men whose minds had derived a peculiar character from the daily contemplation of superior beings and eternal interests. Not content with acknowledging, in general terms, an overruling Providence, they habitually ascribed every event to the will of the Great Being, for whose power nothing 45 was too vast, for whose inspection nothing was too minute. To know him, to serve him, to enjoy him, was with them the great end of existence. They rejected with contempt the ceremonious homage which other sects substituted for the pure worship of the soul. Instead of catching occasional glimpses of the Deity 50 through an obscuring veil, they aspired to gaze full on his intolerable brightness, and to commune with him face to face. Hence originated their contempt for terrestrial distinctions. The difference between the greatest and the meanest of mankind seemed to vanish, when compared with the boundless interval which 55 separated the whole race from him on whom their own eyes were constantly fixed. They recognized no title to superiority but his favour; and, confident of that favour, they despised all the accomplishments and all the dignities of the world. If they were unacquainted with the works of philosophers and poets, they 60 were deeply read in the oracles of God. If their names were not found in the registers of heralds, they were recorded in the Book of Life. If their steps were not accompanied by a splendid train of menials, legions of ministering angels had charge over them. Their palaces were houses not made with hands; their diadems 65

crowns of glory which should never fade away. On the rich and
the eloquent, on nobles and priests, they looked down with contempt: for they esteemed themselves rich in a more precious
treasure, and eloquent in a more sublime language, nobles by the
70 right of an earlier creation, and priests by the imposition of a
mightier hand. The very meanest of them was a being to whose
fate a mysterious and terrible importance belonged, on whose
slightest action the spirits of light and darkness looked with
anxious interest, who had been destined, before heaven and earth
75 were created, to enjoy a felicity which should continue when
heaven and earth should have passed away. Events which short-
sighted politicians ascribed to earthly causes, had been ordained
on his account. For his sake empires had risen, and flourished,
and decayed. For his sake the Almighty had proclaimed his will
80 by the pen of the Evangelist, and the harp of the prophet. He
had been wrested by no common deliverer from the grasp of no
common foe. He had been ransomed by the sweat of no vulgar
agony, by the blood of no earthly sacrifice. It was for him that
the sun had been darkened, that the rocks had been rent, that
85 the dead had risen, that all nature had shuddered at the sufferings
of her expiring God.

4. Thus the Puritan was made up of two different men, the
one all self-abasement, penitence, gratitude, passion, the other
proud, calm, inflexible, sagacious. He prostrated himself in the
90 dust before his Maker: but he set his foot on the neck of his
king. In his devotional retirement, he prayed with convulsions,
and groans, and tears. He was half-maddened by glorious or
terrible illusions. He heard the lyres of angels or the tempting
whispers of fiends. He caught a gleam of the Beatific Vision, or
95 woke screaming from dreams of everlasting fire. Like Vane,[1] he
thought himself intrusted with the sceptre of the millennial year.
Like Fleetwood,[2] he cried in the bitterness of his soul that God
had hid his face from him. But when he took his seat in the council, or girt on his sword for war, these tempestuous workings of
100 the soul had left no perceptible trace behind them. People who

---

[1] Sir Henry Vane (1613–1662), English Puritan statesman.
[2] Probably Charles Fleetwood (d. 1692), Puritan soldier and politician,
at one time proposed as successor to Cromwell.

saw nothing of the godly but their uncouth visages, and heard nothing from them but their groans and their whining hymns, might laugh at them. But those had little reason to laugh who encountered them in the hall of debate or in the field of battle. These fanatics brought to civil and military affairs a coolness of 105 judgement and an immutability of purpose which some writers have thought inconsistent with their religious zeal, but which were in fact the necessary effects of it. The intensity of their feelings on one subject made them tranquil on every other. One overpowering sentiment had subjected to itself pity and hatred, 110 ambition and fear. Death had lost its terrors and pleasure its charms. They had their smiles and their tears, their raptures and their sorrows, but not for the things of this world. Enthusiasm had made them Stoics, had cleared their minds from every vulgar passion and prejudice, and raised them above the influence of 115 danger and of corruption. It sometimes might lead them to pursue unwise ends, but never to choose unwise means. They went through the world, like Sir Artegal's [3] iron man Talus with his flail, crushing and trampling down oppressors, mingling with human beings, but having neither part nor lot in human in- 120 firmities, insensible to fatigue, to pleasure, and to pain, not to be pierced by any weapon, not to be withstood by any barrier.

5. Such we believe to have been the character of the Puritans. We perceive the absurdity of their manners. We dislike the sullen gloom of their domestic habits. We acknowledge that the tone of 125 their minds was often injured by straining after things too high for mortal reach: and we know that, in spite of their hatred of Popery, they too often fell into the worst vices of that bad system, intolerance and extravagant austerity, that they had their ancho-rites and their crusades, their Dunstans and their De Montforts, 130 their Dominics and their Escobars. Yet, when all circumstances are taken into consideration, we do not hesitate to pronounce them a brave, a wise, an honest, and an useful body.

※※※※※※※※※

Macaulay's prose is perhaps the most *dazzling* in our language.

[3] Character in Spenser's *Faerie Queene,* representing justice.

In these days of carelessness, hearty crudity, and studied lowness of speech and writing, it comes as something of a shock to discover prose in which every clause, every phrase, indeed every single word is selected and placed not only in order to convey a meaning but also in order to make a pattern of rhythms, cadences, sounds, and grammatical structures. The variety of Macaulay's sentences is matched by their perfection of form. Often the effect of reading them aloud can be almost hypnotic; but they must nevertheless be read so, for here the *art* of writing attains a peak of perfection that overlooks, like Mount Everest, the territory ahead and behind. Every shape of the formal sentence appears with majestic clarity, in the purest outline. One does not expect a modern writer to imitate Macaulay; but no student who has really *heard* his cadences will ever write a bad sentence. Nor is the brilliance of form attained by any sacrifice of content: this prose is packed with information, reference, and idea.

Macaulay's punctuation is frequently for the ear, rather than structural, not because he neglects structure but because the structure of his sentences is so perfect that few can fail to be aware of it. Let us examine meaning, structure, and, finally, punctuation. Begin by reading the passage aloud, twice. Underline every unfamiliar word, and then look them all up in a good dictionary.

1.   What word in the first sentence indicates the central idea of Par. 1? How is that word made more specific in the second sentence? And at what point is the development of "odious and ridiculous" finally qualified?

2.   You must know that from about 1560 to 1640 the Puritans were ridiculed, tolerated, persecuted, and feared as their power grew, in England. They were in power from 1640 to 1660; and then again they were ridiculed, defamed, and persecuted until religious tolerance was established after the "bloodless revolution" of 1688. When did the ridicule described in Par. 1 occur?

3.   Paragraph 2 deals further with the superficial limitations of the Puritans. But examine the two uses of "regret"; can they be considered ironic? sarcastic? mocking? apologetic?

4.   The reference to *The Merchant of Venice* (lines 36–40) reveals the subtlety beneath the elegance of this prose; for whereas the comparison of the homely, rugged Puritans to the

leaden casket of truth is fairly obvious, one might not note that
Charles the First was beheaded by the Puritans, or recall that,
of Charles the Second, the poet Rochester wrote—and pinned on
the King's door:

> Here lies our sovereign Lord, the King
> Whose word no man relies on,
> Who never said a foolish thing
> And never did a wise one.

You may study these facts and write a short essay about them.

5.   Paragraph 3 is developed from what two key words in the
first sentence? Make a list of the qualities and attributes of the
Deity that are set against the mundane, the time-bound, and
the inferior, indicating where the contrast is fully stated, where
merely implied. For example, lines 43–52 contrast the Puritans'
notion of their own relation to God with their notions of *whose*
relation to God? Clues are "ceremonious homage" and "occasional glimpses." Identify contrasts built in terms of light, size,
distance, rank, learning, servants, buildings, crowns, wealth.

6.   Rising through these examples, Macaulay reaches his climax
with references to the Crucifixion; identify them. Since the point
of view in the paragraph is both Macaulay's and the Puritans',
you need to determine how the two are related before you venture
to define exactly the *attitude* of author to subject in lines 76–86.
Macaulay later says he has represented the Puritans with "perfect
candor." Does this preclude any ironies or reservations in his
tone? Are there such reservations or ironies to be detected?

7.   Define the shift in point of view between Pars. 3 and 4. Tone
is also involved, but here it depends on the changed point of view.

8.   How does the "Thus" beginning Par. 4 relate to the system
of contrasts in Par. 3? Specifically, does it relate to the idea or the
form? As a transitional word, does this "Thus" demand too much
thought of the reader? In what following sentence is the answer
to this question made perfectly clear? Note how lines 91–98
develop one side, lines 98–122 develop the other, of this contrast.

9.   (a) Whose point of view does "fanatics" (105) represent?
(b) "Necessary effects" (108) means "inevitable results." How
does Macaulay justify this phrase? (c) Is it explained by the

central theme of the paragraph? (d) What sentence explains it specifically?

10. Find out what "enthusiasm" (113) meant in the 18th century, especially in reference to religious belief. Stoics, of course, are the exact opposites of enthusiasts. Can the brilliant antithesis, "Enthusiasm had made them Stoics," be logically justified? Does the following abstract and metaphorical explanation satisfy you? "Enthusiasm" can be an excellent topic for an essay in definition or for a research paper.

11. What specific points in this selection are generalized and commented upon in the conclusion?

12. Parallelism and balance are the foundations of Macaulay's style. Here he works up to them: the first sentence of the selection has none; the second only the pairing of "odious and ridiculous"; the third and fourth, again, only one parallelism each. Lines 10–12 contain three clauses beginning with "they," and for variation a fourth with a different subject. With lines 14–18 we come to a sustained parallel structure, making an elaborate compound subject; identify the elegant variation, within this parallelism, introduced in the seventh member.

13. Paragraph 2 opens with a different parallelism—a simple subject modified by a series of relative clauses; mark each. Re-read the rest of the passage aloud, and then mark with a colored pencil all the different kinds of parallelism that appear, both within and among sentences. Do not worry about the precise line between parallelism and balance: for example, in lines 66–71 the two devices are fused. Explain how.

To demonstrate the usefulness of these devices try rewriting such a passage as lines 14–18 into separate sentences:

> The ostentatious simplicity of their dress was ridiculed by satirists and dramatists. Their sour aspect was mocked. Their nasal twang was imitated. . . .

and so on. Either content must be sacrificed or repetition will become unbearably tedious. Parallelism, as we shall frequently note, is *the* great economizer.

14. Note lines 59–63. While Macaulay balances two sentences here in almost perfect correspondence, he modulates his four *references* from the literal to the figurative. Explain the steps.

15. Let us now see where Macaulay's punctuation differs from today's.

In line 9, the comma sets off a prepositional phrase—"at the time"—from the element it modifies (It is an adverb of time, modifying "were exposed.") Structurally it is quite unnecessary. Macaulay's structure, as we have said, is perfectly obvious. He introduces the comma to make us pause and therefore break the sentence into two balanced cadences—explain why it serves to charm the ear rather than indicate the sense.

16. Similar commas to emphasize cadences, for oral reading, appear in lines 31, 35, 39, and 52. Look for further examples. You should find at least *nine*.

The comma in line 77, coming between the subject and verb, would never appear in good formal prose today. Macaulay uses it to maintain the balance of paired cadences which prevails in the paragraph.

17. By way of confirming these observations, look at certain places where such commas *might* have been inserted and explain why they were not: line 21 after "ridicule," line 59 after "accomplishments," line 111 after "terrors."

18. For an even more emphatic division than the semicolon, Macaulay uses the colon, as in line 68—or in the famous sentence, lines 89–91, where only a comma is needed for structure. Find one more example.

19. Find a *restrictive* and a *non-restrictive* modifier punctuated according to the rule described on page 10, question 17.

20. Macaulay can be imitated superficially, and you will find it both amusing and useful to turn out sonorous, balanced cadences. Try a paragraph, in this style, about some campus group. Do not mind if in this instance your style is more imaginative than your content.

Gibbon

LYTTON STRACHEY

1. Happiness is the word that immediately rises to the mind at the thought of Edward Gibbon: and happiness in its widest connotation—including good fortune as well as enjoyment. Good fortune, indeed, followed him
5 from the cradle to the grave in the most tactful way possible; occasionally it appeared to fail him; but its absence always turned out to be a blessing in disguise. Out of a family of seven he alone had the luck to survive—but only with difficulty; and the maladies of his childhood opened his mind to the pleasures of
10 study and literature. His mother died; but her place was taken by a devoted aunt, whose care brought him through the dangerous years of adolescence to a vigorous manhood. His misadventures at Oxford saved him from becoming a don. His exile to Lausanne, by giving him a command of the French language,
15 initiated him into European culture, and at the same time enabled him to lay the foundations of his scholarship. His father married again; but his stepmother remained childless and became one of his dearest friends. He fell in love; the match was forbidden; and he escaped the dubious joys of domestic life with the future
20 Madame Necker.[1] While he was allowed to travel on the Continent, it seemed doubtful for some time whether his father would have the resources or the generosity to send him over the

[1] Suzanne Carchod, a Swiss girl to whom Gibbon was engaged, married the famous banker, economist, and statesman, Jacques Necker (1732–1804), became the mother of the famous Madame de Staël, and pushed her husband without mercy to make him satisfy her own ambitions.

Alps into Italy. His fate hung in the balance; but at last his father
produced the necessary five hundred pounds and, in the autumn
of 1764, Rome saw her historian. His father died at exactly the 25
right moment, and left him exactly the right amount of money.
At the age of thirty-three Gibbon found himself his own master,
with a fortune just sufficient to support him as an English gentleman of leisure and fashion. For ten years he lived in London, a
member of Parliament, a placeman, and a diner-out, and during 30
those ten years he produced the first three volumes of his History.
After that he lost his place, failed to obtain another, and, finding
his income unequal to his expenses, returned to Lausanne, where
he took up his residence in the house of a friend, overlooking the
Lake of Geneva. It was the final step in his career, and no less 35
fortunate than all the others. In Lausanne he was rich once more,
he was famous, he enjoyed a delightful combination of retirement
and society. Before another ten years were out he had completed
his History; and in ease, dignity, and absolute satisfaction his
work in this world was accomplished.   40

2. One sees in such a life an epitome of the blessings of the
eighteenth century—the wonderful μηδὲν ἄγαν [2] of that most
balmy time—the rich fruit opening slowly on the sun-warmed wall,
and coming inevitably to its delicious perfection. It is difficult to
imagine, at any other period in history, such a combination of 45
varied qualities, so beautifully balanced—the profound scholar
who was also a brilliant man of the world—the votary of cosmo-
politan culture, who never for a moment ceased to be a supremely
English 'character.' The ten years of Gibbon's life in London
afford an astonishing spectacle of interacting energies. By what 50
strange power did he succeed in producing a masterpiece of
enormous erudition and perfect form, while he was leading the
gay life of a man about town, spending his evenings at White's or
Boodle's or the Club, attending Parliament, oscillating between
his house in Bentinck Street, his country cottage at Hampton 55
Court, and his little establishment at Brighton, spending his sum-
mers in Bath or Paris, and even, at odd moments, doing a little
work at the Board of Trade, to show that his place was not entirely a sinecure? Such a triumph could only have been achieved

[2] "Nothing too much."

60 by the sweet reasonableness of the eighteenth century. 'Monsieur
Gibbon n'est point mon homme,' [3] said Rousseau. Decidedly! The
prophet of the coming age of sentiment and romance could have
nothing in common with such a nature. It was not that the historian was a mere frigid observer of the golden mean—far from
65 it. He was full of fire and feeling. His youth had been at moments
riotous—night after night he had reeled hallooing down St.
James's Street. Old age did not diminish the natural warmth of
his affections; the beautiful letter—a model of its kind—written of
the death of his aunt, in his fiftieth year, is a proof of it. But the
70 fire and the feeling were controlled and co-ordinated. Boswell
was a Rousseau-ite, one of the first of the Romantics, an inveterate
sentimentalist, and nothing could be more complete than the contrast between his career and Gibbon's. He, too, achieved a glorious triumph; but it was by dint of sheer force of native genius
75 asserting itself over the extravagance and disorder of an agitated
life—a life which, after a desperate struggle, seemed to end at last
in darkness and shipwreck. With Gibbon there was never any
struggle: everything came naturally to him—learning and dissipa-
tion, industry and indolence, affection and scepticism—in the
80 correct proportions; and he enjoyed himself up to the very end.
    3. To complete the picture one must notice another antithesis:
the wit, the genius, the massive intellect, were housed in a physical mold that was ridiculous. A little figure, extraordinarily
rotund, met the eye, surmounted by a top-heavy head, with a
85 button nose, planted amid a vast expanse of cheek and ear, and
chin upon chin rolling downward. Nor was this appearance only;
the odd shape reflected something in the inner man. Mr. Gibbon,
it was noticed, was always slightly overdressed; his favourite
wear was a flowered velvet. He was a little vain, a little pompous;
90 at the first moment one almost laughed; then one forgot everything under the fascination of that even flow of admirably intelligent, exquisitely turned, and most amusing sentences. Among all
his other merits this obviously ludicrous egotism took its place.
The astonishing creature was able to make a virtue even of
95 absurdity. Without that touch of nature he would have run the

    [3] "Monsieur Gibbon is not a man for me."

risk of being too much of a good thing; as it was there was no such danger; he was preposterous and a human being.

4. It is not difficult to envisage the character and the figure; what seems strange, and remote, and hard to grasp is the connection between this individual and the decline and fall of the Roman Empire. The paradox, indeed, is so complete as to be almost romantic. At a given moment—October 15, 1764—at a given place—the Capitoline Hill, outside the church of Aracoeli—the impact occurred between the serried centuries of Rome and Edward Gibbon. His life, his work, his fame, his place in the history of civilisation, followed from that circumstance. The point of his achievement lay precisely in the extreme improbability of it. The utter incongruity of those combining elements produced the masterpiece—the gigantic ruin of Europe through a thousand years, mirrored in the mind of an eighteenth-century English gentleman.

5. How was the miracle accomplished? Needless to say, Gibbon was a great artist—one of those rare spirits, with whom a vital and penetrating imagination and a supreme capacity for general conceptions express themselves instinctively in an appropriate form. That the question has ever been not only asked but seriously debated, whether History was an art, is certainly one of the curiosities of human ineptitude. What else can it possibly be? It is obvious that History is not a science: it is obvious that History is not the accumulation of facts, but the relation of them. Only the pedantry of incomplete academic persons could have given birth to such a monstrous supposition. Facts relating to the past, when they are collected without art, are compilations; and compilations, no doubt, may be useful; but they are no more History than butter, eggs, salt and herbs are an omelette. That Gibbon was a great artist, therefore, is implied in the statement that he was a great historian; but what is interesting is the particular nature of his artistry. His whole genius was pre-eminently classical; order, lucidity, balance, precision—the great classical qualities—dominate his work; and his History is chiefly remarkable as one of the supreme monuments of Classic Art in European literature.

6. 'L'ordre est ce qu'il y a de plus rare dans les opérations de
l'esprit.' [4] Gibbon's work is a magnificent illustration of the splen-
135 did dictum of Fénelon. He brought order out of the enormous
chaos of his subject—a truly stupendous achievement! With characteristic good fortune, indeed, the material with which he had
to cope was still just not too voluminous to be digested by a
single extremely competent mind. In the following century even
140 a Gibbon would have collapsed under the accumulated mass of
knowledge at his disposal. As it was, by dint of a superb construc-
tive vision, a serene self-confidence, a very acute judgment, and
an astonishing facility in the manipulation of material, he was
able to dominate the known facts. To dominate, nothing more;
145 anything else would have been foreign to his purpose. He was a
classicist; and his object was not comprehension but illumination.
He drove a straight, firm road through the vast unexplored forest
of Roman history; his readers could follow with easy pleasure
along the wonderful way; they might glance, as far as their eyes
150 could reach, into the entangled recesses on either side of them;
but they were not invited to stop, or wander, or camp out, or
make friends with the natives; they must be content to look and
to pass on.

7. It is clear that Gibbon's central problem was the one of
155 exclusion: how much, and what, was he to leave out? This was
largely a question of scale—always one of the major difficulties in
literary composition—and it appears from several passages in the
Autobiographies that Gibbon paid particular attention to it. . . .
Even with the scale of the History he was not altogether satisfied;
160 the chapters on Christianity, he thought, might, with further
labour, have been considerably reduced. But, even more funda-
mental than the element of scale, there was something else that,
in reality, conditioned the whole treatment of his material, the
whole scope and nature of his History; and that was the style in
165 which it was written. The style once fixed, everything else followed. Gibbon was well aware of this. He wrote his first chapter
three times over, his second and third twice; then at last he was
satisfied, and after that he wrote on without a hitch. In particular
the problem of exclusion was solved. Gibbon's style is probably

[4] Roughly, "Order is the rarest power of the mind."

the most exclusive in literature. By its very nature it bars out a 170
great multitude of human energies. It makes sympathy impossible, it takes no cognisance of passion, it turns its back upon
religion with a withering smile. But that was just what was
wanted. Classic beauty came instead. By the penetrating influence of style—automatically, inevitably—lucidity, balance and 175
precision were everywhere introduced; and the miracle of order
was established over the chaos of a thousand years.

❋❋❋❋❋❋❋❋❋❋❋

1. "Order is the rarest power of the mind." Strachey reminds
us how wonderfully Gibbon's vast undertaking illustrates this
French dictum. Indeed, order is one of a writer's first considerations. He must decide *how* to present *what* he knows. Most
writers follow some sort of plan or outline; the beginning writer
will find it most necessary for organizing his ideas.

Read Strachey's essay on Gibbon, noting the main idea in each
paragraph. Then divide each paragraph into its components. You
will, in effect, be doing what Strachey probably did when he was
organizing his essay. Note too how one paragraph leads to another. Strachey talks of the events of Gibbon's life in Par. 1, of
Gibbon as an example of his times in Par. 2, of Gibbon's figure
and mannerisms in Par. 3, of his huge work in Par. 4, and so on.
How are the ideas of one paragraph developed so that they lead
smoothly to the ideas of the next? List the words and phrases
that link one paragraph to the next.

2. In the first paragraph Strachey sketches the main events of
Gibbon's life. What idea mentioned in the first sentence unites
the events Strachey recalls? How are this idea and its two sub-
ideas developed in the paragraph? This use of a device to tie the
facts of Gibbon's life together corresponds to the way that a
sustaining parallelism ties ideas or words together.

3. Strachey places Gibbon in relation to two very famous 18th
century figures. Rousseau was the apostle of instinct, nature, and
spontaneity, who believed that civilization warped and thwarted
the essential goodness of Natural Man. James Boswell, like Gibbon a lover of London society, was afflicted with terrible melancholy, paralyzing fears of death, and the heavy burden of a

disapproving father. Gibbon differs from each of these men in a radically different way. What is the area of the distinction, in each case?

4. How many of the six terms in lines 78–79 have been concretely exemplified in the previous paragraphs? How many have been generally stated? Which is developed in the following paragraph? Is the balance of the three pairs as meaningful as it is formal?

5. How does the picture of Gibbon in Par. 3 sustain the generalizations we have just examined in Par. 2? Is there any contradiction indicating that the former is an oversimplification? We may note here a point where some slight straining-for-effect shows: the adverb *most* (92) is there to balance *admirably* and *exquisitely,* but it does not really contribute anything to the meaning. Look for similar shortcomings in lines 92–97. Consider, further, the "paradox" (101) of the next paragraph. Since the 18th century continually looked back to the classical qualities it saw in Greece and Rome, modeling its prose and its statesmanship after them, where is the "utter incongruity" of Gibbon's choosing to write about Rome? Write a paragraph discussing and explaining these and other discrepancies in the selection. You might take as your theme the question whether the attempt to write in the grand manner of Macaulay has not led Strachey to set up parallelisms, antitheses, and balances of ideas which do not seem to be sustained by the evidence.

6. Paragraph 6 has some loose and some very careful diction. What is the value of *magnificent* (134), *splendid* (134–5), and *enormous* and *stupendous* (135–6)? Under what circumstances can superlatives be *ine*ffective? Comment on the adjectives in lines 141–143 with this point in mind.

7. Now consider *digest* (138), *dominate* (144), and *illumination* (146). How do the latter two relate to each other? What, precisely, do the words mean here? How does the idea of "classicist" connect them?

8. Gibbon described his theme as a display of "the triumph of barbarism and Christianity" over the Roman Empire. What reflection does such a thesis cast upon the statement that "his object was not comprehension"? A less epigrammatic analysis says that Gibbon equates the decline of Rome with the loss of

individual liberty under a succession of imperial tyrannies. Does this involve "comprehension"?

9. What central thought under the sustained metaphor of lines 147–153 defines *classicist?* While such figurative language is arresting, does it *prove* anything? Discuss.

10. Is *scale* or *exclusion* (155–156) the larger classification? If a writer, with a scarcity of facts, had to "work up" his subject by invention, would *scale* still be a problem for him? Would *exclusion?*

11. Strachey in lines 170–173 applies his word "exclusion" figuratively rather than literally. That is, attitudes rather than data are being excluded. It appears, for example, that an attitude toward religion is conveyed, so that it is a question of substitution rather than exclusion here. Define the attitudes conveyed and excluded. What word in the paragraph indicates the area of these matters?

12. Strachey is a modern stylist in the line of descent from Macaulay. As you read this selection aloud you will find that although it is formally akin to its ancestor it is not so brilliant, so sonorous, so spectacular. Nor does it attempt to be. More relaxed in tone and manner, Strachey's writing appears more thoughtful and more intimately engaged with its subject. On the other hand, he sometimes seems to strain for effects that Macaulay achieves with offhand ease. Try reading the two selections aloud in order to see these differences.

13. The dash is used to indicate an abrupt and generally non-grammatical jump and, in pairs, like parentheses or paired commas, to set off a word or phrase that interrupts the subject-verb-object sequence. Strachey uses the dash for emphasis, that is, to suggest that the thought is about take an arresting turn. On the whole he would do better without it, for it repeatedly obscures the symmetry of his sentences and hints that his language needs propping up with tricks. In line 3 a comma would do very well, as in line 8 and in lines 42–43. In lines 46–47 the dashes seriously obscure the structure of the sentence because they appear to enclose a parenthetical element, whereas the true form would better emerge were the second dash replaced by a comma. Note also that the comma after *culture* (48) should be balanced by one after *scholar* (46). Or should they both be omitted? That is, are the "who" clauses restrictive or non-restrictive? Your ear

should tell you. (For discussion of rule see p. 10.) Read them
aloud to demonstrate. Examine the other dashes in the selection
and decide which, if any, are essential.

14.   In lines 50–59 we begin with a Macaulayesque flourish of
"enormous erudition and perfect form," but thereafter the balance and parallelism thin out. With some effort you might rewrite
this sentence more in the manner of Macaulay. Try it. Hint:
semicolons could be used to link the parallel forms like *spending,
attending,* and *oscillating.*

15.   The semicolons in lines 86, 88, 89, 90, 96, and 97 come between
independent clauses not connected by conjunctions (*and* or *but*).
Those in lines 129 and 130 separate large elements which contain
commas. What function is served by the semicolon in line 176?

Rome in Power and Decay

EDWARD GIBBON

1. 'The greatness of Rome (such is the language of the historian) was founded on the rare and almost incredible alliance of virtue and of fortune. The long period of her infancy was employed in a laborious struggle against the tribes of Italy, the neighbours and enemies of the 5 rising city. In the strength and ardour of youth she sustained the storms of war, carried her victorious arms beyond the seas and the mountains, and brought home triumphal laurels from every country of the globe. At length, verging towards old age, and sometimes conquering by the terror only of her name, she sought 10 the blessings of ease and tranquillity. The VENERABLE CITY, which had trampled on the necks of the fiercest nations, and established a system of laws, the perpetual guardians of justice and freedom, was content, like a wise and wealthy parent, to devolve on the Cæsars, her favourite sons, the care of governing her ample patri- 15 mony. A secure and profound peace, such as had been once enjoyed in the reign of Numa,[1] succeeded to the tumults of a republic; while Rome was still adored as the queen of the earth, and the subject nations still reverenced the name of the people and the majesty of the senate. But this native splendour (con- 20 tinues Ammianus[2]) is degraded and sullied by the conduct of some nobles, who, unmindful of their own dignity and of that of their country, assume an unbounded licence of vice and folly. They contend with each other in the empty vanity of titles and surnames, and curiously select or invent the most lofty and 25

From *The Decline and Fall of the Roman Empire.*
[1] According to legend, the second king of Rome.
[2] The historian whom Gibbon is following very closely in this passage.

sonorous appellations—Reburrus or Fabunius, Pagonius or Tar-
rasius—which may impress the ears of the vulgar with astonish-
ment and respect. From a vain ambition of perpetuating their
memory, they affect to multiply their likeness in statues of bronze
30 and marble; nor are they satisfied unless those statues are covered
with plates of gold; an honourable distinction, first granted to
Acilius the consul, after he had subdued by his arms and counsels
the power of king Antiochus. The ostentation of displaying, of
magnifying perhaps, the rent-roll of the estates which they pos-
35 sess in all the provinces, from the rising to the setting sun, pro-
vokes the just resentment of every man who recollects that their
poor and invincible ancestors were not distinguished from the
meanest of the soldiers by the delicacy of their food or the splendour of their apparel. But the modern nobles measure their rank
40 and consequence according to the loftiness of their chariots, and
the weighty magnificence of their dress. Their long robes of silk
and purple float in the wind; and as they are agitated, by art or
accident, they occasionally discover the under garments, the rich
tunics, embroidered with the figures of various animals. Followed
45 by a train of fifty servants, and tearing up the pavement, they
move along the streets with the same impetuous speed as if they
travelled with post-horses; and the example of the senators is
boldly imitated by the matrons and ladies, whose covered car-
riages are continually driving round the immense space of the
50 city and suburbs. Whenever these persons of high distinction
condescend to visit the public baths, they assume, on their en-
trance, a tone of loud and insolent command, and appropriate
to their own use the conveniences which were designed for the
Roman people. If, in these places of mixed and general resort,
55 they meet any of the infamous ministers of their pleasures, they
express their affection by a tender embrace, while they proudly
decline the salutations of their fellow-citizens, who are not permitted to aspire above the honour of kissing their hands or their
knees. As soon as they have indulged themselves in the refresh-
60 ment of the bath, they resume their rings and the other ensigns
of their dignity, select from their private wardrobe of the finest
linen, such as might suffice for a dozen persons, the garments the
most agreeable to their fancy, and maintain till their departure

the same haughty demeanour, which perhaps might have been
excused in the great Marcellus after the conquest of Syracuse. 65
Sometimes indeed these heroes undertake more arduous achievements: they visit their estates in Italy, and procure themselves,
by the toil of servile hands, the amusements of the chase. If at
any time, but more especially on a hot day, they have courage to
sail in their painted galleys from the Lucrine lake to their elegant 70
villas on the sea-coast of Puteoli and Caieta, they compare their
own expeditions to the marches of Cæsar and Alexander. Yet
should a fly presume to settle on the silken folds of their gilded
umbrellas, should a sunbeam penetrate through some unguarded
and imperceptible chink, they deplore their intolerable hardships, 75
and lament in affected language that they were not born in the
land of the Cimmerians, the regions of eternal darkness. In these
journeys into the country the whole body of the household marches
with their master. In the same manner as the cavalry and infantry,
the heavy and the light armed troops, the advanced guard and 80
the rear, are marshalled by the skill of their military leaders, so
the domestic officers, who bear a rod as an ensign of authority,
distribute and arrange the numerous train of slaves and attend-
ants. The baggage and wardrobe move in the front, and are
immediately followed by a multitude of cooks and inferior min- 85
isters employed in the service of the kitchens and of the table.
The main body is composed of a promiscuous crowd of slaves,
increased by the accidental concourse of idle or dependent
plebeians. The rear is closed by the favourite band of eunuchs,
distributed from age to youth, according to the order of seniority. 90
Their numbers and their deformity excite the horror of the indignant spectators, who are ready to execrate the memory of
Semiramis [3] for the cruel art which she invented of frustrating
the purposes of nature, and of blasting in the bud the hopes of
future generations. In the exercise of domestic jurisdiction the 95
nobles of Rome express an exquisite sensibility for any personal
injury, and a contemptuous indifference for the rest of the human
species. When they have called for warm water, if a slave has
been tardy in his obedience, he is instantly chastised with three
hundred lashes; but should the same slave commit a wilful mur- 100

[3] Reputed founder of Babylon.

der, the master will mildly observe that he is a worthless fellow,
but that if he repeats the offence he shall not escape punishment.
Hospitality was formerly the virtue of the Romans; and every
stranger who could plead either merit or misfortune was relieved
105 or rewarded by their generosity. At present, if a foreigner, perhaps of no contemptible rank, is introduced to one of the proud
and wealthy senators, he is welcomed indeed in the first audience with such warm professions and such kind inquiries, that he
retires enchanted with the affability of his illustrious friend, and
110 full of regret that he had so long delayed his journey to Rome,
the native seat of manners as well as of empire. Secure of a
favourable reception, he repeats his visit the ensuing day, and is
mortified by the discovery that his person, his name, and his
country are already forgotten. If he still has resolution to per-
115 severe, he is gradually numbered in the train of dependents, and
obtains the permission to pay his assiduous and unprofitable court
to a haughty patron, incapable of gratitude or friendship, who
scarcely deigns to remark his presence, his departure, or his return. Whenever the rich prepare a solemn and popular entertain-
120 ment, whenever they celebrate with profuse and pernicious
luxury their private banquets, the choice of the guests is the
subject of anxious deliberation. The modest, the sober, and the
learned are seldom preferred; and the nomenclators, who are
commonly swayed by interested motives, have the address to
125 insert in the list of invitations the obscure names of the most
worthless of mankind. But the frequent and familiar companions
of the great are those parasites who practise the most useful of all
arts, the art of flattery; who eagerly applaud each word and every
action of their immortal patron; gaze with rapture on his marble
130 columns and variegated pavements, and strenuously praise the
pomp and elegance which he is taught to consider as a part
of his personal merit. At the Roman tables the birds, the *squirrels,*
or the fish, which appear of an uncommon size, are contemplated
with curious attention; a pair of scales is accurately applied to
135 ascertain their real weight; and, while the more rational guests
are disgusted by the vain and tedious repetition, notaries are
summoned to attest by an authentic record the truth of such a
marvellous event. Another method of introduction into the

houses and society of the great is derived from the profession of
gaming, or, as it is more politely styled, of play. The confederates 140
are united by a strict and indissoluble bond of friendship, or
rather of conspiracy; a superior degree of skill in the *Tesserarian*
art (which may be interpreted the game of dice and tables) is a
sure road to wealth and reputation. A master of that sublime
science, who in a supper or assembly is placed below a magis- 145
trate, displays in his countenance the surprise and indignation
which Cato might be supposed to feel when he was refused the
prætorship by the votes of a capricious people. The acquisition
of knowledge seldom engages the curiosity of the nobles, who
abhor the fatigue and disdain the advantages of study; and the 150
only books which they peruse are the Satires of Juvenal, and the
verbose and fabulous histories of Marius Maximus. The libraries
which they have inherited from their fathers are secluded, like
dreary sepulchres, from the light of day. But the costly instruments of the theatre, flutes, and enormous lyres, and hydraulic 155
organs, are constructed for their use; and the harmony of vocal
and instrumental music is incessantly repeated in the palaces of
Rome. In those palaces sound is preferred to sense, and the care
of the body to that of the mind. It is allowed as a salutary maxim,
that the light and frivolous suspicion of a contagious malady is 160
of sufficient weight to excuse the visits of the most intimate
friends; and even the servants who are despatched to make the
decent inquiries are not suffered to return home till they have
undergone the ceremony of a previous ablution. Yet this selfish
and unmanly delicacy occasionally yields to the more imperious 165
passion of avarice. The prospect of gain will urge a rich and
gouty senator as far as Spoleto; every sentiment of arrogance and
dignity is subdued by the hopes of an inheritance, or even of a
legacy; and a wealthy childless citizen is the most powerful of
the Romans. The art of obtaining the signature of a favourable 170
testament, and sometimes of hastening the moment of its execu-
tion, is perfectly understood; and it has happened that in the same
house, though in different apartments, a husband and a wife
with the laudable design of overreaching each other, have summoned their respective lawyers, to declare at the same time their 175
mutual but contradictory intentions. The distress which follows

and chastises extravagant luxury often reduces the great to the use of the most humiliating expedients. When they desire to borrow, they employ the base and supplicating style of the slave in
180 the comedy; but when they are called upon to pay, they assume the royal and tragic declamation of the grandsons of Hercules. If the demand is repeated, they readily procure some trusty sycophant, instructed to maintain a charge of poison, or magic, against the insolent creditor, who is seldom released from prison till he
185 has signed a discharge of the whole debt. These vices, which degrade the moral character of the Romans, are mixed with a puerile superstition that disgraces their understanding. They listen with confidence to the predictions of haruspices, who pretend to read in the entrails of victims the signs of future greatness
190 and prosperity; and there are many who do not presume either to bathe or to die, or to appear in public, till they have diligently consulted, according to the rules of astrology, the situation of Mercury and the aspect of the moon. It is singular enough that this vain credulity may often be discovered among the profane
195 sceptics who impiously doubt or deny the existence of a celestial power.'

※※※※※※※※※※

With Edward Gibbon we come to a richer prose than Macaulay's—grander, more sonorous, more subtly tuned. Not quite as shiny as Macaulay's, it is solider and richer.

1. Paragraphs, being convenient divisions of larger units, are apt to be scaled in some relation to the size of the larger units which they divide. Gibbon's *Decline and Fall* is tremendous; its chapters are tremendous; and consequently its paragraphs are often as long as the chapters in shorter books. Yet if they seem formidable, remember that the relief we get from paragraph divisions is really a crutch—that to the deeply interested reader such aids are unimportant. Considered as a complete essay, this selection could be divided into nine paragraphs. Find the divisions and decide whether there are effective transitions from topic to topic. How many of your paragraphs are introduced by *topic sentences* which state their theme? For example, a

paragraph might begin with "But the frequent and familiar companions . . ." (126); or with "The acquisition of knowledge . . ." (148).

2. Having read this passage aloud several times, you will want to give particular attention to the diction, for many words are unfamiliar and several familiar ones are used in strange ways. Check on: *devolve* (14), *curiously* (25), *vulgar* (27), *affect* (29), *ostentation* (33), *meanest* (38), *discover* (43), *tearing* (45), *post-haste* (47), *condescend* (51), *ensigns* (60), *demeanour* (64), *promiscuous* (87), *execrate* (92), *exquisite* (96), *sensibility* (96), *remark* (118), *pernicious luxury* (120), *nomenclators* (123), *address* (124), *curious* (134), *verbose, fabulous* (152), *suffered* (163), *imperious* (165), *expedient* (178), *sycophant* (182), *haruspices* (188).

3. You may have been warned against starting sentences with *and* or *but*. Note how often Gibbon does this. For what purpose, do you think?

4. The *irony* mentioned by Strachey appears in several parts of this passage. Underline and explain the ironic words in lines 66–72. What about "almost incredible" (3): would this be called ironic or perhaps sardonic? Discuss also the effect of *marvellous* (138), *sublime* (144), *laudable* (174), "either to bathe or to die" (190–191).

5. Since Gibbon writes long sentences with many subordinate clauses and modifiers, we may begin by examining his punctuation of the *restrictive* and *non-restrictive* modifier, which is guided by his exquisite ear. The term VENERABLE CITY (11) sufficiently identifies Rome so that the *which* clause after it is additional, *non-restrictive* information; therefore we pause after CITY, and there is a comma. But *every man* (36) is not sufficiently identified, and so the voice carries the cadence on, without pause but rather with rising inflection, perhaps all the way to *soldiers*. This modifying clause is essential to the meaning (i.e. *restrictive*) and must not be set off with a comma. Note the punctuation and the proper oral reading in similar situations in lines 57, 64, 82, 149, 152–3, and 176, where Gibbon's commas are properly inserted or omitted. Look for further examples of both types of modifiers; they do not have to be clauses.

6. Now let us verify the perfection of Gibbon's sentence structure by finding situations where he has punctuated to indicate the flow and balance of his cadences *rather* than the structure or syntax of his sentences. The point is that the structure is so obvious as to be unmistakable. In line 12, the comma divides a compound predicate, namely the two verbs *trample* and *established* of the single subject, *which*. The pause thus demanded after *nations* violates the syntax (because the *and* connects the two parts of a compound predicate and the absence of the comma signals this fact to the reader) but produces a remarkably sonorous sentence, made up of a long series of cadences, each of slightly different length. A more striking example appears in the next sentence: the *while* clause, modifying *succeeded* is strictly subordinate and would never be set off by a comma except that here Gibbon wishes to force a dramatic pause right in the middle of his sentence. A still bolder example appears in lines 28–33, where the second semicolon comes before an *appositive* (which is normally set off by a comma) rather than a new clause; the effect is to divide the sentence into three symmetrical and sonorous parts rather than to indicate grammatical relation. Identify further situations where a comma is placed between the verbs of a compound predicate, between compound modifiers, and compound subjective complements; also further semicolons which are introduced strictly for the ear.

7. What effect is achieved by the use of a comma rather than a semicolon in line 130? More important—why is there *not* a comma after *patron,* in line 129, instead of the semicolon?

8. Strachey organized his first paragraph (p. 20) around the idea of Gibbon's happiness; Gibbon uses comparable general terms in Sen. 1. What are they? What further device does Gibbon use in the first 20 lines?

9. What is the antecedent of *such,* in line 62? Identify a demonstrative, a personal, a possessive, and a reflexive pronoun in lines 66–68.

10. Gibbon varies his sentence patterns widely; and the methods are easy to identify: Subject-verb-object order is occasionally inverted, the object coming first; numerous sentences begin with modifiers or a series of modifiers. In a section of about 50 lines, make a count of how many sentences begin with the subject,

how many with modifiers, how many in other ways. Begin by marking all the subjects, verbs, and objects (or complements) with three colors. Your instructor may choose to spend an hour helping with this task.

11. An example of a formal balance may be seen in this sentence (178–181):

When they desire to borrow, they employ the base and supplicating style of the slave in the comedy; but when they are called upon to pay, they assume the royal and tragic declamation of the grandsons of Hercules.

Observe that this balance involves two introductory adverbial clauses, two pairs of adjectives, two similar prepositional phrases, *and* two kinds of dramatic performance, of which only one is specifically named. Identify each of these items in the sentence. Notice also that variation—which is as essential as pattern and uniformity—is carefully introduced: What word after the semicolon is a variation of "style"?

12. Strachey says that Gibbon's main problem was one of "exclusion." He has confined and restricted his material by presenting it as a series of *typical* circumstances and incidents. Now, the relation of the general to the specific varies from detail to detail: "the empty vanity of titles and surnames" (24) covers a multitude of specific cases; displaying the rent-roll of provincial estates, we may guess, is taken from few or even a single specific instance; whereas the complaint of the noble when a fly (73) settled on the folds of his garment is probably taken from a single quoted incident. Note the consistent mode of generalization, and identify other instances in the text where the source would seem to be a single example, or a number of examples.

13. If you undertake to describe a group, an institution, a segment of society, in the manner of Gibbon, you will have to gather a substantial list of facts, order them according to some simple and reasonable plan, and describe them in a stately and dignified language. This will not be easy, but it will be worth the effort, for when you can write sentences like Gibbon's, no matter how unnatural they may seem in the twentieth century (and indeed they are—you will imitate him only for practice), you will be well on the way to developing a style of your own.

A Journey to the Western Islands

SAMUEL JOHNSON

1. The general conversation of the Islanders has nothing particular. I did not meet with the inquisitiveness of which I have read, and suspect the judgment to have been rashly made. A stranger of curiosity comes into a place where a stranger is seldom seen: he importunes the people with questions, of which they cannot guess the motive, and gazes with surprise on things which they, having had them always before their eyes, do not suspect of any thing wonderful. He appears to them like some being of another world, and then thinks it peculiar that they take their turn to inquire whence he comes, and whither he is going.

2. The Islands were long unfurnished with instruction for youth, and none but the sons of gentlemen could have any literature. There are now parochial schools, to which the lord of every manor pays a certain stipend. Here the children are taught to read; but by the rule of their institution, they teach only *English,* so that the natives read a language which they may never use or understand. If a parish, which often happens, contains several Islands, the school being but in one, cannot assist the rest. This is the state of *Col,* which, however, is more enlightened than some other places; for the deficiency is supplied by a young gentleman, who, for his own improvement, travels every year on foot over the Highlands to the session at Aberdeen; and at his return, during the vacation, teaches to read and write in his native Island.

3. In *Sky* there are two grammar schools, where boarders are taken to be regularly educated. The price of board is from three pounds, to four pounds ten shillings a year, and that of instruc-

38

tion is half a crown a quarter. But the scholars are birds of
passage, who live at school only in the summer; for in winter 30
provisions cannot be made for any considerable number in one
place. This periodical dispersion impresses strongly the scarcity
of these countries.

4. Having heard of no boarding-school for ladies nearer than
Inverness, I suppose their education is generally domestick. The 35
elder daughters of the higher families are sent into the world,
and may contribute by their acquisitions to the improvement of
the rest.

✳✳✳✳✳✳✳✳✳✳✳

Read the selection aloud; then answer the following questions.

1. What connection is assumed between *conversation* and *inquisitiveness* (2–3)? What is the *judgment* to which he refers
(4) and why does Johnson conclude that it was rashly made?
What might be said of his own judgment in this respect?

2. Is the rest of Par. 1 an elaboration on "inquisitiveness" only,
or can it be understood as also relating to "conversation"? Explain.

3. This development in lines 4–11 is an excellent example of
Samuel Johnson's famous power of rational analysis. It was, indeed, the special characteristic of his extraordinary conversation.
Rational analysis (or, simply, logic) depends on the premises and
the data at its disposal. It would be an interesting exercise to
try out a different set of assumptions—for Johnson here is reasoning largely from assumptions—and see how different *and* effective
a development of the first paragraph you can compose. The first
step is to identify and discuss the assumptions—a good task for
the first assignment on this selection.

4. There seems to be a considerable jump to Par. 2. What
thought of Par. 1 is carried into the next?

5. Explain the difficult sentence, line 32.

6. Johnson's sentences are considerably less magnificent than
Gibbon's or Macaulay's, but we can detect in them uses of punc-

tuation for sound rather than for structure. The comma in line 3, separating (as do Gibbon and Macaulay) a compound verb in a simple sentence, is unnecessary; Johnson has used it to emphasize his two cadences. The second sentence (4–8) is carefully balanced for the ear. Why does the comma before *and* (6) *not* violate the rule against placing a comma between compound verbs of a simple sentence?

7.   Is the third sentence punctuated for the ear or for structure? Explain how the comma in line 13 serves *both* functions.

8.   In line 16, according to modern practice, there should be a comma after *but* or none after *institution*. Explain how you can tell that Johnson has been guided there by ear rather than by structure.

9.   The following sentence,

> If a parish, which often happens, contains several Islands, the school being but in one, cannot assist the rest. (18–20)

is made of what we have called cadences—that is rhythmical units—rather than sense units. Read aloud, its pleasing effect is obvious. Yet here is a sacrifice of clarity, particularly where a subject is dislocated from its verb. Identify this subject and its verb. Now see whether you can rewrite the sentence, maintaining a pleasant rhythmical pattern and at the same time making the sense emerge much more effectively.

10.   You can find more places where punctuation serves rhythm rather than structure. Point them out and try your hand at re-composing them.

The Post Office Pen

1. Up to now, nobody has breathed a word in defense of the dip pens Postmaster General Summerfield is ousting from post offices across the nation, and if we don't speak up the pens will go out thinking they didn't have a friend in the world. (Nobody said much when the mailboxes were made as garish as beer advertisements, or when the noble series of Presidential profiles on our postage stamps gave way to an ill-engraved gallery of lifeless mugs, but let it pass, let it pass.) We liked the old pens; the ink flowed from the nibs dark and luminous, the faint scratching was an agreeable accompaniment to composition, the cork holder felt airy and suave between the fingers, and even the most abject handwriting took on an angular distinction. We are thinking especially of the square-tipped nib, though the bowl-shaped, too, induced more real penmanship than any flow-forever, jet-styled pen. True, some post-office pens were splayed, split, and encrusted, and some wells dry, but seeing a herd of scrawny cattle we do not curse the suffering animals. Few people are fit to tend a cow, and fewer are competent to hold a pen. To seize, to press, to frown and crush was for many the exercise of their certificated literacy.

2. The pens, like modern poetry and Dean Acheson, were abused in a tone of impregnable smugness. We once overheard, in a Vermont post office, a woman rest the case for democracy on their wretchedness. "Compare these pens with the bank's," she instructed the child with her. "The Post Office is a state-run monopoly; you take what it gives you. The banks operate in a competitive system, and have to please their customers." The bank, as will happen in Vermont, was right across the street, and we found there the ball-point instruments usual in local temples

30 of deposit, insultingly chained to their tuberous sockets. We hope
the child's conversion to the free way of life did not hinge on this
lesson alone. Ball-point pens began as a vulgar novelty for sub-
aqueous scribes. The industry's publicists have shown great vigor,
and thanks to them ink may become as quaint a liquid to the next
35 generation as kerosene is to this, but their product still unrolls
a pale, dull line, whose total lack of the thin-and-thick elements
that quicken calligraphy is not redeemed by an erratic splotchiness.

3. Perhaps the inverse ratio between beauty and efficiency is
40 rigid and not to be bucked. The candle was a graceful, ardent,
and numinous method of illumination, but fluorescent tubes in
gawky casings are no doubt easier, in the optometrical sense, on
the eyes. We consent to hideous brightness. However, it seems
that Progress, in order to maintain the appearance of itself, must
45 sacrifice to the dumb god Era its own best fruits. The roll-top desk
was the most functional desk ever devised; Functionalism swept
it away. The customary resident of that desk, the dip pen with
metal nib, retained the eloquence of the goose quill and saved the
geese. When Summerfield moved, the geese stood idly by.

※※※※※※※※※※※

The *New Yorker* magazine's editorial page has specialized in
the art of treating small incidents and common facts of life with
a linguistic imagination that turns them into little gems of insight
and entertainment. These exercises demonstrate how the play of
the cultivated mind depends upon as well as expresses itself
through *language*. *New Yorker* language is succinct, specific, yet
always rich in its own sort of reference.

1.   Linguistic adventurousness appears in the ignorance of the
unlettered, the slang of the tough, the jargon of trades and skills;
it is often most conscious and most imaginative, however, in the
practice of the cultivated man and the writer. Where, in this
selection, do you find the first bold evidence of linguistic adventurousness? Why such a descent into "vulgar" speech? Is the
word suggestive enough or colorful enough to merit defense as
the best possible word for the situation? What sort of suggestions
does it involve?

2.   *Airy* and *suave* (11–12) reveal different sorts of inventiveness. What particular meaning of *airy* is involved? The use of *suave* is particularly imaginative; define its full (but precise!) meaning here. Which of the several meanings of *distinction* (13) applies here? What about *real* (15)? What is *certificated literacy* (20)? Why, exactly, call banks *temples* (29)?—identify at least two meanings, both somewhat pejorative. Is the chain an insult, really, or evidence of something else? What literal aspect of *tuber* is drawn upon (30); what fanciful? Explain *quaint* (34) and *quicken* (37). What is the pun or joke on *easier* (42)? Hint: It is used literally whereas it is usually used figuratively. Discover the reference to Eros in line 45.

Ardent and *numinous* (40–41) are almost poetic; what about *gawky?* What is the effect of the mixture?

3.   Development in this essay proceeds through a series of imaginative flights which amuse by their outrageousness but delight by their aptness. The reader is in a contest with the writer's skills of surprise and deception. The comparison in lines 15–18 is preposterous, to be sure; its tone is almost mock-biblical; yet it makes a point. Is this point a matter of tone or, perhaps, idea? Or will it not bear close examination? Can it be said to introduce an *intentional* note of unreason into the piece—in order to account for the writer's affection for the old pens? What other function does such a note of unreason serve? Write a brief paragraph discussing the connection of this sentence with the following one. Is it reasonable?

4.   Dean Acheson, Assistant Secretary of State under President Roosevelt and Secretary of State under President Truman (1949–1953), was fiercely assailed by members of the other party. What *point* does the comparison in lines 21–22 make? Note especially the value of *impregnable*.

5.   What *is* the "case for democracy" made in lines 24–27, and why exactly does the writer reject it? The ball-point pen was once advertized as writing under water—a clever stunt, because nobody wants to write under water, and therefore the absurdity of the claim made people remember the instrument. In just what sense, then, are we to take "vulgar novelty" (32)?

6.   What is guilty of the "erratic splotchiness" of line 37?

7.   Between "hideous brightness" (43) and "hideous func-

tionalism" (implied but unstated) we have the "dumb god Era" contradicting himself. Explain the charge, which is little more than hinted in the passage. What tone does the capital on Functionalism (46) establish?

8. What is the difference between the two *geese* of the last lines? Consider both literal and figurative meanings. Compare with the questions on *easier* (42) and *temples* (29).

9. Finally, where is the ratio between beauty and efficiency "inverse" and where "direct" in this piece?

10. After studying the above questions, you will see that this prose has layers of reference and subtlety. If not as magnificent as Gibbon's, it is more tightly packed, more concrete, and more suave in its rhythms. Reread it aloud; then let us examine the relations of sound and sense to punctuation.

The long sentence, lines 9–13, is made of five independent clauses of similar form. Why, then, is the first clause followed by a semicolon? Identify a difference both in substance and in form that sets it off from the rest. What might Macaulay or Gibbon have used instead of that semicolon? Count the syllables in each of the five clauses and you will discover a pattern that accounts, in part, for the pleasing movement of the sentence as it is read aloud.

The following two sentences are as carefully punctuated as Macaulay's; is there any conflict between sound and sense? Does the restrictive—non-restrictive distinction account for the absence of commas around "seeing a herd of scrawny cattle" (17)? Identify a restrictive and a non-restrictive clause in lines 35–38, both properly punctuated. (See page 10 for rules governing these clauses.)

Notice that this writer always places a comma before the final element of a series (". . . some post-office pens were splayed, split, and encrusted . . ." line 16). This practice makes the omission of the comma after "frown" ("To seize, to press, to frown and crush was for many the exercise of their certificated literary.") *meaningful* and *useful;* tell precisely what it indicates.

One comma in Par. 2 violates the general rule of not separating the two verbs of a compound predicate. Locate it and decide whether it is indeed necessary—or confusing. Note compound predicate adjectives (40) and another compound verb (48), not separated by commas; note compound direct objects similarly treated in this sentence that you are now reading.

Topic: Try your hand at exploring the overtones—personal, social, aesthetic, economic—of some small item in the contemporary scene. You need not expect to achieve the range and penetration of an observer like the author of this sketch, but you can take a fresh look at something and make some original comments. Clothes, eating habits, decorations, buildings may give you a topic. You do not have to be entirely reasonable, but where you give way to fantasy or exaggeration you must have a reason. Where the *New Yorker* piece is most unreasonable there is most reason, *if* you see what the author is really talking about.

The Return of the Native

THOMAS HARDY

A face on which time makes but little impression.

1. A Saturday after-
noon in November was approaching the time of twilight, and the
vast tract of unenclosed wild known as Egdon Heath embrowned
itself moment by moment. Overhead the hollow stretch of whitish
5 cloud shutting out the sky was as a tent which had the whole
heath for its floor.

2. The heaven being spread with this pallid screen and the earth
with the darkest vegetation, their meeting-line at the horizon
was clearly marked. In such contrast the heath wore the appear-
10 ance of an instalment of night which had taken up its place before
its astronomical hour was come: darkness had to a great extent
arrived hereon, while day stood distinct in the sky. Looking up-
wards, a furze-cutter would have been inclined to continue work;
looking down, he would have decided to finish his faggot and
15 go home. The distant rims of the world and of the firmament
seemed to be a division in time no less than a division in matter.
The face of the heath by its mere complexion added half an hour
to evening; it could in like manner retard the dawn, sadden noon,
anticipate the frowning of storms scarcely generated, and in-
20 tensify the opacity of a moonless midnight to a cause of shaking
and dread.

3. In fact, precisely at this transitional point of its nightly roll
into darkness the great and particular glory of the Egdon waste
began, and nobody could be said to understand the heath who
25 had not been there at such a time. It could best be felt when it
could not clearly be seen, its complete effect and explanation

From *The Return of the Native.*

lying in this and the succeeding hours before the next dawn: then, and only then, did it tell its true tale. The spot was, indeed, a near relation of night, and when night showed itself an apparent tendency to gravitate together could be perceived in its shades and the scene. The sombre stretch of rounds and hollows seemed to rise and meet the evening gloom in pure sympathy, the heath exhaling darkness as rapidly as the heavens precipitated it. And so the obscurity in the air and the obscurity in the land closed together in a black fraternization towards which each advanced half-way.

4. The place became full of a watchful intentness now; for when other things sank brooding to sleep the heath appeared slowly to awake and listen. Every night its Titanic form seemed to await something; but it had waited thus, unmoved, during so many centuries, through the crises of so many things, that it could only be imagined to await one last crisis—the final overthrow.

5. It was a spot which returned upon the memory of those who loved it with an aspect of peculiar and kindly congruity. Smiling champaigns of flowers and fruit hardly do this, for they are permanently harmonious only with an existence of better reputation as to its issues than the present. Twilight combined with the scenery of Egdon Heath to evolve a thing majestic without severity, impressive without showiness, emphatic in its admonitions, grand in its simplicity. The qualifications which frequently invest the façade of a prison with far more dignity than is found in the façade of a palace double its size lent to this heath a sublimity in which spots renowned for beauty of the accepted kind are utterly wanting. Fair prospects wed happily with fair times; but alas, if times be not fair! Men have oftener suffered from the mockery of a place too smiling for their reason than from the oppression of surroundings oversadly tinged. Haggard Egdon appealed to a subtler and scarcer instinct, to a more recently learnt emotion, than that which responds to the sort of beauty called charming and fair.

6. Indeed, it is a question if the exclusive reign of this orthodox beauty is not approaching its last quarter. The new Vale of Tempe may be a gaunt waste in Thule: human souls may find themselves in closer and closer harmony with external things

⁶⁵ wearing a sombreness distasteful to our race when it was young.
The time seems near, if it has not actually arrived, when the
chastened sublimity of a moor, a sea, or a mountain will be all of
nature that is absolutely in keeping with the moods of the more
thinking among mankind. And ultimately, to the commonest
⁷⁰ tourist, spots like Iceland may become what the vineyards and
myrtle-gardens of South Europe are to him now; and Heidelberg
and Baden be passed unheeded as he hastens from the Alps to
the sand-dunes of Scheveningen.

7. The most thorough-going ascetic could feel that he had a
⁷⁵ natural right to wander on Egdon: he was keeping within the
line of legitimate indulgence when he laid himself open to influences such as these. Colours and beauties so far subdued were,
at least, the birthright of all. Only in summer days of highest
feather did its mood touch the level of gaiety. Intensity was more
⁸⁰ usually reached by way of the solemn than by way of the
brilliant, and such a sort of intensity was often arrived at during
winter darkness, tempests, and mists. Then Egdon was aroused to
reciprocity; for the storm was its lover, and the wind its friend.
Then it became the home of strange phantoms; and it was found
⁸⁵ to be the hitherto unrecognized original of those wild regions of
obscurity which are vaguely felt to be compassing us about in
midnight dreams of flight and disaster, and are never thought of
after the dream till revived by scenes like this.

8. It was at present a place perfectly accordant with man's
⁹⁰ nature—neither ghastly, hateful, nor ugly: neither commonplace,
unmeaning, nor tame; but, like man, slighted and enduring; and
withal singularly colossal and mysterious in its swarthy monot-
ony. As with some persons who have long lived apart, solitude
seemed to look out of its countenance. It had a lonely face, sug-
⁹⁵ gesting tragical possibilities.

9. This obscure, obsolete, superseded country figures in Domesday. Its condition is recorded therein as that of heathy, furzy,
briary wilderness—'Bruaria.' Then follows the length and breadth
in leagues; and, though some uncertainty exists as to the exact
¹⁰⁰ extent of this ancient lineal measure, it appears from the figures
that the area of Egdon down to the present day has but little
diminished. 'Turbaria Bruaria'—the right of cutting heath-turf—

occurs in charters relating to the district. 'Overgrown with heth
and mosse,' says Leland of the same dark sweep of country.

10. Here at least were intelligible facts regarding landscape— 105
far-reaching proofs productive of genuine satisfaction. The un-
tameable, Ishmaelitish thing that Egdon now was it always had
been. Civilization was its enemy; and ever since the beginning
of vegetation its soil had worn the same antique brown dress, the
natural and invariable garment of the particular formation. In its 110
venerable one coat lay a certain vein of satire on human vanity
in clothes. A person on a heath in raiment of modern cut and
colours has more or less an anomalous look. We seem to want the
oldest and simplest human clothing where the clothing of the
earth is so primitive.   115

11. To recline on a stump of thorn in the central valley of
Egdon, between afternoon and night, as now, where the eye could
reach nothing of the world outside the summits and shoulders
of heathland which filled the whole circumference of its glance,
and to know that everything around and underneath had been 120
from prehistoric times as unaltered as the stars overhead, gave
ballast to the mind adrift on change, and harassed by the irre-
pressible New. The great inviolate place had an ancient permanence which the sea cannot claim. Who can say of a particular sea
that it is old? Distilled by the sun, kneaded by the moon, it is 125
renewed in a year, in a day, or in an hour. The sea changed, the
fields changed, the rivers, the villages, and the people changed,
yet Egdon remained. Those surfaces were neither so steep as to
be destructible by weather, nor so flat as to be the victims of
floods and deposits. With the exception of an aged highway, and 130
a still more aged barrow presently to be referred to—themselves
almost crystallized to natural products by long continuance—even
the trifling irregularities were not caused by pickaxe, plough, or
spade, but remained as the very finger-touches of the last
geological change.   135

12. The above-mentioned highway traversed the lower levels
of the heath, from one horizon to another. In many portions of
its course it overlaid an old vicinal way, which branched from
the great Western road of the Romans, the Via Iceniana, or Ike-
nild Street, hard by. On the evening under consideration it would 140

have been noticed that, though the gloom had increased sufficiently to confuse the minor features of the heath, the white
surface of the road remained almost as clear as ever.

※※※※※※※※※※

This opening passage of a famous novel is a mood piece of
extraordinary power and significance for the story, because the
setting it presents is not only physical but also spiritual and symbolic. Playing on the images of light and dark as symbols of good
and evil, thought and force, hope and despair, Hardy suggests
that in the relation of man to the universe there are profound
complexities and ambiguities.

To be more concrete (since concreteness is a central theme of
this textbook), let us say that Hardy begins with the familiar
opposition of earth-heaven, nature-spirit, man-God and by use of
his symbols subtly modulates the standard dualism to the point
where there is more darkness above, more light below, before we
have come to the end of the chapter of which the present selection is the beginning. Hardy does not stop with this simple change,
however, but also suggests a fraternity of purpose between a
darkness above and the darkness below. Out of these symbols, at
which we have merely hinted, grows the novel's profound and
disturbing treatment of human destiny. Is evil, it asks, an expression of Man or of Fate?

We shall examine this passage first for its complex meaning,
then for the stages through which that meaning is developed,
and then for the formal order of the sentences and their punctuation, in order to see how form and content are, as in all great
writing, inseparable.

1. Read the whole passage aloud, trying to capture the
rhythms of the thought as it flows in sentence and paragraph.
Before the second reading, look up the following words: *heath,
furze, faggot, firmament, opacity, gravitate, exhale, precipitate,
fraternization, intentness, congruity, champaigns, admonition,
invest, prospect, tinged, haggard, gaunt, chasten, ascetic, reciprocity, original* (as noun), *venerable, raiment, anomalous,
inviolate,* and *vicinal.* Identify these proper names and references:
Titan, Vale of Tempe, Thule, Scheveningen, Domesday Book,
Leland, and Ishmael.

2.   In the first four paragraphs of this passage we may trace in detail how layers of meaning can be produced by figurative or symbolic language. The opposition of earth and sky in this twilight scene is complicated by words that move between suggestions of humanity and un-humanity, of purpose and mere force, of rationality and mere change. Let us look at some of them: In line 3 *embrowned itself* suggests purpose or at least self-direction, whereas the terms *tent* (5) and *pallid screen* (7) are strictly non-human and lifeless. With *instalment* (10), the heath is drawn toward the lifeless and mechanical aspects of the sky; this impression lasts until the major turn of *face* in line 17. The turn is quickly enriched by the human aspects of *complexion* (17) and *anticipate* (19) for the heath and *frowning of storms* for the sky.

The personification becomes dramatic with "tell its true tale" (28) and proceeds through an ambiguous mixture of un-human terms like *tendency* and *gravitate* to the powerful images of the last two sentences in the paragraph (31–36). Discuss these terms and figures in some detail, showing how the human and non-human play upon each other. For example, consider the human and non-human aspects of *closed* in line 35! You will of course have to give most attention to the effect of *fraternization* (35) and the question of what *sort* of relation is suggested by the term. Study this through Par. 4, pointing toward an explanation of "final overthrow" (42). Again, of what by whom? Shakespeare's Othello says, "And when I love thee not, Chaos is come again." Milton in *Paradise Lost* speaks of Chaos as "the womb of nature and perhaps her grave." These references will start you toward an explanation of what Hardy suggests; but it will be only a start. Refer to "Titan"; for what "final overthrow" were the Titans waiting? Did it come? Can all these references be combined for an explanation?

It may help in your approach to the problem if you realize that, in the Greek myth, the old Titans were overthrown by Zeus, who continues to rule the lesser gods, and men. Hardy assumes that Zeus is roughly equivalent to Order, which under another cosmology (i.e. an explanation of the world) is the opposite of a primordial Chaos—the imposition of form upon formlessness. That "form" prevails today as man's destiny or fate—the Order in which man finds himself and in which he must live—and Hardy means to explore it in his novel. You will not have missed the point that this Order, as expressed in the heath, points toward tragedy.

3. Paragraph 5: We may define or elucidate an idea in many ways. By comparison and contrast we show likeness and unlikeness, and both serve to *place* or define a thing, for definition is the setting of limits or outlines (literally "ends"). Here the term "kindly congruity" (44) gives a quality of the heath that is more precisely located by a later term of opposition, namely "mockery" in line 56. How does the positive "congruity" move toward the negative "mockery"? Show the steps that take us from one to the other.

4. Define the exact nature of the *response to beauty*—which constitutes a definition of beauty—that is merely implied in Par. 5.

5. How is "congruity" (44) linked to "harmony" (64)?

6. Write an explanation of the difference in function of Pars. 5 and 6. If Par. 5 develops a definition of beauty, what does Par. 6 do with this definition?

7. In Par. 7 we come upon a development of the beauty theme that could easily be overlooked. It begins with *ascetic* (74) and goes on through *indulgence* (76) and *influences* (76). Explain the development and show how much farther it is carried through the paragraph. You must begin by establishing the full meaning of *ascetic*.

At least in line 78 implies a plea or an attempt to wring a concession in an argument. Who is speaking to whom about what?

8. Does Par. 8, after you have read and reread the whole selection, seem to be more about man or the heath?

9. Paragraphs 9–10: *Obsolete* and *superseded*, if they apply in some figurative way to man, have rather far-reaching intentions. Was the heath less obsolete in the time of William the Conqueror? If so, how? How do you account for the human metaphor, *Ishmaelitish*, used to enrich the non-humanity of the heath? What is the effect of this paradox at this point in the exposition? What words in Par. 10 further link the heath to the human condition?

10. We have seen this selection move from more-or-less objective description (Par. 1), to ambiguous personification of heath and sky (Pars. 2, 3), with a minor climax at the end of Par. 4, in

which the animation of the heath has been complete. In Pars. 5, 6, 7, the theme of beauty is developed to suggest that the heath reflects not only certain basic and enduring human qualities but also certain attitudes peculiar to *modern* man. Paragraph 8 restates the theme that the heath is an image of man's nature and destiny. Paragraphs 9 and 10 assert its hostility to civilization and vanity; and the two final paragraphs seem, without now personifying the heath, to make it at once an enduring symbol of man's elemental self and a setting against which his impermanent frailties will enact some austere retribution or failure. Test this analysis against your own reading of the passage.

11.   You may prepare an oral or written analysis of one or two of these paragraphs, in which you discuss the particular words that determine its literal and figurative or symbolic effects. Or you may write an essay discussing each separate idea or concept that is represented by the heath.

PUNCTUATION:

Hardy's punctuation is orthodox, modern, economical, and scrupulously adjusted to his oral cadences, which are as carefully wrought as his ideas.

12.   The elements, "known as Egdon Heath" (3), "shutting out the sky" (5), and "which had the whole heath for its floor" (5) are presented, by the absence of commas, as *restrictive* modifiers. Consider what changes in meaning would occur if these modifiers were enclosed by commas. Test the difference in each case by reading aloud. Which of the three modifiers could as well be punctuated—and read—as non-restrictive?

13.   In line 7, why must there be no comma after *screen?* Read aloud to test.

14.   Is the *which* clause in line 10 restrictive? Test by reading aloud.

15.   Hardy's "economy" in using the comma appears strikingly in lines 17, 18; especially in 23, 29, 38, and in 35. Account for each of these situations and show the special effects that are due to the punctuation. Note how by contrast these uses give the commas in lines 28 and 29 an unusual effectiveness.

16.   With the preceding hints to work from, prepare a careful

analysis of the punctuation in lines 39 to 73, demonstrating 1) the general economy, 2) the close observance of the basic rules of syntax (e.g. why there is no comma after "size" in line 52), and 3) the special effectiveness that the punctuation achieves, when it does appear, in the midst of this general economy. Consider thus the quite unnecessary commas in lines 83 and 122 (after "change").

17. The semicolon is here used by Hardy:
    1) to connect independent clauses when there is no conjunction and a period would separate them too absolutely,
    2) to set off a compound clause with greater emphasis than a comma would achieve, and
    3) to separate compound clauses which themselves contain commas.
Find the examples of these uses in the selection.
The colon is used:
    1) to indicate some sort of equivalency in what is to follow, and
    2) to make a dramatic link between independent clauses.
Find examples of these uses in the selection.
    Note that a long sentence does not necessarily require a semicolon, and that Hardy does not use one if the sentence makes a single statement rather than having a contrast or a pairing or a repetition of ideas. Explain the absence of semicolons in the sentences, lines 116–123, 140–143, and 50–54, and 79–82.

18. Pattern and variation play through the forms of parallelism. In lines 12–21 we may see how they operate. The first sentence is parallel except for the added "and go home" at the end; up to that point the two halves contain identical elements. The second sentence reveals a perfect balance between "a division in time" and "a division in matter." This is enough of perfect parallelism, for the moment, and so with the following sentence Hardy introduces a more complex pattern: before the semicolon there is a simple form of "Face . . . added . . . hour"; after it the predicate is fourfold—"it could . . . retard . . . sadden . . . anticipate . . . and intensify." The *objects* of these four verbs are of steadily increasing length except for one striking variation. What is it? Now if Hardy had put "sadden noon" first in the series, he would have had a uniformly increasing length of parts. Try read-

ing it aloud in this order. Try a slight rephrasing that keeps *dawn* before *noon* and yet makes the first verb-object the shortest of the four. But Hardy did not do this, and we are probably correct in assuming that he did not do it for a reason, namely to keep his "syllabic increase" from becoming too obvious or too rigid.

Examine the rest of the selection for passages in which similar attention is given to varying the forms of classical rhetoric.

Compare this passage, and others typical of Hardy's style, with the parallelism and balance of lines 126–132 of the selection from Edward Gibbon (p. 32). Notice, in this comparison, the *pairs* of phrases that Gibbon uses so frequently, with perhaps more concern for cadence than for meaning.

19. Now try your hand at developing this technique of syllabic increase. Write a sentence with a series of elements in strictly parallel structure demonstrating it, using one or more of the following situations:

1. A dog runs into a room (you will use a more specific and lively verb than "runs"); what damage does he do to the furniture, the rug, the baby in a play pen, etc.?
2. You watch from your window as the wind gathers momentum before a storm. How does it affect the various trees, plants, flowers in your garden?
3. A comedian tells a joke on stage. Describe the facial changes of various members of the audience.

Among the common situations where parallelism is used are the series of verb-objects or verb-adverbs. For example,

The busy week-end farmer pruned the vines, weeded the radishes, cultivated the asparagus bed, and then climbed upstairs and fell soundly asleep.

and

The little boy greeted his soldier-father with hesitation. He smiled shyly, then shook hands warmly, and finally, all hesitation gone, affectionately climbed on his lap and hugged him.

See whether you can make any improvements in the rhythms and cadences of these sentences.

20. Find other examples of syllabic increase and decrease where Hardy uses parallelism. Are they frequent?

21. After this study, you are perhaps ready to compare Hardy's sentence forms and rhythms with those of Gibbon and Macaulay. Consider this judgment of Hardy's writing:

> If it cannot be as splendid—and resplendent—as a pure style out of the past, it can serve its purposes more richly and variously—and this is a quality of much modern art of every type—music, painting, sculpture, or writing.

Hardy's prose is no less rhythmical but, being less strictly dependent upon balance, parallelism, and antithesis, it is more varied, more closely woven into the texture of his thought, and although less spectacular perhaps more moving and impressive. They are as different, in some ways, as a Greek temple and a modern functional dwelling by Frank Lloyd Wright. Like the forms of modern architecture, Hardy's prose draws upon the resources of many past styles.

****

II

****

Old Mr. Flood

JOSEPH MITCHELL

1. A tough Scotch-Irishman I know, Mr. Hugh G. Flood, a retired house-wrecking contractor, aged ninety-three, often tells people that he is dead set and determined to live until the afternoon of July 27, 1965, when he will be a hundred and fifteen years old. "I don't ask much here below," he says. "I just want to hit a hundred and fifteen. That'll hold me." Mr. Flood is small and wizened. His eyes are watchful and icy-blue, and his face is red, bony, and clean-shaven. He is old-fashioned in appearance. As a rule, he wears a high, stiff collar, a candy-striped shirt, a serge suit, and a derby. A silver watch-chain hangs across his vest. He keeps a flower in his lapel. When I am in the Fulton Fish Market neighborhood, I always drop into the Hartford House, a drowsy waterfront hotel at 309 Pearl Street, where he has a room, to see if he is still alive.

2. Many aged people reconcile themselves to the certainty of death and become tranquil; Mr. Flood is unreconcilable. There are three reasons for this. First, he deeply enjoys living. Second, he comes of a long line of Baptists and has a nagging fear of the hereafter, complicated by the fact that the descriptions of heaven in the Bible are as forbidding to him as those of hell. "I don't really want to go to either one of those places," he says. He broods about religion and reads a chapter of the Bible practically every day. Even so, he goes to church only on Easter. On that day he has several drinks of Scotch for breakfast and then gets in a cab and goes to a Baptist church in Chelsea. For at least a week thereafter he is gloomy and silent. "I'm a God-fearing man," he says,

"and I believe in Jesus Christ crucified, risen, and coming again, but one sermon a year is all I can stand." Third, he is a diet theorist—he calls himself a seafoodetarian—and feels obliged to
30 reach a spectacular age in order to prove his theory. He is convinced that the eating of meat and vegetables shortens life and he maintains that the only sensible food for man, particularly for a man who wants to hit a hundred and fifteen, is fish.

3. To Mr. Flood, the flesh of finfish and shellfish is not only
35 good to eat, it is an elixir. "When I get through tearing a lobster apart, or one of those tender West Coast octopuses," he says, "I feel like I had a drink from the fountain of youth." He eats with relish every kind of seafood, including sea-urchin eggs, blowfish tails, winkles, ink squids, and barndoor skates. He especially likes
40 an ancient Boston breakfast dish—fried cod tongues, cheeks, and sounds, sounds being the gelatinous air bladders along the cod's backbone. The more unusual a dish, the better he likes it. It makes him feel superior to eat something that most people would edge away from. He insists, however, on the plainest of cooking.
45 In his opinion, there are only four first-class fish restaurants in the city—Sweet's and Libby's on Fulton Street, Gage & Tollner's in Brooklyn, and Lundy's in Sheepshead Bay—and even these, he says, are disinclined to let well enough alone. Consequently, he takes most of his meals in Sloppy Louie Morino's, a busy-bee on
50 South Street frequented almost entirely by wholesale fishmongers from Fulton Market, which is across the street. Customarily, when Mr. Flood is ready for lunch, he goes to the stall of one of the big wholesalers, a friend of his, and browses among the bins for half an hour or so. Finally he picks out a fish, or an eel, or
55 a crab, or the wing of a skate, or whatever looks the best that day, buys it, carries it unwrapped to Louie's, and tells the chef precisely how he wants it cooked. Mr. Flood and the chef, a surly old Genoese, are close friends. "I've made quite a study of fish cooks," Mr. Flood says, "and I've decided that old Italians are
60 best. Then comes old colored men, then old mean Yankees, and then old drunk Irishmen. They have to be old; it takes almost a lifetime to learn how to do a thing simply. Even the stove has to be old. If the cook is an awful drunk, so much the better. I don't

think a teetotaler could cook a fish. If he was a mean teetotaler, he might." 65

4. Mr. Flood's attitude toward seafood is not altogether mystical. "Fish," he says, "is the only grub left that the scientists haven't been able to get their hands on and improve. The flounder you eat today hasn't got any more damned vitamins in it than the flounder your great-great-grandaddy ate, and it tastes the 70 same. Everything else has been improved *and* improved *and* improved to such an extent it ain't fit to eat. Consider the egg. When I was a boy on Staten Island, hens ate grit and grasshoppers and scraps from the table and whatever they could scratch out of the ground, and a platter of scrambled eggs was a 75 delight. Then the scientists developed a special egg-laying mash made of old corncobs and sterilized buttermilk, and nowadays you order scrambled eggs and you get a platter of yellow glue, Grade A. Consider the apple. Years ago you could enjoy an apple. Then the scientists took hold and invented chemical fertilizers 80 especially for apple trees, and apples got big and red and shiny and beautiful and absolutely tasteless. As for vegetables, vegetables have been improved until they're downright poisonous. Two-thirds of the population has the stomach jumps, and no wonder." 85

5. Except for bread and butter, sauces, onions, and baked potatoes, Mr. Flood himself has rarely eaten anything but seafood since 1885 and he is in sound shape. For a man past ninety who worked hard in the wet and the wind from boyhood until the age of eighty, he is, in fact, a phenomenon; he has his own teeth, he 90 hears all right, he doesn't wear glasses, his mind seldom wanders, and his appetite is so good that immediately after lunch he begins speculating about what he will have for dinner. He walks cautiously and a little feebly, it is true, but without a stick unless there is snow on the sidewalks. "All I dread is accidents," he said 95 recently. "A broken bone would most likely wind things up for me. Aside from that, I don't fret about my health. I'm immune to the average germ; don't even catch colds; haven't had a cold since 1912. Only reason I caught that one, I went on a toot and it was a pouring-down rainy night in the dead of winter and my 100

shoes were cracked and they let the damp in and I lost my balance a time or two and sloshed around in the gutter and somewhere along the line I mislaid my hat and I'd just had a haircut
and I stood in a draft in one saloon an hour or more and there
105 was a poor fellow next to me sneezing his head off and when I
got home I crawled into a bed that was beside an open window
like a fool and passed out with my wet clothes on, shoes and all.
Also, I'd spent the night before sitting up on a train and hadn't
slept a wink and my resistance was low. If the good Lord can
110 just see His way clear to protect me from accidents, no stumbling
on the stairs, no hell-fired automobiles bearing down on me in
the dark, no broken bones, I'll hit a hundred and fifteen easy."

✳✳✳✳✳✳✳✳✳✳

Joseph Mitchell assumes that his reader shares his own highly
cultivated and sophisticated taste. His accomplished manner
marks him as a professional *writer* with an eye for the unfamiliar;
but he also makes this piece seem a labor of love. Thus we become involved with Joseph Mitchell's interest in Mr. Flood
without being swamped by his emotions. The latter, indeed, are
so carefully withheld and so cautiously presented that we are
soon considerably engaged in discovering them.

1.   The first paragraph has a mass of fact words but very few
explanatory ones. The latter give us something of the author's
opinions, but only *something* of them; there are three such words;
find them and explain how much of the writer's personal opinions
and/or feelings they reveal. Then mark the fact words, like
retired, small, wizened, watchful. Do some of them contain an
element of explanation or opinion?

2.   Mitchell begins with an extraordinary fact ("I just want to
hit a hundred and fifteen.") and then gives a physical picture
of his subject. From thousands of possible details of appearance,
he has chosen about eleven and packed them into a brief passage.
Two considerations apply here: one must not give a detail that
will produce a false total image in the reader's mind; the writer
must proceed from the whole to the parts with extreme care. On
these principles, account for the *order* of the first seven facts,

beginning with "small," and then for the selection and order of
the facts that follow the explanatory "old-fashioned."

3. Pursue this question of facts and explanatory words
through the rest of the selection, noting not only their relative
frequencies, but also the amount of personal feeling and opinion
revealed by the explanatory words.

4. Is the writer inside Mr. Flood's mind, completely outside, or
partly inside? This is the vital and interesting question of point
of view—vital because it determines the tone of a piece and because it must be consistently handled, interesting because it is a
key to understanding literary method. Where, how, and how far
does the author get into Mr. Flood's mind?

(a) Is there any penetration of it in Par. 1?

(b) In Par. 2 we have information about what he *thinks.* List
the words (or underline them) that indicate that it is *thought:
unreconcilable, enjoys, nagging fear,* etc.; there are four or five
more. Now, do these words take us among Mr. Flood's thoughts
or are they based on the writer's *observation* and *hearing?*

(c) In Par. 3, lines 42–44, we come to a crux:

The more unusual a dish, the better he likes it. It makes him
feel superior to eat something that most people would edge
away from.

Does the writer *infer* these facts, does he know them from evidence, or has he stepped into Mr. Flood's mind? Paragraphs 4
and 5 represent which minds? Mark the words in each that reveal
the quality or idiosyncrasy of the two minds.

5. These lines (42–44) make it clear that Mr. Flood regards
himself as something of a character and a phenomenon. There
is, indeed, a strong dash of pose and even of vanity in his personality. Identify the points, later in the selection, where this fact
is developed. Certainly in his remarks on cooks (58–65). Do
you agree? Where else? There are at least two major examples.

6. We are well into Par. 5 before the writer uses an overall term
of judgment: "phenomenon"—and even this word is carefully
limited in its application. Is it a moral judgment, or what?

7. Concrete fact and author's interpretations are, if we may
resort to superlatives, ultimate poles of good and bad writing.
Facts speak for themselves. When an author tells us how to feel

without giving us the concrete evidence or motive for such feeling, probably we do not respond. The ultimate point of concreteness comes in the drama, where the author makes no comment at all, but provides only the characters' words. (There may be abundant stage directions, of course, but these do not affect our case.) The same absolute concreteness is approached in some novels where all information comes through the eyes and minds of the characters.

The ultimate point of interpretation and subjectivity appears in such a sentence as:

> The mother, heartbroken at the loss of her only child, mourned for several days and then killed herself.

Here, surely, is a tragic situation, but just as surely it is impossible for us to respond to this description of it, because we have no concrete evidence, no facts that serve to individualize the mother and her feelings.

Most writing is somewhere between these extremes. The average writer's temptation is always to neglect the facts and overdo the interpretations. Good writers withhold their opinions until the reader is eager to know them and indeed finds himself trying to discover what the writer "really thinks" about a character or a situation.

Doubtless you have observed that a central aspect of your interest in this selection is your curiosity about the author's opinion of Mr. Flood. And not only is it partly withheld—it is also a complex and an unusual opinion. This selection is, we might say, dedicated to an ideal of individuality. It is without cant, pose, or pretense: Mr. Flood fascinates the author because he is so entirely individual. He is an entity, integral and dense with life, even though a considerable part of his personality is a pose or, to put it more kindly, an achievement of which he is conscious and proud. You may write an essay on some aspect of this matter: the extent to which all characters are acting a part, the gap between the "true" self and the image one attempts to fill, or between the successful public self and the felt personal self. The essay must somehow be loaded with facts, for it is only with facts—and the most carefully chosen words—that you can make your points vivid and interesting.

Across the Prairies

MARK TWAIN

1. Along about an hour after breakfast we saw the first prairie-dog villages, the first antelope, and the first wolf. If I remember rightly, this latter was the regular *cayote* (pronounced ky-*o*-te) of the farther deserts. And if it *was*, he was not a pretty creature, or respectable 5 either, for I got well acquainted with his race afterward, and can speak with confidence. The cayote is a long, slim, sick and sorry-looking skeleton, with a gray wolf-skin stretched over it, a tolerably bushy tail that forever sags down with a despairing expression of forsakenness and misery, a furtive and evil eye, and 10 a long, sharp face, with slightly lifted lip and exposed teeth. He has a general slinking expression all over. The cayote is a living, breathing allegory of Want. He is *always* hungry. He is always poor, out of luck and friendless. The meanest creatures despise him and even the fleas would desert him for a velocipede. He is 15 so spiritless and cowardly that even while his exposed teeth are pretending a threat, the rest of his face is apologizing for it. And he is *so* homely!—so scrawny, and ribby, and coarse-haired, and pitiful.

2. When he sees you he lifts his lip and lets a flash of his teeth 20 out, and then turns a little out of the course he was pursuing, depresses his head a bit, and strikes a long, soft-footed trot through the sage-brush, glancing over his shoulder at you, from time to time, till he is about out of easy pistol range, and then he stops and takes a deliberate survey of you; he will trot fifty 25 yards and stop again—another fifty and stop again; and finally the gray of his gliding body blends with the gray of the sage-brush,

From *Roughing It.*

and he disappears. All this is when you make no demonstration
against him; but if you do, he develops a livelier interest in his
30 journey, and instantly electrifies his heels and puts such a deal
of real estate between himself and your weapon, that by the time
you have raised the hammer you see that you need a minie rifle,
and by the time you have got him in line you need a rifled
cannon, and by the time you have "drawn a bead" on him you see
35 well enough that nothing but an unusually long-winded streak of
lightning could reach him where he is now. But if you start a
swift-footed dog after him, you will enjoy it ever so much—
especially if it is a dog that has a good opinion of himself and
has been brought up to think he knows something about speed.
40 The cayote will go swinging gently off on that deceitful trot of
his, and every little while he will smile a fraudful smile over his
shoulder that will fill that dog entirely full of encouragement
and worldly ambition, and make him lay his head still lower to
the ground, and stretch his neck further to the front, and pant
45 more fiercely, and stick his tail out straighter behind, and move
his furious legs with a yet wilder frenzy, and leave a broader
and broader, and higher and denser cloud of desert sand smoking
behind, and marking his long wake across the level plain! And
all this time the dog is only a short twenty feet behind the cayote,
50 and to save the soul of him he cannot understand why it is that
he cannot get perceptibly closer; and he begins to get aggravated,
and it makes him madder and madder to see how gently the
cayote glides along and never pants or sweats or ceases to smile;
and he grows still more and more incensed to see how shamefully
55 he has been taken in by an entire stranger, and what an ignoble
swindle that long, calm, soft-footed trot is; and next he notices
that he is getting fagged, and that the cayote actually has to
slacken speed a little to keep from running away from him—and
then that town-dog is mad in earnest, and he begins to strain
60 and weep and swear, and paw the sand higher than ever, and
reach for the cayote with concentrated and desperate energy.
This "spurt" finds him six feet behind the gliding enemy, and two
miles from his friends. And then, in the instant that a wild new
hope is lighting up his face, the cayote turns and smiles blandly
65 upon him once more, and with a something about it which seems

to say: "Well, I shall have to tear myself away from you, bub—business is business, and it will not do for me to be fooling along this way all day"—and forthwith there is a rushing sound, and the sudden splitting of a long crack through the atmosphere, and behold that dog is solitary and alone in the midst of a vast solitude.

3. It makes his head swim. He stops, and looks all around; climbs the nearest sand-mound, and gazes into the distance; shakes his head reflectively, and then, without a word, he turns and jogs along back to his train, and takes up a humble position under the hindmost wagon, and feels unspeakably mean, and looks ashamed, and hangs his tail at half-mast for a week. And for as much as a year after that, whenever there is a great hue and cry after a cayote, that dog will merely glance in that direction without emotion, and apparently observe to himself, "I believe I do not wish any of the pie."

4. The cayote lives chiefly in the most desolate and forbidding deserts, along with the lizard, the jackass rabbit and the raven, and gets an uncertain and precarious living, and earns it. He seems to subsist almost wholly on the carcasses of oxen, mules, and horses that have dropped out of emigrant trains and died, and upon windfalls of carrion, and occasional legacies of offal bequeathed to him by white men who have been opulent enough to have something better to butcher than condemned army bacon. He will eat anything in the world that his first cousins, the desert-frequenting tribes of Indians, will, and they will eat anything they can bite. It is a curious fact that these latter are the only creatures known to history who will eat nitro-glycerine and ask for more if they survive.

5. The cayote of the deserts beyond the Rocky Mountains has a peculiarly hard time of it, owing to the fact that his relations, the Indians, are just as apt to be the first to detect a seductive scent on the desert breeze, and follow the fragrance to the late ox it emanated from, as he is himself; and when this occurs he has to content himself with sitting off at a little distance watching those people strip off and dig out everything edible, and walk off with it. Then he and the waiting ravens explore the skeleton and polish the bones. It is considered that the cayote, and the obscene

bird, and the Indian of the desert, testify their blood kinship
105 with each other in that they live together in the waste places of
the earth on terms of perfect confidence and friendship, while
hating all other creatures and yearning to assist at their funerals.
He does not mind going a hundred miles to breakfast, and a
hundred and fifty to dinner, because he is sure to have three or
110 four days between meals, and he can just as well be traveling and
looking at the scenery as lying around doing nothing and adding
to the burdens of his parents.

6. We soon learned to recognize the sharp, vicious bark of the
cayote as it came across the murky plain at night to disturb our
115 dreams among the mail-sacks; and remembering his forlorn
aspect and his hard fortune, made shift to wish him the blessed
novelty of a long day's good luck and a limitless larder the
morrow.

※※※※※※※※※※※

Humorous writing depends for its effects on surprise, whether
it be from incongruity, exaggeration, or understatement. Mark
Twain here already writes as an American spokesman to the
world; at the height of his career he became the most famous
American. This position gave him the opportunity to parade himself under various guises, while the contrast between the serious
and the extreme or ridiculous gave him further resources of fun-
making. One of his favorite guises was that of a man who hates
the whole human race but sets forth his objections in such whimsical language that no one can take the matter seriously when
the manner is so diverting. The *play* of Mark Twain's language
shimmers over incongruities of manner and matter.

1. The coyote (as it is now spelled) lives on carrion, like the
jackal and the hyena of Africa; like kites, vultures, and buzzards,
these creatures are repulsive. Mark Twain surprises us by trans-
posing this repulsiveness into another key; the process begins
with the word "respectable" (5) and is carried along with
"sorry-looking" (8) and "despairing expression of forsakenness and misery" (9–10). Define the characteristics thus substituted for repulsiveness and show how they are developed and

elaborated by other terms in the next four lines. Then show where Twain leaves this path for ridiculous exaggeration.

2. Which of the elements of humor that we have listed is involved in the transition from Par. 1 to Par. 2?

3. The theme of Par. 2 can be put in a word: *speed*. Mark the divisions of the development of this theme and comment on the *order* followed; there is a principle that takes you from the first to the second division; what shift of substance and method goes with the third division?

4. The long sentence, lines 20–28, is loosely composed, with "and then . . . and then . . . and finally," as a child might tell a story. Is this carelessness, or for the ear, or has it some relation to the subject? Does the length of the next sentence (28–36) have the same quality?

5. Now, with the anecdote of the dog, we can identify more of the surprises that make humor. There is, first, a change of attitude toward the coyote; define it. There is also an incongruous *moral* attitude attributed to the dog; it begins with "fraudful," line 41, mark the words in which it is extended. What seems to be the author's attitude toward the dog? It will take some defining.

6. How does the *moral* attitude (Ques. 5) lead into or prepare for "weep" and "swear," (59–60) and how do these words contribute to the humor?

7. In a number of instances Twain places a comma before the second half of a compound predicate in order to emphasize the humorous rhythms of his prose. Identify these commas; they are numerous in the selection.

8. Does Par. 3 detract from the unity of the piece? Or does it contribute to the description of the coyote? Or does it serve another aspect of the whole piece?

9. Paragraph 4 introduces what third major theme on the coyote? Define the figurative thread that extends through "windfalls . . . legacies . . . bequeathed . . . opulent" (87–88).

10. Mark the words and phrases in Par. 4 which contribute to your image of Mark Twain, rather than to that of the coyote.

What new prejudice of the author becomes the substance of the next paragraph? Does it shock you?

11.   Just when it seems that Twain is more interested in the Indian than in the coyote, he returns to his original theme in the last sentence of Par. 5. But here is the sentence more about the coyote, or the author? What two themes of the previous paragraphs does it touch upon?

12.   Edward Gibbon would as soon undress in public as write some of the sentences in Par. 2; yet he is far from humorless. Reading aloud passages from Gibbon and Twain may give you material for a short essay comparing their personal and social worlds.

13.   In the two following poems, one of which even has some of the humorous irrationality found in Twain, machines are treated in much the same way that Twain treats the coyote. Write an essay exploring the similarities and/or differences of treatment in the three pieces.

Alternatively, use your study of them to guide you in writing your own theme about an animal or machine. Try to connect the subject to your own experiences by using Twain's device of describing its characteristics in human terms. Explore the thing's "emotions" or "feelings": How does a pony that carries children in a circle all day feel about his passengers? What does your car feel when you "operate" on it? What does the huge IBM machine think of the people who constantly feed it questions? What does a dog on a hunting trip think about?

Stephen Spender's poem is much more lyrical, intense, and romantic than an essay based on these suggestions would be. If you want to be more intense, choose a subject about which you have strong feelings and serious thoughts (perhaps a skyscraper or ocean liner).

THE EGG AND THE MACHINE

ROBERT FROST

He gave the solid rail a hateful kick.
From far away there came an answering tick
And then another tick. He knew the code:
His hate had roused an engine up the road.
He wished when he had had the track alone

He had attacked it with a club or stone
And bent some rail wide open like a switch
So as to wreck the engine in the ditch.
Too late though, now, he had himself to thank.
Its click was rising to a nearer clank.
Here it came breasting like a horse in skirts.
(He stood well back for fear of scalding squirts.)
Then for a moment all there was was size
Confusion and a roar that drowned the cries
He raised against the gods in the machine.
Then once again the sandbank lay serene.
The traveler's eye picked up a turtle trail,
Between the dotted feet a streak of tail,
And followed it to where he made out vague
But certain signs of buried turtle's egg;
And probing with one finger not too rough,
He found suspicious sand, and sure enough,
The pocket of a little turtle mine.
If there was one egg in it there were nine,
Torpedo-like, with shell of gritty leather
All packed in sand to wait the trump together.
"You'd better not disturb me any more,"
He told the distance, "I am armed for war.
The next machine that has the power to pass
Will get this plasm in its goggle glass."

THE EXPRESS

STEPHEN SPENDER

After the first powerful plain manifesto
The black statement of pistons, without more fuss
But gliding like a queen, she leaves the station.
Without bowing and with restrained unconcern
She passes the houses which humbly crowd outside,
The gasworks and at last the heavy page
Of death, printed by gravestones in the cemetery.
Beyond the town there lies the open country
Where, gathering speed, she acquires mystery,
The luminous self-possession of ships on ocean.
It is now she begins to sing—at first quite low
Then loud, and at last with a jazzy madness—

The song of her whistle screaming at curves,
Of deafening tunnels, brakes, innumerable bolts.
And always light, aerial, underneath
Goes the elate meter of her wheels.
Steaming through metal landscape on her lines
She plunges new eras of wild happiness
Where speed throws up strange shapes, broad curves
And parallels clean like the steel of guns.
At last, further than Edinburgh or Rome,
Beyond the crest of the world, she reaches night
Where only a low streamline brightness
Of phosphorus on the tossing hills is white.
Ah, like a comet through flames she moves entranced
Wrapt in her music no bird song, no, nor bough
Breaking with honey buds, shall ever equal.

The Green Donkey-Driver

ROBERT LOUIS STEVENSON

1. The bell of Monastier was just striking nine as I got quit of these preliminary troubles and descended the hill through the common. As long as I was within sight of the windows, a secret shame and the fear of some laughable defeat withheld me from tampering with Modestine. She tripped along upon her four small hoofs with a sober daintiness of gait; from time to time she shook her ears or her tail; and she looked so small under the bundle that my mind misgave me. We got across the ford without difficulty—there was no doubt about the matter, she was docility itself—and once on the other bank, where the road begins to mount through pine-woods, I took in my right hand the unhallowed staff, and with a quaking spirit applied it to the donkey. Modestine brisked up her pace for perhaps three steps, and then relapsed into her former minuet. Another application had the same effect, and so with the third. I am worthy the name of an Englishman, and it goes against my conscience to lay my hand rudely on a female. I desisted, and looked her all over from head to foot; the poor brute's knees were trembling and her breathing was distressed; it was plain that she could go no faster on a hill. God forbid, thought I, that I should brutalise this innocent creature; let her go at her own pace, and let me patiently follow.

2. What that pace was, there is no word mean enough to describe; it was something as much slower than a walk as a walk is slower than a run; it kept me hanging on each foot for an incredible length of time; in five minutes it exhausted the spirit and set up a fever in all the muscles of the leg. And yet I had to keep

From *Travels With a Donkey*.

73

close at hand and measure my advance exactly upon hers; for if I dropped a few yards into the rear, or went on a few yards ahead, 30 Modestine came instantly to a halt and began to browse. The thought that this was to last from here to Alais nearly broke my heart. Of all conceivable journeys, this promised to be the most tedious. I tried to tell myself it was a lovely day; I tried to charm my foreboding spirit with tobacco; but I had a vision ever present 35 to me of the long, long roads, up hill and down dale, and a pair of figures ever infinitesimally moving, foot by foot, a yard to the minute, and, like things enchanted in a nightmare, approaching no nearer to the goal.

3. In the mean time there came up behind us a tall peasant, 40 perhaps forty years of age, of an ironical snuffy countenance, and arrayed in the green tail-coat of the country. He overtook us hand over hand, and stopped to consider our pitiful advance.

"Your donkey," says he, "is very old?"

I told him, I believed not.

45 Then, he supposed, we had come far.

I told him, we had but newly left Monastier.

"*Et vous marchez comme ça!*" cried he; and, throwing back his head, he laughed long and heartily. I watched him, half prepared to feel offended, until he had satisfied his mirth; and then, "You 50 must have no pity on these animals," said he; and, plucking a switch out of a thicket, he began to lace Modestine about the stern-works, uttering a cry. The rogue pricked up her ears and broke into a good round pace, which she kept up without flagging, and without exhibiting the least symptom of distress, as long as the 55 peasant kept beside us. Her former panting and shaking had been, I regret to say, a piece of comedy.

4. My *deus ex machina,* before he left me, supplied some excellent, if inhumane, advice; presented me with the switch, which he declared she would feel more tenderly than my cane; and 60 finally taught me the true cry or masonic word of donkey-drivers, "Proot!" All the time, he regarded me with a comical incredulous air, which was embarrassing to confront; and smiled over my donkey-driving, as I might have smiled over his orthography, or his green tail-coat. But it was not my turn for the moment. . . .

65 5. I hurried over my midday meal, and was early forth again.

But, alas, as we climbed the interminable hill upon the other side, "Proot!" seemed to have lost its virtue. I prooted like a lion, I prooted mellifluously like a sucking-dove; but Modestine would be neither softened nor intimidated. She held doggedly to her pace; nothing but a blow would move her, and that only for a second. I must follow at her heels, incessantly belabouring. A moment's pause in this ignoble toil, and she relapsed into her own private gait. I think I never heard of any one in as mean a situation. I must reach the lake of Bouchet, where I meant to camp, before sundown, and, to have even a hope of this, I must instantly maltreat this uncomplaining animal. The sound of my own blows sickened me. Once, when I looked at her, she had a faint resemblance to a lady of my acquaintance who formerly loaded me with kindness; and this increased my horror of my cruelty.

6. To make matters worse, we encountered another donkey, ranging at will upon the roadside; and this other donkey chanced to be a gentleman. He and Modestine met nickering for joy, and I had to separate the pair and beat down their young romance with a renewed and feverish bastinado. If the other donkey had had the heart of a male under his hide, he would have fallen upon me tooth and hoof; and this was a kind of consolation—he was plainly unworthy of Modestine's affection. But the incident saddened me, as did everything that spoke of my donkey's sex.

7. It was blazing hot up the valley, windless, with vehement sun upon my shoulders; and I had to labour so consistently with my stick that the sweat ran into my eyes. Every five minutes, too, the pack, the basket, and the pilot-coat would take an ugly slew to one side or the other; and I had to stop Modestine, just when I had got her to a tolerable pace of about two miles an hour, to tug, push, shoulder, and readjust the load. And at last, in the village of Ussel, saddle and all, the whole hypothec turned round and grovelled in the dust below the donkey's belly. She, none better pleased, incontinently drew up and seemed to smile; and a party of one man, two women, and two children came up, and, standing round me in a half-circle, encouraged her by their example.

8. I had the devil's own trouble to get the thing righted; and the instant I had done so, without hesitation, it toppled and fell down upon the other side. Judge if I was hot! And yet not a hand

was offered to assist me. The man, indeed, told me I ought to
105 have a package of a different shape. I suggested, if he knew nothing better to the point in my predicament, he might hold his
tongue. And the good-natured dog agreed with me smilingly. It
was the most despicable fix. I must plainly content myself with the
pack for Modestine, and take the following items for my own
110 share of the portage: a cane, a quart flask, a pilot-jacket heavily
weighted in the pockets, two pounds of black bread, and an open
basket full of meats and bottles. I believe I may say I am not
devoid of greatness of soul; for I did not recoil from this infamous
burden. I disposed it, Heaven knows how, so as to be mildly
115 portable, and then proceeded to steer Modestine through the
village. She tried, as was indeed her invariable habit, to enter
every house and every courtyard in the whole length; and, en-
cumbered as I was, without a hand to help myself, no words can
render an idea of my difficulties. A priest, with six or seven others,
120 was examining a church in process of repair, and he and his
acolytes laughed loudly as they saw my plight. I remembered
having laughed myself when I had seen good men struggling with
adversity in the person of a jackass, and the recollection filled
me with penitence. That was in my old light days, before this
125 trouble came upon me. God knows at least that I shall never laugh
again, thought I. But O, what a cruel thing is a farce to those engaged in it!

✳✳✳✳✳✳✳✳✳✳✳

1. The tone of this piece, which is rather special, can be located in the words, the phrases, and the ideas.
Certain words have a special tone. What do the following tell
about the writer's attitude toward *himself* and his *subject?*

> got quit (2)
> secret shame (4)
> laughable defeat (5)
> tampering (5)
> looked so small (8)
> mind misgave me (8–9)
> unhallowed staff (12)
> quaking spirit (13)

How does the idea introduced by "secret shame" appear in the remaining items on the list? More than the writer's exasperation with the animal is portrayed by these terms—his fear of something in himself and also of something other than either of these two. What are they? How nearly does "shame" describe the emotion? What overtones do the words that follow add to "shame"?

2.   What gait or movement of a donkey can be called a *minuet?*

3.   Now a further set of terms:

"rudely on a female" (17) closely followed by "poor brute"
"it was plain (20)
"innocent creature" (21)

Through these we have come to a point where the narrator has *assumed a moral position* with respect to his donkey. Define it in a sentence, not neglecting the cause of it, imbedded in "secret shame," which makes it ludicrous.

4.   The reversal that follows requires two passages. Give each a title. At what points in Par. 3 does the author *tell* us about Modestine's treachery? Try your hand at a *dramatic*, concrete rendition of the same facts. Has the author's explanation weakened the effect of his story compared to what he might have achieved with more concrete facts?

5.   As the donkey regains the upper hand in Par. 5, the author returns to

ignoble toil (72)
private gait (73
mean situation (73)
uncomplaining animal (76)

and

resemblance to a lady (77–78)

which recall the tone of what earlier passages? Show precisely where the tone corresponds, where it diverges, and where it adds to the tone of the passage depending upon "secret shame."

6.   Adjectives modify nouns, pronouns. The adjectives in Par. 1 are *preliminary, secret, laughable, four, small, sober, small, other, unhallowed, quaking, three, former, another, same, poor, plain, innocent.* Which are *predicate* adjectives? Define one.

Trembling and *distressed* (19) are participles, which are forms of a verb ending in *-ed* or *-ing*. They may be considered verbs or adjectives; the difference is generally obvious, but sometimes not. Here *trembling* is probably part of the verb, whereas *distressed* is an adjective. Can you state the difference that justifies the classification? Underline the rest of the words ending in *-ed* or *-ing* and decide whether they are parts of the verb or adjectives.

Underline once the adjectives in Pars. 2–5, twice the predicate adjectives.

7.   It has been said frequently that "the adjective is the enemy of the noun," that is, that the force of a strong word is weakened by a modifier. The most obvious instance is *very*, which generally weakens the word it is intended to intensify. Examine all the adjectives you have marked and decide whether any of them weakens the effect of the noun it modifies. Your instructor may ask you to go through the whole selection for this exercise. You will learn a good deal about writing from such a close scrutiny of modifiers.

8.   Compare and contrast Stevenson's humor with Mark Twain's. The differences are great; try to put your finger exactly on the similarities.

9.   "Mixed emotions" have been irreverently defined as seeing one's mother-in-law going over a cliff in one's new Cadillac. Stevenson has given us a much subtler, but still comical exercise in mixed emotions. Notice that he maintains a dual attitude toward himself as well as toward the donkey and the various spectators. The duality of attitude toward himself is controlled by his careful management of a dual point of view in *time:* he is *in* the experience, and he is regarding it also from the perspective that corresponds, roughly, to that of his reader. You may write your essay about a predicament in which you found yourself at some time, giving special attention to discovering and maintaining just the right balance between how you felt then and how you feel as you tell about it.

Ross As Editor

JAMES THURBER

1. One afternoon
Sherwood Anderson was brought into Ross's office and introduced
to the editor. On such occasions, when there was time, Ross was
briefed by one of us as to the nature and stature of a visiting
author's work—not that it ever did much good. Ross stood in awe 5
and reverence of no writer. He had been through too much with
too many of them. I am sure that, after the introduction, he said,
"Hi, Anderson," in his large freewheeling way, and then launched
into whatever came into his mind. This meeting was notable for
one of his reckless literary pronouncements: "There hasn't been a 10
good short story writer in America, Anderson, since O. Henry
died." I wasn't there and I don't know how this affected Anderson,
but he later sold Ross five short stories.

2. I was present, though, when Ross met Paul Nash, having
ushered the English painter into the editor's office myself one 15
morning in 1931. The day before, I had explained to Ross that
Nash was on his way to Pittsburgh to serve as one of the three
foreign judges of the annual Carnegie Exhibition of Modern Art,
but had stopped over in New York to meet Otto Soglow, Milt
Gross, and other favorite cartoonists of his, for he was easily 20
admirer-in-chief of American comic art and artists. I had also told
Ross that Nash was a keen collector of human curiosa, and had
long wanted to talk with the editor of the *New Yorker.*

3. "Hi, Nash," Ross began. "There are only two phony arts,
painting and music." Nash was a man of humor and imagination, 25
whose eyes twinkled, and never darkened, when outrageous

opinion raised its aggressive head. He was pretty good at holding untenable positions himself. When Nash and I finally left Ross's office, the Englishman said, "He is like your skyscrapers. They are
30 unbelievable, but there they are."

4.   Ross's knowledge of the two phony arts was, it is safe to say, flimsy. I never heard of his going to a show of paintings, and he would have been as unhappy at a symphony concert as at a lecture on dialectical materialism. He had certainly encountered
35 modern painting in colored reproductions and on the walls of the apartments of some of his friends and acquaintances, but he must have viewed them disconsolately, as if they were jumbled paragraphs of prose that needed straightening out. Nobody ever heard him sing, or even hum, a single bar of any song, and whistling set
40 his teeth on edge. "His mind is uncluttered by culture," said a man at the Players Club, during one of those impromptu panel discussions of Harold Ross that often began when writers and artists got together. "That's why he can give prose and pictures the benefit of the clearest concentration of any editor in the world." It
45 wasn't as simple as that, for there was more than clear concentration behind the scowl and the searchlight glare that he turned on manuscripts, proofs, and drawings. He had a sound sense, a unique, almost intuitive perception of what was wrong with something, incomplete or out of balance, understated or overem-
50 phasized. He reminded me of an army scout riding at the head of a troop of cavalry who suddenly raises his hand in a green and silent valley and says, "Indians," although to the ordinary eye and ear there is no faintest sign or sound of anything alarming. Some of us writers were devoted to him, a few disliked him heartily,
55 others came out of his office after conferences as from a side show, a juggling act, or a dentist's office, but almost everybody would rather have had the benefit of his criticism than that of any other editor on earth. His opinions were voluble, stabbing, and grinding, but they succeeded somehow in refreshing your knowledge of
60 yourself and renewing your interest in your work.

5. Having a manuscript under Ross's scrutiny was like putting your car in the hands of a skilled mechanic, not an automotive engineer with a bachelor of science degree, but a guy who knows what makes a motor go, and sputter, and wheeze, and sometimes

come to a dead stop; a man with an ear for the faintest body 65
squeak as well as the loudest engine rattle. When you first gazed,
appalled, upon an uncorrected proof of one of your stories or
articles, each margin had a thicket of queries and complaints—
one writer got a hundred and forty-four on one profile. It was as
though you beheld the works of your car spread all over the gar- 70
age floor, and the job of getting the thing together again and
making it work seemed impossible. Then you realized that Ross
was trying to make your Model T or old Stutz Bearcat into a
Cadillac or Rolls-Royce. He was at work with the tools of his
unflagging perfectionism, and, after an exchange of growls or 75
snarls, you set to work to join him in his enterprise.

6. Ross's marginal questions and comments were sometimes
mere quibbling or hairsplitting, and a few of them invariably
revealed his profound ignorance in certain areas of life and learning and literature, while others betrayed his pet and petty preju- 80
dices. You had to wade through these and ignore them, as you
did his occasional brief marginal essays on unrelated or completely irrelevant subjects. One or two of his trusted associate
editors would sometimes intercept a proof and cross out the im-
pertinent and immaterial Rossisms, but I always insisted that they 85
be left in, for they were the stains and labels of a Ross that never
ceased to amuse me.

7. The blurs and imperfections his scout's eye always caught
drew from his pencil such designations as *unclear, repetition,
cliché, ellipsis,* and now and then blunter words. He knew when 90
you had tired and were writing carelessly, and when you were
"just monkeying around here," or going out on a limb, or writing
fancy, or showing off. His "Who he?" became famous not only in
the office but outside, and ten years ago was the title of a piece
on Ross written by Henry Pringle. Joe Liebling once had "Who 95
he?" painted on the door of his office, to the bewilderment of
strangers who wondered what kind of business Liebling could be
in. Sometimes this query put a careful finger on someone who had
not been clearly identified, and at other times it showed up the
gaps in Ross's knowledge of historical, contemporary, or literary 100
figures. (He once said that only two names were familiar to every
reader in the civilized world: Houdini and Sherlock Holmes.)

8. I remember that Ross once told me, after reading a casual of mine, "You must have dropped about eight lines out of this in
105 your final rewrite." The thing ran smoothly enough, it seemed to me when I reread it in his office, but I went back and checked my next to last draft. Ross had been wrong, I had dropped only seven lines.

✳✳✳✳✳✳✳✳✳✳✳✳

This selection is by one of the great humorists of our time, about the most famous American magazine editor of the century —Harold Ross of the *New Yorker* magazine. As in Joseph Mitchell's account of Mr. Flood (p. 59), we are interested in both author and subject; but here there is a sense of actuality— of history—that adds weight to every word. For both Ross and Thurber are legends of the twentieth-century cult of personality: every word, gesture, action of the Great Ones is sought out and treasured.

1. List the *unnamed* qualities of Ross that are indicated by Thurber's details of evidence in the first three paragraphs: (he is shy, tactless, impulsive . . . What else?) Match the concrete details with the general qualities.

2. Why is it "safe to say" (31)?

3. What is the precise force of *disconsolately* in line 37?

4. Describe the picture evoked by "impromptu panel discussions" (41); what word in the phrase is most striking and effective?

5. A keynote of Ross's character is struck early, with, "He had been through too much with too many of them." (6–7) To what extent does this sentence reveal Ross's own words and attitude toward writers, to what extent Thurber's amused interpretation of Ross's manner? How does *freewheeling* relate to *reckless* (8, 10)? This question may require some research (hint: look at the automobile advertisements for 1928–30); the two words comment on precisely what aspect of Ross?

6. To what key term in the previous sentence does the analogy

of the army scout (50–53) refer? Exactly how good is it as a comment on the phrase? You may find that it is much better than appears at first glance. Next, look through the selection to find words and phrases which modify or influence this scout image to make it partly comic. If, for example, you actually see Ross as the scout, holding up his hand and saying, "Indians," why is the picture amusing? Why is it apt?

7.   From the scout analogy, we proceed in Par. 5 to see Ross as a mechanic. Are any of the comic elements carried over into this image? What word in this paragraph enriches the idea introduced by *disconsolately* (37)?

8.   We have been conducted through an apparently rambling series of facts, anecdotes, colorful descriptive terms, and humorous analogies; straight reporting takes over for *most* of Par. 6— and again for *most* of Par. 7. In each case, what deflects the author from his straight reporting?

9.   You should now be able to analyze this selection in terms of Ross's characteristic of *eccentricity* and *talent*. List the actions reported, the personal and intellectual qualities exhibited, the effects of Ross on his business and social environment and the rôle of Thurber as associate and interpreter. Is the treatment orderly or disorderly? Is there, that is, a systematic building up of a picture—or does the writer merely let his associations carry him at random?

10.   With a piece that provides such insight into the painstaking labors of professional writers, it will be rewarding to scrutinize some of Thurber's terms and explain exactly what they mean and suggest: *dialectical materialism* (33), *curiosa* (22), *darkened* (26), *uncluttered* (40), *searchight glare* (46), *stabbing, grinding* (58), *guy* (63), *complaints* (68), *unflagging perfectionism* (75), *stains and labels* (86), *out on a limb* (92), and *writing fancy* (92). Find specific terms or incidents to illustrate each of the three points in

        . . . others came out of his office after conferences as from
        a side show, a juggling act, or a dentist's office (55–56).

11.   Thurber's punctuation is in general perfectly formal but here and there somewhat loose to match a studied informality of style. This sentence, for example, uses the simple conjunction *and* in-

stead of an adverb that would indicate the logic of his thought
more exactly:

> I wasn't there and I don't know how this affected Anderson,
> but he later sold Ross five short stories.

What causal relation is left for the reader to infer? What informality of punctuation in this sentence blends with this informality
of manner?

The non-structural comma between compound elements
appears today, much as it did in the eighteenth century, in positions where emphasis calls for a break in the flow of the sentence.
Examples here occur only in lines 18, 22, and 26. Show why the
commas in lines 8, 24, 75, 78, 85, 94, and 99 do *not* fall in this
category.

In line 107 there is a comma where strict punctuation would
demand what? Why has Thurber used the comma?

12.   It takes a lifetime to be able to write like James Thurber,
plus a special talent, plus an enormous range of experience. But
you can do a sketch of someone you know well *if* you will study
him closely enough to gather a substantial array of facts. Then if
you plan to emulate Thurber further you will have to think about
your own attitude and just how much of it you will reveal from
paragraph to paragraph of your essay. If you have a good subject
and gather your facts conscientiously, you will probably find that
you are engaged in a longer essay than you had expected.

Lulu

ISAK DINESEN

1. Lulu was a young antelope of the bushbuck tribe, which is perhaps the prettiest of all the African antelopes. They are a little bigger than the fallow-deer; they live in the woods, or in the bush, and are shy and fugitive, so that they are not seen as often as the antelopes of the 5 plains. But the Ngong Hills, and the surrounding country, were good places for bushbuck, and if you had your camp in the hills, and were out hunting in the early morning, or at sunset, you would see them come out of the bush into the glades, and as the rays of the sun fell upon them their coats shone red as copper. 10 The male has a pair of delicately turned horns.

2. Lulu became a member of my household in this way:

3. I drove one morning from the farm to Nairobi. My mill on the farm had burnt down a short time before, and I had had to drive into town many times to get the insurance settled and paid 15 out; in this early morning I had my head filled with figures and estimates. As I came driving along the Ngong Road a little group of Kikuyu children shouted to me from the roadside, and I saw that they were holding a very small bushbuck up for me to see. I knew that they would have found the fawn in the bush, and that 20 now they wanted to sell it to me, but I was late for an appointment in Nairobi, and I had no thought for this sort of thing, so I drove on.

4. When I was coming back in the evening and was driving past the same place, there was again a great shout from the side 25 of the road and the small party was still there, a little tired and

disappointed, for they may have tried to sell the fawn to other people passing by in the course of the day, but keen now to get the deal through before the sun was down, and they held up the
30 fawn high to tempt me. But I had had a long day in town, and some adversity about the insurance, so that I did not care to stop or talk, and I just drove on past them. I did not even think of them when I was back in my house, and dined and went to bed.

5. The moment that I had fallen asleep I was woken up again
35 by a great feeling of terror. The picture of the boys and the small buck, which had now collected and taken shape, stood out before me, clearly, as if it had been painted, and I sat up in bed as appalled as if someone had been trying to choke me. What, I thought, would become of the fawn in the hands of the captors
40 who had stood with it in the heat of the long day, and had held it up by its joined legs? It was surely too young to eat on its own. I myself had driven past it twice on the same day, like the priest and the Levite in one, and had given no thought to it, and now, at this moment, where was it? I got up in a real panic and woke
45 up all my houseboys. I told them that the fawn must be found and brought me in the morning, or they would all of them get their dismissal from my service. They were immediately up to the idea. Two of my boys had been in the car with me the same day, and had not shown the slightest interest in the children or the fawn;
50 now they came forward, and gave the others a long list of details of the place and the hour and of the family of the boys. It was a moonlight night; my people all took off and spread in the landscape in a lively discussion of the situation; I heard them expatiating on the fact that they were all to be dismissed in case the
55 bushbuck were not found.

6. Early next morning when Farah brought me in my tea, Juma came in with him and carried the fawn in his arms. It was a female, and we named her Lulu, which I was told was the Swaheli word for a pearl.

60 7. Lulu by that time was only as big as a cat, with large quiet purple eyes. She had such delicate legs that you feared they would not bear being folded up and unfolded again, as she lay down and rose up. Her ears were smooth as silk and exceedingly expressive.

Her nose was as black as a truffle. Her diminutive hoofs gave her all the air of a young Chinese lady of the old school, with laced feet. It was a rare experience to hold such a perfect thing in your hands.

8. Lulu soon adapted herself to the house and its inhabitants and behaved as if she were at home. During the first weeks the polished floors in the rooms were a problem in her life, and when she got outside the carpets her legs went away from her to all four sides; it looked catastrophic but she did not let it worry her much and in the end she learnt to walk on the bare floors with a sound like a succession of little angry finger-taps. She was extraordinarily neat in all her habits. She was headstrong already as a child, but when I stopped her from doing the things she wanted to do, she behaved as if she said: Anything rather than a scene.

9. Kamante brought her up on a sucking-bottle, and he also shut her up at night, for we had to be careful of her as the leopards were up round the house after nightfall. So she held to him and followed him about. From time to time when he did not do what she wanted, she gave his thin legs a hard butt with her young head, and she was so pretty that you could not help, when you looked upon the two together, seeing them as a new paradoxical illustration to the tale of the Beauty and the Beast. On the strength of this great beauty and gracefulness, Lulu obtained for herself a commanding position in the house, and was treated with respect by all. . . .

10. Now my dogs understood Lulu's power and position in the house. The arrogance of the great hunters was like water with her. She pushed them away from the milk-bowl and from their favourite places in front of the fire. I had tied a small bell on a rein round Lulu's neck, and there came a time when the dogs, when they heard the jingle of it approaching through the rooms, would get up resignedly from their warm beds by the fireplace, and go and lie down in some other part of the room. Still nobody could be of a gentler demeanour than Lulu was when she came and lay down, in the manner of a perfect lady who demurely gathers her skirts about her and will be in no one's way. She drank the milk with a polite, pernickety mien, as if she had been pressed by an

overkind hostess. She insisted on being scratched behind the ears, in a pretty forbearing way, like a young wife who pertly permits her husband a caress.

11. When Lulu grew up and stood in the flower of her young
105 loveliness she was a slim delicately rounded doe, from her nose to her toes unbelievably beautiful. She looked like a minutely painted illustration to Heine's song of the wise and gentle gazelles by the flow of the river Ganges.

12. But Lulu was not really gentle, she had the so-called devil
110 in her. She had, to the highest degree, the feminine trait of appearing to be exclusively on the defensive, concentrated on guarding the integrity of her being, when she was really, with every force in her, bent upon the offensive. Against whom? Against the whole world. Her moods grew beyond control or computation,
115 and she would go for my horse, if he displeased her. I remembered old Hagenbeck in Hamburg, who had said that of all animal races, the carnivora included, the deer are the least to be relied on, and that you may trust a leopard, but if you trust a young stag, sooner or later he falls upon you in the rear.

120 13. Lulu was the pride of the house even when she behaved like a real shameless young coquette; but we did not make her happy. Sometimes she walked away from the house for hours, or for a whole afternoon. Sometimes when the spirit came upon her and her discontent with her surroundings reached a climax, she
125 would perform, for the satisfaction of her own heart, on the lawn in front of the house, a war-dance, which looked like a brief zigzagged prayer to Satan.

14. "Oh Lulu," I thought, "I know that you are marvellously strong and that you can leap higher than your own height. You
130 are furious with us now, you wish that we were all dead, and indeed we should be so if you could be bothered to kill us. But the trouble is not as you think now, that we have put up obstacles too high for you to jump, and how could we possibly do that, you great leaper? It is that we have put up no obstacles at all. The
135 great strength is in you, Lulu, and the obstacles are within you as well, and the thing is, that the fullness of time has not yet come."

15. One evening Lulu did not come home and we looked out

for her in vain for a week. This was a hard blow to us all. A clear
note had gone out of the house and it seemed no better than other 140
houses. I thought of the leopards by the river and one evening I
talked about them to Kamante.

16. As usual he waited some time before he answered, to digest
my lack of insight. It was not till a few days later that he approached me upon the matter. "You believe that Lulu is dead, 145
Msabu," he said.

17. I did not like to say so straight out, but I told him I was
wondering why she did not come back.

18. "Lulu," said Kamante, "is not dead. But she is married."

19. This was pleasant, surprising, news, and I asked him how 150
he knew of it.

20. "Oh yes," he said, "she is married. She lives in the forest
with her *bwana*,"—her husband, or master. "But she has not forgotten the people; most mornings she is coming back to the house.
I lay out crushed maize to her at the back of the kitchen, then 155
just before the sun comes up, she walks round there from the
woods and eats it. Her husband is with her, but he is afraid of
the people because he has never known them. He stands below
the big white tree by the other side of the lawn. But up to the
houses he dare not come."   160

21. I told Kamante to come and fetch me when he next saw
Lulu. A few days later before sunrise he came and called me out.

22. It was a lovely morning. The last stars withdrew while we
were waiting, the sky was clear and serene but the world in which
we walked was sombre still, and profoundly silent. The grass was 165
wet; down by the trees where the ground sloped it gleamed with
the dew like dim silver. The air of the morning was cold, it had
that twinge in it which in Northern countries means that the frost
is not far away. However often you make the experience,—I
thought,—it is still impossible to believe, in this coolness and 170
shade, that the heat of the sun and the glare of the sky, in a few
hours' time, will be hard to bear. The grey mist lay upon the hills,
strangely taking shape from them; it would be bitterly cold on the
Buffalo if they were about there now, grazing on the hillside, as
in a cloud.   175

23. The great vault over our heads was gradually filled with

clarity like a glass with wine. Suddenly, gently, the summits of the hill caught the first sunlight and blushed. And slowly, as the earth leaned towards the sun, the grassy slopes at the foot of the
180 mountain turned a delicate gold, and the Masai woods lower down. And now the tops of the tall trees in the forest, on our side of the river, blushed like copper. This was the hour for the flight of the big, purple wood-pigeons which roosted by the other side of the river and came over to feed on the Cape-chestnuts in my
185 forest. They were here only for a short season in the year. The birds came surprisingly fast, like a cavalry attack of the air. For this reason the morning pigeon-shooting on the farm was popular with my friends in Nairobi; to be out by the house in time, just as the sun rose, they used to come out so early that they rounded
190 my drive with the lamps of their cars still lighted.

24. Standing like this in the limpid shadow, looking up towards the golden heights and the clear sky, you would get the feeling that you were in reality walking along the bottom of the Sea, with the currents running by you, and were gazing up towards
195 the surface of the Ocean.

25. A bird began to sing, and then I heard, a little way off in the forest, the tinkling of a bell. Yes, it was a joy, Lulu was back, and about in her old places! It came nearer, I could follow her movements by its rhythm; she was walking, stopping, walking on
200 again. A turning round one of the boys' huts brought her upon us. It suddenly became an unusual and amusing thing to see a bush-buck so close to the house. She stood immovable now, she seemed to be prepared for the sight of Kamante, but not for that of me. But she did not make off, she looked at me without fear and with-
205 out any remembrance of our skirmishes of the past or of her own ingratitude in running away without warning.

26. Lulu of the woods was a superior, independent being, a change of heart had come upon her, she was in possession. If I had happened to have known a young princess in exile, and while
210 she was still a pretender to the throne, and had met her again in her full queenly estate after she had come into her rights, our meeting would have had the same character. Lulu showed no more meanness of heart than King Louis Philippe did, when he declared that the King of France did not remember the grudges

of the Duke of Orleans. She was now the complete Lulu. The 215
spirit of offensive had gone from her; for whom, and why, should
she attack? She was standing quietly on her divine rights. She
remembered me enough to feel that I was nothing to be afraid of.
For a minute she gazed at me; her purple smoky eyes were absolutely without expression and did not wink, and I remembered 220
that the Gods or Goddesses never wink, and felt that I was face
to face with the ox-eyed Hera. She lightly nipped a leaf of grass
as she passed me, made one pretty little leap, and walked on to
the back of the kitchen, where Kamante had spread maize on the
ground.   225

✳✳✳✳✳✳✳✳✳✳

Isak Dinesen (pen name of Baroness Karen Blixen) writes a
gentle, relaxed, figurative kind of prose. She is not arguing with
the reader, not trying to convince him of anything, but sharing
her impressions and insights into Africa and its inhabitants. Her
fluid prose is filled with figures—comparisons, analogies, metaphors, similes—that reveal the quality of the author's very original
sensibility. One might not notice these figures upon first reading,
and this is as it should be. Thus the reader is not overcome by
technique and can concentrate on the experience of knowing the
quality of the author's mind.

1.   Make an outline of this selection. You will be able to identify
at least four main sections—perhaps five. Then each main division
can be sub-divided.

2.   The information in Par. 1 about the bushbuck tribe is of
three types: some of it *characterizes* Lulu, some *contrasts* with
that about Lulu, and some is just additional information about
the tribe that the author finds interesting. Identify each.

3.   How does the description in lines 13–55 add to the relaxed,
unhurried tone of the piece? What other purposes might it have?

4. (a) Go through the essay marking all the similes and metaphors. (Remember that a metaphor is a compressed simile. In the
metaphor the comparison is implied—a marble brow. In the simile
the comparison is explicit and generally contains the word *like* or
as—a brow white as marble.)

(b) Now try changing the similes into metaphors. For example, in line 10 we could say "their copper coats shone." Often a metaphor is a more powerful figure than a simile. Is this the case in the example above? How does the change affect the rhythm of the sentence?

5.   What figure of speech is used in lines 64–66? in lines 98–99? in lines 104–105?

6.   Similes and metaphors become personification when the non-human is compared to the human. Identify the personifications in this piece.

7.   "Language is fossil poetry," says Ralph Waldo Emerson in "The Poet." He means, of course, that virtually all the abstract or general words we use today, and many of the concrete ones, were originally metaphors—they represented an abstract or general idea by a natural, physical appearance. For example, *right* is etymologically *straight, wrong* is *twisted, spirit* is *wind*. We know ourselves that metaphors which we hear over and over are no longer felt as metaphors. Such is the case with words like *sunset, daybreak,* and *skyscraper*. This is part of the growth of language. Comment on the degree of metaphor still apparent in the following italicized words: (You may have to check on the etymology in a good dictionary.)

I had my *head* filled with figures and estimates (16–17)
She was *headstrong* (75)
Flower of her young loveliness (104–105)
This was a *hard blow* to us all (139)
A *clear note* had gone out of the house (139–140)
The great *vault* over our heads (176)
The summits of the hill *caught* the first sunlight and *blushed* (178)
The earth *leaned* towards the sun (179)
A *change of heart* had come upon her (208)

8.   Of course not all comparisons or analogies are metaphors or similes. Much depends on the words that connect the two ideas or things compared. Study the comparisons in lines 191–195. What words could you change to make this a simile?

9.   While some stylistic devices might more properly be examined in connection with poetry, a good prose writer will know

and use them for various effects. What device is used in each of the following, and how does it affect the passage: *beyond control or computation* (114), *smooth as silk* (63), *tops of the tall trees* (181), *from her nose to her toes* (105–106), *moonlight night* (52).

10. What does Isak Dinesen reveal about the natives in lines 48–52? In lines 143–145? |

11. How does the vocative passage of Par. 14 prepare for what comes later? If you rewrote this paragraph in the expository tone of the rest of the selection, would anything be gained in the new version? Which would be more dramatic? More effective?

12. Explain *paradoxical* (84).

13. Conventions of punctuation differ among the Western nations. There appear in this selection some Danish uses of the comma that do not appear in conventional English.

In line 22 we should have a semicolon after *thing. So* is not a conjunction but a conjunctive adverb. Other conjunctive adverbs, which are always preceded by a semicolon when they introduce a clause, are *thus, therefore, hence, however, then, nevertheless,* and *afterwards.*

Note other examples of this improper comma, as well as the comma simply joining two independent clauses, which is considered even more irregular and improper in standard English practice, in lines 109, 167, 198, 202, 204, 207.

What accounts for the superfluous comma in line 165? Find several other such commas in the selection. For example, lines 48, 50, 95.

14. A very few places in this selection reveal that the author, even though an extraordinary writer, is not native English or American: *woken* (34), *woke* (44), *spread in* (52), the sentence lines 75–77, *make* (169), and *which* (183)—we generally use *that* for a restrictive clause. Explain how these situations stretch the native idiom. Can you find others?

The Character of the American Indian

FRANCIS PARKMAN

1. Of the Indian character, much has been written foolishly, and credulously believed. By the rhapsodies of poets, the cant of sentimentalists, and the extravagance of some who should have known better, a counter-
5 feit image has been tricked out, which might seek in vain for its likeness through every corner of the habitable earth; an image bearing no more resemblance to its original than the monarch of the tragedy and the hero of the epic poem bear to their living prototypes in the palace and the camp. The shadows of his wilder-
10 ness home, and the darker mantle of his own inscrutable reserve, have made the Indian warrior a wonder and a mystery. Yet to the eye of rational observation there is nothing unintelligible in him. He is full, it is true, of contradiction. He deems himself the centre of greatness and renown; his pride is proof against the fiercest
15 torments of fire and steel; and yet the same man would beg for a dram of whiskey, or pick up a crust of bread thrown to him like a dog, from the tent door of the traveller. At one moment, he is wary and cautious to the verge of cowardice; at the next, he abandons himself to a very insanity of recklessness; and the
20 habitual self-restraint which throws an impenetrable veil over emotion is joined to the unbridled passions of a madman or a beast.

2. Such inconsistencies, strange as they seem in our eyes, when viewed under a novel aspect, are but the ordinary incidents of
25 humanity. The qualities of the mind are not uniform in their ac-tion through all the relations of life. With different men, and dif-ferent races of men, pride, valor, prudence, have different forms

From *The Conspiracy of Pontiac*.

of manifestation, and where in one instance they lie dormant, in
another they are keenly awake. The conjunction of greatness and
littleness, meanness and pride, is older than the days of the 30
patriarchs; and such antiquated phenomena, displayed under a
new form in the unreflecting, undisciplined mind of a savage, call
for no special wonder, but should rather be classed with the other
enigmas of the fathomless human heart. The dissecting knife of a
Rochefoucault might lay bare matters of no less curious observa- 35
tion in the breast of every man.

3. Nature has stamped the Indian with a hard and stern
physiognomy. Ambition, revenge, envy, jealousy, are his ruling
passions; and his cold temperament is little exposed to those
effeminate vices which are the bane of milder races. With him 40
revenge is an overpowering instinct; nay, more, it is a point of
honor and a duty. His pride sets all language at defiance. He
loathes the thought of coercion; and few of his race have ever
stooped to discharge a menial office. A wild love of liberty, an
utter intolerance of control, lie at the basis of his character, and 45
fire his whole existence. Yet, in spite of this haughty independence, he is a devout hero-worshipper; and high achievement in
war or policy touches a chord to which his nature never fails to
respond. He looks up with admiring reverence to the sages and
heroes of his tribe; and it is this principle, joined to the respect for 50
age springing from the patriarchal element in his social system,
which, beyond all others, contributes union and harmony to the
erratic members of an Indian community. With him the love of
glory kindles into a burning passion; and to allay its cravings, he
will dare cold and famine, fire, tempest, torture, and death itself. 55

4. These generous traits are overcast by much that is dark, cold,
and sinister, by sleepless distrust, and rankling jealousy. Treacher-
ous himself, he is always suspicious of treachery in others. Brave
as he is,—and few of mankind are braver,—he will vent his passion by a secret stab rather than an open blow. His warfare is 60
full of ambuscade and stratagem; and he never rushes into battle
with that joyous self-abandonment with which the warriors of the
Gothic races flung themselves into the ranks of their enemies. In
his feasts and his drinking bouts we find none of that robust and
full-toned mirth which reigned at the rude carousals of our bar- 65

baric ancestry. He is never jovial in his cups, and maudlin sorrow
or maniacal rage is the sole result of his potations.

5. Over all emotion he throws the veil of an iron self-control,
originating in a peculiar form of pride, and fostered by rigorous
70 discipline from childhood upward. He is trained to conceal passion, and not to subdue it. The inscrutable warrior is aptly imaged
by the hackneyed figure of a volcano covered with snow; and no
man can say when or where the wild-fire will burst forth. This
shallow self-mastery serves to give dignity to public deliberation,
75 and harmony to social life. Wrangling and quarrel are strangers
to an Indian dwelling; and while an assembly of the ancient Gauls
was garrulous as a convocation of magpies, a Roman senate might
have taken a lesson from the grave solemnity of an Indian council.
In the midst of his family and friends, he hides affections, by na-
80 ture none of the most tender, under a mask of icy coldness; and
in the torturing fires of his enemy, the haughty sufferer maintains
to the last his look of grim defiance.

6. His intellect is as peculiar as his moral organization. Among
all savages, the powers of perception preponderate over those of
85 reason and analysis; but this is more especially the case with the
Indian. An acute judge of character, at least of such parts of it as
his experience enables him to comprehend; keen to a proverb in
all exercises of war and the chase, he seldom traces effects to their
causes, or follows out actions to their remote results. Though a
90 close observer of external nature, he no sooner attempts to account for her phenomena than he involves himself in the most
ridiculous absurdities; and quite content with these puerilities, he
has not the least desire to push his inquiries further. His curiosity,
abundantly active within its own narrow circle, is dead to all
95 things else; and to attempt rousing it from its torpor is but a
bootless task. He seldom takes cognizance of general or abstract
ideas; and his language has scarcely the power to express them,
except through the medium of figures drawn from the external
world, and often highly picturesque and forcible. The absence of
100 reflection makes him grossly improvident, and unfits him for
pursuing any complicated scheme of war or policy.

7. Some races of men seem moulded in wax, soft and melting,
at once plastic and feeble. Some races, like some metals, combine

the greatest flexibility with the greatest strength. But the Indian
is hewn out of a rock. You can rarely change the form without de- 105
struction of the substance. Races of inferior energy have possessed
a power of expansion and assimilation to which he is a stranger;
and it is this fixed and rigid quality which has proved his ruin.
He will not learn the arts of civilization, and he and his forest
must perish together. The stern, unchanging features of his mind 110
excite our admiration from their very immutability; and we look
with deep interest on the fate of this irreclaimable son of the
wilderness, the child who will not be weaned from the breast of
his rugged mother. And our interest increases when we discern in
the unhappy wanderer the germs of heroic virtues mingled 115
among his vices,—a hand bountiful to bestow as it is rapacious to
seize, and even in extremest famine, imparting its last morsel to
a fellow-sufferer; a heart which, strong in friendship as in hate,
thinks it not too much to lay down life for its chosen comrade; a
soul true to its own idea of honor, and burning with an un- 120
quenchable thirst for greatness and renown.

✳✳✳✳✳✳✳✳✳✳✳

Parkman is one of the great American stylists, in the grand manner. Here we have a piece that just touches the fringes of flam-
boyance. It is clearly meant to make a virtuoso impression, and it
does. Few matters in our history have been more variously represented and more violently disputed than the character of the
Indian.

1. Look up the following words, unless you are quite sure of
them. Notice the derivations particularly of those marked with an
asterisk (*). Par. 1: *credulously, rhapsodies, *cant, sentimentalists, tricked out, prototypes, mantle.* Par. 2: *novel aspect, incidents, prudence, *dormant, meanness, fathomless, Rochefoucault,
curious.* Par. 3: *physiognomy, coercion, menial, sages, patriarchal.*
Par. 4: *rankling, ambuscade, stratagem, *carousals, *maudlin,
potations, cups. Par. 5: *hackneyed, *inscrutable, garrulous.*
Par. 6: *preponderate, puerilities, bootless, cognizance, torpor,
improvident.* Par. 7: *immutability, rapacious.*

2. Read the selection aloud, perhaps twice. Determine whether

Parkman punctuates for structure, as in the best modern practice, or for rhythm, as Macaulay and Gibbon do. Good evidence is to be found in the first and third sentences, particularly the latter, where what purpose guides the punctuation? Make a careful analysis of the rest of Par. 1 to identify the elements of *balance* and proportion in Parkman's sentences. Indicate places where the semicolon is used to separate units of rhythm, particularly in lines 13–22. Note throughout the first paragraph (and indeed the whole selection) how carefully Parkman employs the device of syllabic increase: in a series of phrases or clauses, each one tends to be a trifle longer than the previous one.

3.   Parkman's method may be determined fairly easily with a précis: write a sentence describing the central thought of each paragraph; then see whether your sentence is substantially covered by a summary sentence in the paragraph.

4.   Note that Par. 2 presents generalizations about Man which provide the moral setting for Parkman's analysis of the Indian. Thus the *inconsistencies* set forth in Par. 1 are related to Man by the first two sentences of Par. 2. Write a paragraph carefully explaining how the particular characteristics of the Indian are, for Parkman, related to Man.

5.   There may be an inconsistency or a problem in Parkman's analysis: examine the *causes* of the Indian's character implied in Par. 2:

> The qualities of the mind are not uniform in their action through all the relations of life. With different men, and different races of men, pride, valor, prudence, have different forms of manifestation, and where in one instance they lie dormant, in another they are keenly awake.

alongside what is implied in Par. 3:

> Nature has stamped the Indian with a hard and stern physiognomy.

You may note that the first approach is through the word "qualities," whereas the second turns on "stamped," which casts into metaphor a perhaps different notion of how a man is formed. That which is stamped has received a total, permanent impression.

It looks as if "the mind" is a *constant* which exhibits different facets in different situations, but the word "race" suggests that these differences are inherited. And what cause is implied by "nature" (37)? Parkman presently seems to attempt to neutralize this contradiction by reverting to the earlier notion of a constant "mind" of which some aspects are, as he says, "dormant" (28). Explain this notion of "dormant" and discuss the question whether it solves the problem; for it raises a doubt, namely, how can we be sure of the *existence* of traits that remain "dormant"? Now look at the metaphors in Par. 7, not only the wax, the metal, and the rock, but also "moulded" and "hewn." Do these support the racial or the cultural theory of temperament?

6. Do the four traits, "Ambition, revenge, envy, jealousy," (38) account for the further qualities named in Par. 3? In the entire selection?

7. Explain the difference between "concealing" and "subduing" passion (70–71). The theme of Par. 5, "shallow self-mastery," is tinged with contempt. But is the self-mastery shallow when the Indian is under physical torture? (Where else in the selection is this quality discussed or suggested?) What, then, is shallow? In short, are there qualities that Parkman seems to value more highly than courage? Where does generosity stand in this scale of values?

8. How do the uses of "nature" in line 90 and line 37 differ?

9. The strength of this prose is perhaps an aspect of the limitation of its penetration. The Indian is set forth on an *extremely* high level of generalization; not only is there just one Indian, but he also has traits of the most general sort. The individual does not appear. Such distance lends itself to grand, spectacular periods (i.e. sentences), but what of Parkman's charge that the Indian of literature is a "counterfeit image"? You may explore this issue by reading Edmund Wilson's *Apologies to the Iroquois*, 1960 (see next selection), where you will find perhaps the opposite extreme of concreteness in a style that differs equally from Parkman's. Write an essay comparing the literary methods—diction, style, level of abstraction, quality and character of ideas—of the two writers.

10. Or you might write an essay exploring the sources of so-called "racial temperaments." (See Par. 3 and Question 5). Are they caused by "nature" or by *environment,* or by *culture* (which is, of course, social environment)? This is a question that can occupy the rest of your life as an anthropologist, sociologist, or

psychologist. For your assignment you may write an essay comparing certain individuals of your acquaintance whose attitudes and ideas differ sharply. Are they racial, social, environmental? At the opposite extreme you can look into some of the writings of the modern anthropologists like Margaret Mead or Ruth Benedict. Or you can look up the theory of Hippolyte Taine on climate and character. In short, you can roam at will from close personal observation of people to the most hypothetical speculations about man and society.

Apologies to the Iroquois

EDMUND WILSON

1. Standing Arrow
commenced our interview by getting a little tough—understand-
ably, in view of the fact that on first meeting him I had chal-
lenged him rather sharply—but he soon began exerting charm.
Though he had a slight cast in one eye, his features were rather 5
fine, and reminded one of portraits of the youthful Napoleon. He
had also, as I could see, some of the qualities of the Mussolinian
spellbinder. He used gestures of a kind, I thought, unusual on the
part of an Indian, which might have been picked up from the
Canadian French and which seemed to show experience in public 10
speaking. When I talked later to another Mohawk—not one of
Standing Arrow's followers—of the leader's persuasive powers, he
answered, "He's got a touch of the hypnotist. People go to him
prejudiced against him and come away completely convinced."
Another Mohawk, who disapproved of him, told me that his elo- 15
quence in English—of which his command was imperfect—was
nothing to his eloquence in Mohawk: "When he talks to me, as
long as he's there, I can't disagree with anything he says." I felt
something of this myself. I had heard about Standing Arrow some
unfavorable things, yet I found myself won over in contact with 20
him. He appealed to the imagination.
2. While Standing Arrow was reading the statement, another
Indian entered the shack. I had noticed him, on my arrival, fast
asleep in the back seat of a car, which he filled with a compact
lump. He was dark, broad-shouldered, and stocky, somewhat for- 25
midable-looking, with his strongly cut features, which recalled the

From *Apologies to the Iroquois,* by Edmund Wilson. Published by Farrar,
Straus and Cudahy, Inc. Reprinted by permission of the author.

cigar-store Indian but seemed rather made of iron than of wood,
and his piercing eyes open on a crack. He shook hands with me,
then sat down and listened. Soon he said to me, "I will talk to him
30 in my own language." They spoke Mohawk for a minute or two,
then Standing Arrow turned to me: "You say you're a magazine
writer. Can you show me your credentials?" I had not provided
myself with any, but I managed to reassure them. The dark man
became quite friendly—I was to see him twice after that. I found
35 he had a sly, Indian, deadpan humor. He was a worker in "high
steel," and told me with pride that he had not only worked on the
Empire State Building but had even been employed on the tower.
A good many of the Mohawk Indians, if not the majority of them,
are steel-and-iron workers. They are equipped with what one Mo-
40 hawk described to me as "an uncanny sense of balance" and an
astonishing coolness in working at heights, which evidently derive
from their earlier life, from threading forests and scaling mountains, from canoeing in streams rough with rapids. A very important factor is, undoubtedly, their habit, in walking, of putting one
45 foot in front of the other, instead of straddling, as, when they see
our tracks in the snow, we seem to them to do. They do not need
to make an effort in walking a narrow beam. That this aptitude
of the Iroquois was well developed before modern engineering
was known is shown by a passage in an early English book, John
50 Lawson's "History of Carolina," published in 1709: "They will
walk over deep brooks and creeks," he writes of the Tuscaroras,
"on the smallest poles, and that without any fear or concern. Nay,
an *Indian* will walk on the ridge of a barn or house and look down
the gable-end, and spit upon the ground, as unconcerned as if he
55 was walking on *terra firma*." And today—it is a proof of the per-
sistence of their strength—they have found in the construction of
bridges, high buildings, and power-line towers an incongruous
opportunity for exercising their traditional self-control, their muscular coördination, and their indifference to physical danger. The
60 story of the Iroquois's development as experts in this occupation,
the crews for which had hitherto been largely made up of old
sailing-ship men trained in climbing the rigging—has already been
admirably told in an article by Mr. Joseph Mitchell, "The Mohawks in High Steel." He has described how, suspended at

dizzying heights on exiguous platforms of plank, they toss red-hot 65
rivets to one another and pound them into place with pneumatic
hammers. In the construction of the Quebec Bridge, which crosses
the St. Lawrence River, says Mitchell, a span at one time collapsed and thirty-five Indians were killed, but this, far from dis-
couraging the Mohawks, proved to stimulate their interest in the 70
work. It had before seemed hardly more dangerous than the tim-
ber rafting in which they had been previously employed; now it
gave them a feeling of achievement, of having faced and survived
an ordeal, such as their early hunting and fighting had given
them. The only characteristic, it seems, that makes them rather 75
unreliable from the employer's point of view is their tendency
suddenly to desert the job—regardless of money considerations—
and go on to some other alluring project, no matter how far away,
the rumor of which has reached them.

✳✳✳✳✳✳✳✳✳✳✳

Here is a bit of contemporary writing that is about as different
from Parkman's as it could be. It differs in tone, rhythms, level of
diction, concreteness, and method. The author is one of America's
most distinguished Men of Letters—if we use that term to designate the professional writer who has touched on a range of subjects in a variety of genres. Edmund Wilson, novelist, essayist, re-
porter, critic, and historian, stands out as an American Man of
Letters, a formulator and leader of opinion, a prime force of
American intellect. Our selection, from a book on the Six Nations
of the Iroquois today, is reporting at its best.

"Apologies" in the title is explained by the fact that Wilson deals
with the way that the United States and various States have continually violated their treaties with the Indians. Violations of the
Iroquois' rights in New York State are the main theme of this
book. Standing Arrow is an Indian leader and representative in
the dispute.

1. Underline the words in Par. 1 which designate *qualities* of
Standing Arrow (5 or 6 words), aspects of his *appearance* (2 or
3 words), and *actions* (2 words). Which word indicates the
theme of the paragraph?

2. How do Wilson's references to the "youthful Napoleon" and to the "Mussolinian spellbinder" concern Standing Arrow?

3. What does the author accomplish by mentioning what others said or thought of Standing Arrow, in lines 11–18?

4. Wilson's language is clear, compact, and economical. Thus he is able to give us quite a good idea of the people he writes about in just a sentence or two. He uses words and phrases that describe both physical appearance and inner qualities of the person. Illustrate this statement by examining his description of the dark Indian.

5. What characteristics of the Indian in general, the traditional Indian, does Wilson examine in this selection? What individual differences does he indicate in his descriptions of Standing Arrow and the dark Indian? Do the individual differences explain the general or traditional idea of the Indian, or do they conflict with the traditional idea? If there is a conflict, what reasons are given for it?

6. Wilson uses the now common technique of achieving interest and closeness by placing himself squarely in the midst of the material and letting his reader watch him discover it. Identify passages in which he is in the center of the action. Wilson's moving back and forth in time (11 and 34), while maintaining the personal viewpoint, serves other purposes in the selection. How many such purposes can you identify and define?

7. "Derive" (41) is either used loosely or was chosen with some care in order to acknowledge but not involve the Theory of Evolution too elaborately in the passage. Which? The essential question is whether species (or traits) evolve in response to environment, or by accident. Now explain whether, and how, "aptitude" and "developed" (47–48) are true to the implications of "derive." It may be that one is and one is not. Does "factor" (44) indicate cause or effect in the Evolutionary frame of reference? Identify other words and phrases that suggest the Theory of Evolution and evaluate their appropriateness for the context. This may be a small research question, or your instructor may explain the issues involved.

8. Explain and justify "incongruous" (57), and "exiguous" (65).

9. Define the tone established by the phrase "getting a little tough" (2). Then explain the precise meaning of "exerting" and show how it not only sharpens the meaning but also slightly alters the tone of "getting tough." If this question appears difficult, consider the implications of the fact that even the New York *Times* might headline a "Get Tough Policy" with Cuba or Russia; the term, in short, has a status other than its use in vulgar or common speech.

10. Sentences are simple, compound, complex and compound-complex. Let us look at some samples:

Lines 18–19, a simple sentence, with subject-verb-object-phrase:

I felt something of this myself.

Line 21, a simple sentence, with subject-verb-prepositional-phrase:

He appealed to the imagination.

Lines 13–14, a simple sentence with a compound predicate:

People go to him prejudiced against him and come away completely convinced.

Note that there is no comma between the two parts of the compound predicate.

Lines 19–21, a compound sentence with two independent clauses:

I had heard about Standing Arrow some unfavorable things, yet I found myself won over in contact with him.

Won in this sentence is an objective complement to the object *myself*.

Lines 6–8, a complex sentence: a main clause ("He had some . . .") with a subordinate clause modifying some word in the main clause. Here it is "as I could see," which modifies *had*:

He had also, as I could see, some of the qualities of the Mussolinian spellbinder.

Lines 5–6, a complex sentence in which the main clause has a simple subject with a compound predicate. The subordinate clause is an adverb modifying the verb *were*:

Though he had a slight cast in one eye, his features were rather fine, and reminded one of portraits of the youthful Napoleon.

Structure does not always indicate logic; for example, in line 64 ff., the main clause is, "He has described . . ." followed by a "how" clause which is here a noun clause, the direct object of "described," with a compound predicate, "toss . . . and pound," —and all this is the object of "says Mitchell"! Lines 67–71 are compound-complex: identify the three independent clauses and the one subordinate clause.

11. Write a comparison of Parkman's and Wilson's treatments of the Indian. Consider each writer's aims, methods, evidence, reliability, scale, and whatever other aspects you consider significant. The effect of your analysis depends very largely on the categories you choose to explore. If you choose to contrast the *tones* of the two selections, do so in terms of sentence structure. You will find this a very profitable exercise.

The Wonderful World of Toots Shor

JOHN BAINBRIDGE

1. Even a man who possesses the required reverence for sports, friendship, and drinking will never get into the Shorian society if he doesn't have what the members call "class." It is the indispensable qualification, but even Shor finds it hard to define it precisely. "Class is a thing when a guy does everything decent," he once said. Though resisting definition in words, class is demonstrable in actions. When Larry MacPhail, who had had a falling out with Shor, was president of the Yankees, he let it be known among members of the team that he didn't look with particular favor on their eating at Shor's. One day, MacPhail asked Joe DiMaggio to have dinner with him that evening. "Thank you, but I can't make it," DiMaggio said. "I'm having dinner with Toots." DiMaggio's action, which was duplicated under less poignant conditions by a number of other Yankee players, is often cited at Shor's as an eloquent illustration of class, one important element of which is loyalty. Outward modesty is another. Practically no one around Shor's, including the leader, suffers from holding a meagre opinion of himself, but exterior self-effacement is de rigueur. Shor sets the tone for public unpretentiousness by, for example, always calling himself a saloonkeeper instead of a restaurateur. His habit of lowrating himself in public is contagious, but though it is widely emulated, it has never been matched. On a recent afternoon, he was having a drink with Charles Berns, one of the original partners of "21," and a few other friends. Berns remarked that he had decided early in life that he was qualified for two occupations—running

a shoeshine stand and running a restaurant. "I like to eat, so I became a restaurant man," Berns said. "Look at the high-tony bum," Shor said. "He's a restaurant man. Me, I'm nothing but a crummy saloonkeeper. I'm just a common, ordinary filthy bum." No one present tried to top that. In private, Shor is less harsh with himself, but even then he adheres to tribal etiquette by prefacing any remarks that might be considered boastful with the phrase "I ain't braggin', but . . ." After showing a visitor around his restaurant one day, Shor said, "I ain't braggin', but I think I got the best joint in New York, and to me New York is America."

2. Openhandedness, particularly under pressure, is also an essential attribute of class. Jack Kearns, the fight promoter, gave a practical demonstration of this one Friday night in Shor's after the fights in Madison Square Garden. A young fighter managed by Kearns had made a good showing at the Garden, and Kearns wanted to celebrate by treating the sportswriters and some of his other friends to drinks. Being low on cash, he borrowed a hundred dollars from Shor. "What class!" Shor says. "He borrows a hundred from me so he can pick up the tabs in my joint." Class also calls for a certain spiritual generosity. During the period when Shor and MacPhail were not on speaking terms, the head of the Yankees saw to it that Shor never failed to receive his customary large allotment of World Series tickets whenever the Yankees were in the contest. "That was a classy thing to do," Shor says. Class has mysterious shadings. When Shor's wife went to the hospital to have her first child, Sherman Billingsley, whom Shor has regarded for twenty years as his natural enemy, sent her flowers, an act that was interpreted by some of Shor's objectively minded friends as one, like MacPhail's, that transcended pettiness and was therefore quite classy. Shor, who is the society's supreme arbiter of what constitutes class, puts a contrary interpretation on Billingsley's bouquet. "To me, that don't denote class," Shor says. "The way things are, it would have been classier if Sherm didn't send anything." A while ago, Shor began hearing reports that Billingsley had become so anxious to make up that he had appointed a Broadway columnist to try to negotiate a reconciliation. At the same time, Shor learned that Billingsley had asked a couple of people, as a personal favor, not to go to Shor's. That

ended hope for a settlement. "I don't mind a knocker," Shor said, 65
"but I got no time for a sneak-knocker." Shor does not, however, make it a rule to withhold the accolade from a man solely
because he dislikes him. "I don't like him, but the bastard's got
class," he has remarked of a Hollywood figure. To thus rise above
personal prejudice is regarded in itself as a classy thing to do. 70
"Class" is plainly a very flexible term, the application of which is
apparently determined as much by emotional as by ratiocinative
processes.

3. The highest compliment that a Shorian can bestow on anyone is to say, "He's a champion with class." In the lexicon of the 75
society, a champion is a person who stands at the top of his profession, whether it is sports, theatre, business, politics, or any
other field, including saloonkeeping. Champions are comparatively
plentiful; champions with class are scarce. It is possible for a
champion who has class to lose it by committing a social or profes- 80
sional error, and be reduced to the rank of plain champion. That
happened to a well-known prizefighter whom Shor at one time
rated at the top but whose performance in one important bout he
found wanting. Conversely, it is possible for a champion without
class to become a champion with. Joe DiMaggio is Shor's favorite 85
example of a champion who acquired class. "When Joe came up to
the Yankees, people thought he was surly," Shor has said. "He
wasn't. The kid was shy. He just didn't know how to talk to people. But he made up his mind to be sociable, and he kept drivin'
at makin' friends. He *attained* class." Some people, Shor feels, are 90
born with class and go on to become champions with class, a
category in which he places Franklin D. Roosevelt. Truman has
also enjoyed a high rating. As a token of esteem, Shor, along with
two of his friends, presented the President with a gold watch after
his election. However, some members of the society feel that the 95
President suffered a temporary diminution of class in the fall of
1949, because he didn't go to St. Louis to attend Robert E. Hanne-
gan's [a politician with "class"] funeral. One night, a champion sportswriter with class, who is such an old and trusted
friend of Shor's that he is allowed special freedom, was sitting in 100
the Stork Club talking with [its proprietor] Sherman Billingsley.
Shor's name entered the conversation, and Billingsley said,

"What's he got that I haven't got?" The sportswriter replied, "Class. And Toots is a champion." Shor has been known to repeat
105 this story, but only after making it clear that he is not bragging.

****

Here is a bit of superb reporting on an unbelievable world—which is nevertheless real. It is also an essay in definition.

1. The Shorian society is, throughout this delightful and malicious little book, treated as an anthropologist would treat a primitive society. Its folkways, taboos, ceremonies, and customs are set forth with a garnishing of the language of the academic anthropologist. Perhaps your instructor will tell you something of this science and its language. You may find numerous phrases that reveal this anthropological motif of the book, a motif that establishes the tone—a tone both subtle and ambiguous. Does the author admire this character who lives, lends, and loves with the great ones of journalism, sport, and the theatre? What does he think about the unique Shorian society? If you can find the answer, you will be able to write a short essay explaining just why the anthropological approach is so clever. After reading the selection aloud, make a list of these anthropological terms and references.

2. You are probably safe in assuming that the facts given are indeed facts (Toots himself endorsed the book enthusiastically); the meanings associated with them are strictly products of the writer's craft. Let us examine a few samples: What aspects of Shor are established by the first speech attributed to him (5–6)? This cannot have been Shor's *only* definition of class. Has class, in spite of this sentence, "resisted definition in words"?
Poignant (14) is loaded with ironies. What are they?
The "21" is a very fine New York restaurant, and the word restaurant is certainly not pretentious. What does Shor achieve by calling himself (proprietor of one of the most celebrated spots in New York) "a crummy saloonkeeper"? What does the writer indicate by the anecdote that follows to the end of the paragraph?

3. Is it possible to discern ulterior motives in Larry MacPhail's sending World Series tickets to Shor? When you place Shor's reaction to this beside his reaction to a rival restaurateur's send-

ing flowers to his wife in the hospital, do you discover any ironic
overtones to, ' "Class" is plainly a very flexible term . . .'? Note,
by the way, that this sentence ends with a highly anthropological
flavor.

4.   The phrase "allowed special freedom" (100) refers to the
fact that Shor wants his friends around *all* the time and has been
known to snub and expel a customer (rather, a member of the
society) who has been seen eating at another resturant. Did the
friend in question reward the trust he enjoyed? Who, by the way,
has determined that he was "a *champion* sportswriter with *class*"?

5.   Write a paragraph or short essay on the significance of the
amount of discussion of *class* at Toots's.

6.   We find only one comma in this selection that violates the
general rule by coming between compound verbs. It is in line 81.
Can you justify it? In the following sentence, is the *whom* . . .
clause restrictive or non-restrictive? Test it by several readings-
aloud: but you will find that you have to give careful thought to
the meaning, here, to know *how* to read it aloud.

7.   Toots Shor has written a warm endorsement of the book from
which this selection is taken. Write a short essay on the question
whether this is an illustration of "class" or not.

8.   Make a count of the number of concrete facts in this essay,
then a count of the explanatory generalizations. The relation of
fact to author's interpretation and explanation should be compared with that of Joseph Mitchell's sketch of Mr. Flood. Here, as
there, the author's attitude toward his subject is partly concealed.
In both, the facts seem to "speak for themselves," but it is the
author's skill in choosing them that makes them appear to do so.
Whereas Mitchell is primarily concerned, however, with giving
us the full flavor of Mr. Flood, John Bainbridge *might* be considered as having a quite special reason for veiling his presentation in anthropological clothing that only a certain kind of people
could see through. What might be this reason?

The Lower Middlebrow

RUSSELL LYNES

1. My wife's grandmother, the wife of a distinguished lawyer, once declined to dine with the Cartiers of jewelry fame because they were, as she put it, "in trade." Life for grandmother was relatively simple where
5 social distinctions were concerned, but while there are still a few people who think and act much as she did, the passage of time has eliminated a great deal of that particular kind of snobbishness from American society. We are replacing it with another kind. The old structure of the upper class, the middle class, and the
10 lower class is on the wane. It isn't wealth or family that makes prestige these days. It's high thinking.

2. Our heroes now are not the Carnegies or the Morgans but the intellectuals—the atomic scientists, the cultural historians, the writers, the commentators, the thinkers of global thoughts who,
15 we assume for lack of another faith, know better than anyone else how we should cope with what we call the new resonance of our national destiny. What we want are oracles, and the best substitutes we can find are the intellectuals. Einstein makes headlines as Millikan never did. Toynbee's popularity is to be reckoned with
20 as Spengler's never was. Even Calvert whiskey has selected as Men of Distinction more artists, architects, writers, and commentators than it has industrialists or financiers. What we are headed for is a sort of social structure in which the highbrows are the elite, the middlebrows are the bourgeoisie, and the lowbrows
25 are *hoi polloi*.

3. For the time being this is perhaps largely an urban phe-

nomenon, and the true middlebrow may readily be mistaken in
the small community for a genuine highbrow, but the pattern is
emerging with increasing clarity, and the new distinctions do not
seem to be based either on money or breeding. Some lowbrows 30
are as rich as Billy Rose, and as flamboyant, some as poor as
Rosie O'Grady and as modest. Some middlebrows run industries;
some run the women's auxiliary of the Second Baptist Church.
Some highbrows eat caviar with their Proust; some eat hamburger
when they can afford it. It is true that most highbrows are in the 35
ill-paid professions, notably the academic, and that most middlebrows are at least reasonably well off. Only the lowbrows can
be found in about equal percentages at all financial levels. There
may be a time, of course, when the highbrows will be paid in
accordance with their own estimate of their worth, but that is not 40
likely to happen in any form of society in which creature com-
forts are in greater demand than intellectual uplift. Like poets
they will have to be content mostly with prestige. The middlebrows are influential today, but neither the highbrows nor the
lowbrows like them; and if we ever have intellectual totalitarian- 45
ism, it may well be the lowbrows and the highbrows who will
run things, and the middlebrows who will be exiled in boxcars to
a collecting point probably in the vicinity of Independence, Missouri.

4. While this social shift is still in its early stages, and the di- 50
viding lines are still indistinct and the species not yet frozen, let
us assume a rather lofty position, examine the principal categories, with their subdivisions and splinter groups, and see where
we ourselves are likely to fetch up in the new order.

[Lynes then examines the highbrow and the lowbrow; the for- 55
mer is the academic intellectual, the artistic and literary sophisti-
cate who associates culture with every aspect of daily life; the latter
is unconcerned with "culture"—he wants comfort and enjoyment
and doesn't worry about whether he has good taste or not.
Lynes divides the middlebrows into two groups. The upper mid- 60
dlebrow "straddles the fence between highbrow and middlebrow."
He may be a conscientious publisher, a museum director, or an
art dealer. He appreciates highbrow culture, but caters to lower
middlebrow taste. Next Lynes considers the lower middlebrow:]

65   5. The lower middlebrow ardently believes that he knows what he likes, and yet his taste is constantly susceptible to the pressures that put him in knickerbockers one year and rust-colored slacks the next. Actually he is unsure about almost everything, especially about what he likes. This may explain his pronouncements on
70 taste, which he considers an effete and questionable virtue, and his resentment of the arts; but it may also explain his strength.

6. When America and Americans are characterized by foreigners and highbrows, the middlebrows are likely to emerge as the dominant group in our society—a dreadful mass of insensible
75 back-slappers, given to sentimentality as a prime virtue, the willing victims of slogans and the whims of the bosses, both political and economic. The picture painted by middlebrow exploiters of the middlebrow, such as the advertisers of nationally advertised brands, is strikingly similar to that painted by the highbrow; their
80 attitudes and motives are quite different (the highbrow paints with a snarl, the advertiser with a gleam), but they both make the middlebrow out to be much the same kind of creature. The villain of the highbrow and the hero of the advertisers is envisaged as "the typical American family"—happy little women, happy little
85 children, all spotless or sticky in the jam pot, framed against dimity curtains in the windows or decalcomania flowers on the cupboard doors. Lower-middlebrowism is a world pictured without tragedy, a world of new two-door sedans, and Bendix washers, and reproductions of hunting prints over the living-room mantel. It is a
90 world in which the ingenuity and patience of the housewife are equaled only by the fidelity of her husband and his love of home, pipe, and radio. It is a world that smells of soap. But it is a world of ambition as well, the constant striving for a better way of life —better furniture, bigger refrigerators, more books in the book-
95 case, more evenings at the movies. To the advertisers this is Americanism; to the highbrows this is the dead weight around the neck of progress, the gag in the mouth of art.

7. The lower middlebrows are not like this, of course, and unlike the highbrows and the upper middlebrows, whose numbers
100 are tiny by comparison, they are hard to pin down. They live everywhere, rubbing elbows with lowbrows in apartment houses like vast beehives, in row houses all alike from the outside except

for the planting, in large houses at the ends of gravel driveways, in big cities, in medium cities and suburbs, and in small towns, from Boston to San Francisco, from Seattle to Jacksonville. They are the members of the book clubs who read difficult books along with racy and innocuous ones that are sent along by Messrs. Fadiman, Canby, Beecroft [1] *et al.* They are the course-takers who swell the enrollments of adult education classes in everything from "The Technique of the Short Story" to "Child Care." They are the people who go to hear the lecturers that swarm out from New York lecture bureaus with tales of travel on the Dark Continent and panaceas for saving the world from a fate worse than capitalism. They eat in tea shoppes and hold barbecues in their back yards. They are hell-bent on improving their minds as well as their fortunes. They decorate their homes under the careful guidance of *Good Housekeeping* and the *Ladies' Home Journal,* or, if they are well off, of *House and Garden,* and are subject to fads in furniture so long as these don't depart too radically from the traditional and the safe, from the copy of Colonial and the reproduction of Sheraton. In matters of taste, the lower-middlebrow world is largely dominated by women. They select the furniture, buy the fabrics, pick out the wallpapers, the pictures, the books, the china. Except in the selection of his personal apparel and the car, it is almost *infra dig* for a man to have taste; it is not considered quite manly for the male to express opinions about things which come under the category of "artistic."

8. Nonetheless, as a member of the school board or the hospital board he decides which design shall be accepted when a new building goes up. The lower middlebrows are the organizers of the community fund, the members of the legislature, the park commissioners. They pay their taxes and they demand services in return. There are millions of them, conscientious stabilizers of society, slow to change, slow to panic. But they are not as predictable as either the highbrows or the bosses, political or economic, think they are. They can be led, they can be seduced, but they cannot be pushed around.

[1] Critics employed by book clubs.

※※※※※※※※※

When we speak of concrete and abstract language, we are not speaking of two exclusive categories but of two classifications of language that merge into each other. The most concrete *term* is a proper name, that identifies a single person, place, or thing. A general noun can be made this concrete with a limiting adjective or set of adjectives, for example, "John Smith's spotted pony." Just so, birch trees are more general than the birch tree on the corner of Houston Street. Words like pedestrian, scholar, and accountant are abstract in their identification of a class rather than an individual, but they are nevertheless concrete designations. Notice that the word pedestrian is abstract because it identifies a very limited aspect of certain people; yet all nouns, except perhaps proper names, abstract or classify in the same way: that is why they are useful; that is how we think with them. Words that identify qualities or characteristics are still more abstract. Scientific abstractions such as velocity, mass, energy, inertia, vector are actually instruments of thought that have been very carefully defined. Abstractions such as beauty, sincerity, dignity, and goodness are in varying degrees elusive and slippery; their meanings depend on modifiers and context. Another class of abstractions makes something out of nothing. Such terms *create* an entity, although they appear to identify a quality or aspect of a thing or situation. For example, we read of a "power vacuum," but some close thought will show you that there cannot possibly be such a thing.

The process of abstraction has been set forth somewhat more systematically by a semanticist in a "ladder of abstraction" that indicates the degrees—or, rather, some of them—of abstraction that can prevail in our thinking and speaking about a cow.

The first step at the bottom is the cow known to science, ultimately consisting of atoms, electrons, etc. The characteristics contained in this idea of cow are infinite because at this level the cow is an ever-changing *process*.

Second, there is the cow we perceive, not the word, but the object our senses abstract from the total process.

Next, up the ladder, the name "Bessie" indicates a particular cow.

Fourth, the word "cow" stands for the characteristics which are common to cows in general.

Fifth, we may refer to Bessie as "livestock," thereby abstracting a more limited and particular cluster of characteristics, including those she shares with pigs and goats.

Sixth, Bessie may be considered a "farm asset"; and here she is classed with both animate and inanimate things, and more of her individual characteristics are omitted.

Seventh, she may be called an "asset," with still more of her characteristics omitted.

Finally, if we call her "wealth," we ignore almost all of her characteristic both as individual and as class of animal.[2]

This is as far as the semanticist goes. Can we go further? Yes, suppose we consider Bessie as "prestige." This is an abstraction even from wealth. The ladder we have described, moreover, is only one of many possible ladders of abstraction. Instead of considering Bessie in the aspect of wealth, we might consider her as matter, form, and shape, mounting this ladder finally up to the extreme abstractions of "pattern" and "beauty."

With these ideas in mind, let us examine Lynes's essay. Here you will observe how vivid and concrete terms continually limit, locate, and make specific the abstractions Lynes is using.

1. Suppose Lynes had begun his essay this way:

American social structure is changing: once a society where prestige was based on wealth and family, it is becoming a society where intellectual attainment is the measure of prestige.

This is a perfectly adequate description of Lynes's initial idea. Yet because it is less concrete it is obviously less interesting, less effective. Underline all the concrete words and phrases in Par. 1. Note that there is not a sharp, clear line between the abstract and the concrete but rather a gradation.

2. How do the concrete facts in Sen. 1 affect the *relatively* abstract words like *social distinctions, passage of time, snobbishness, structure, prestige?*

3. Identify the snobbishness in Par. 1. How does being "in trade" relate to the prestige of wealth and family?

4. Write a one-sentence précis of Par. 2. What does Lynes gain by mentioning the Carnegies and the Morgans? Would it not have been just as effective to say instead, "men of wealth"? What do sentences 3, 4, and 5 in Par. 2 add to the paragraph? Would anything be lost by omitting them?

[2] S. I. Hayakawa, *Language in Thought and Action* (New York, 1949), p. 169.

5. Write a general statement of the thesis of Par. 3, being careful to make the proper point about the relation of wealth to one's
"brow" status.

6. The concrete details which fill out Lynes's ideas are always
more than mere fact; they are loaded with humor and innuendo.
Discuss the overtones and innuendoes that accompany the following: Billy Rose, women's auxiliary of the Second Baptist Church,
caviar, Proust, hamburger, and Independence, Missouri. For
example, is it implied that Billy Rose is a lowbrow?

7. Remembering that the line between abstract and concrete
may be somewhat indefinite, go through Par. 3 and mark all the
completely concrete words and phrases (like Rosie O'Grady).
Then mark with a different color or symbol all the words and
phrases that are relatively concrete. Note the extent to which
these more abstract terms depend on the more concrete ones for
their meaning. (For example, ill-paid professions, financial
levels.) Finally, mark the abstract terms. You will find very few
of these in Lynes, and, when used, they are always graphically
explained by more concrete words and phrases.

8. Read sentence 2 in Par. 3 aloud. What effect is achieved by
the presence of a comma after Billy Rose and not after Rosie
O'Grady?

9. Identify at least three parallel constructions in Par. 3.

10. Underline Lynes's "statement of purpose."

11. In his examination of the lower middlebrow, Lynes describes
(a) what the lower middlebrow thinks he is, (b) what others
believe he is, and (c) what he really is. Identify these three
divisions.

12. Note the concrete detail in lines 65–68. Is Lynes assuming
that *all* lower middlebrows wore knickbockers one year and rust-
colored slacks the next? Why does he choose such details?

13. Underline all the specific, concrete details in this description
of the lower middlebrow. Mark all the adjectives in Pars. 6 and 7
and tell how they make the nouns they modify more complete.
How do these adjectives add to the picture of lower middle-
browism?

14.   The highbrow "snarls" his contempt as he "paints" a picture of the middlebrow. Exactly where is the "gleam" in the advertiser's picture? The structure of the sentence will tell you.

15.   Lynes professes complete objectivity in his description of the various "brow" groups. We suggested that there were innuendoes in Par. 3. What words and phrases in Par. 7 *evaluate* the lower middlebrow—that is to say, judge his taste or his conduct? Would you be surprised to know that Lynes describes *all* classes with the same tone?

16.   Lynes's ultimate standards are taste and sincerity. The highbrows predominate in taste, the lowbrows in sincerity. What proportion of these characteristics does the lower middlebrow seem to have? Justify your answer.

17.   To analyze the process of abstraction, write an essay on the sentence: "Mr. Smith owns a factory worth $1,000,000." This looks very simple at first, but in what sense does Mr. Smith own this factory? Can he burn it down if he wants to? Is the factory a building, a process, or a business? If it is either of the latter two, it includes *men*—and how can one "own" men? If there is a strike, a war, or a change in productive techniques, what does Mr. Smith own? Is *worth* a matter of cost, sale, or replacement of the physical plant?—or is it determined by capitalization from profits (i.e. if the annual profit is $50,000, this sum is 5% of $1,000,000)?
   In your essay address yourself specifically to the operation of the process of abstraction *in language*, as it is revealed in the quoted sentence.

18.   Or you may pick a sentence from a book or magazine or editorial to analyze. Or your instructor may supply one for you to work on.

Farewell, My Lovely!

LEE STROUT WHITE *

1. I see by the new Sears Roebuck catalogue that it is still possible to buy an axle for a 1909 Model T Ford, but I am not deceived. The great days have faded, the end is in sight. Only one page in the current catalogue
5 is devoted to parts and accessories for the Model T; yet everyone remembers springtimes when the Ford gadget section was larger than men's clothing, almost as large as household furnishings. The last Model T was built in 1927, and the car is fading from what scholars call the American scene—which is an understate-
10 ment, because to a few million people who grew up with it, the old Ford practically *was* the American scene.

2. It was the miracle God had wrought. And it was patently the sort of thing that could only happen once. Mechanically uncanny, it was like nothing that had ever come to the world
15 before. Flourishing industries rose and fell with it. As a vehicle, it was hardworking, commonplace, heroic; and it often seemed to transmit those qualities to the persons who rode in it. My own generation identifies it with Youth, with its gaudy, irretrievable excitements; before it fades into the mist, I would like to pay it
20 the tribute of the sigh that is not a sob, and set down random entries in a shape somewhat less cumbersome than a Sears Roebuck catalogue.

3. The Model T was distinguished from all other makes of cars by the fact that its transmission was of a type known as planetary
25 —which was half metaphysics, half sheer fiction. Engineers accepted the word "planetary" in its epicyclic sense, but I was

° A collaboration by Richard Lee Strout and E. B. White.
Copyright, 1936, The New Yorker Magazine, Inc.

always conscious that it also meant "wandering," "erratic."
Because of the peculiar nature of this planetary element, there
was always, in Model T, a certain dull rapport between engine
and wheels, and even when the car was in a state known as neu- 30
tral, it trembled with a deep imperative and tended to inch forward. There was never a moment when the bands were not faintly
egging the machine on. In this respect it was like a horse, rolling
the bit on its tongue, and country people brought to it the same
technique they used with draft animals.   35

4. Its most remarkable quality was its rate of acceleration. In
its palmy days the Model T could take off faster than anything on
the road. The reason was simple. To get under way, you simply
hooked the third finger of the right hand around a lever on the
steering column, pulled down hard, and shoved your left foot 40
forcibly against the low-speed pedal. These were simple, positive
motions; the car responded by lunging forward with a roar. After
a few seconds of this turmoil, you took your toe off the pedal,
eased up a mite on the throttle, and the car, possessed of only two
forward speeds, catapulted directly into high with a series of ugly 45
jerks and was off on its glorious errand. The abruptness of this
departure was never equalled in other cars of the period. The
human leg was (and still is) incapable of letting in a clutch with
anything like the forthright abandon that used to send Model T
on its way. Letting in a clutch is a negative, hesitant motion, 50
depending on delicate nervous control; pushing down the Ford
pedal was a simple, country motion—an expansive act, which
came as natural as kicking an old door to make it budge.

5. The driver of the old Model T was a man enthroned. The
car, with top up, stood seven feet high. The driver sat on top of 55
the gas tank, brooding it with his own body. When he wanted
gasoline, he alighted, along with everything else in the front seat;
the seat was pulled off, the metal cap unscrewed, and a wooden
stick thrust down to sound the liquid in the well. There were
always a couple of these sounding sticks kicking around in the 60
ratty sub-cushion regions of a flivver. Refuelling was more of a
social function then, because the driver had to unbend, whether
he wanted to or not. Directly in front of the driver was the wind-

shield—high, uncompromisingly erect. Nobody talked about air
65 resistance, and the four cylinders pushed the car through the
atmosphere with a simple disregard of physical law.

6. There was this about a Model T: the purchaser never
regarded his purchase as a complete, finished product. When you
bought a Ford, you figured you had a start—a vibrant, spirited
70 framework to which could be screwed an almost limitless assort-
ment of decorative and functional hardware. Driving away from
the agency, hugging the new wheel between your knees, you
were already full of creative worry. A Ford was born naked as a
baby, and a flourishing industry grew up out of correcting its
75 rare deficiencies and combatting its fascinating diseases. Those
were the great days of lily-painting. I have been looking at some
old Sears Roebuck catalogues, and they bring everything back
so clear.

7. First you bought a Ruby Safety Reflector for the rear, so that
80 your posterior would glow in another's car's brilliance. Then you
invested thirty-nine cents in some radiator Moto Wings, a popular
ornament which gave the Pegasus touch to the machine and did
something godlike to the owner. For nine cents you bought a
fan-belt guide to keep the belt from slipping off the pulley.

85 8. You bought a radiator compound to stop leaks. This was as
much a part of everybody's equipment as aspirin tablets are of a
medicine cabinet. You bought special oil to prevent chattering,
a clamp-on dash light, a patching outfit, a tool box which you
bolted to the running board, a sun visor, a steering-column brace
90 to keep the column rigid, and a set of emergency containers for
gas, oil, and water—three thin, disc-like cans which reposed in a
case on the running board during long, important journeys—red
for gas, gray for water, green for oil. It was only a beginning.
After the car was about a year old, steps were taken to check the
95 alarming disintegration. (Model T was full of tumors, but they
were benign.) A set of anti-rattlers (ninety-eight cents) was a
popular panacea. You hooked them on to the gas and spark rods,
to the brake pull rod, and to the steering-rod connections. Hood
silencers, of black rubber, were applied to the fluttering hood.
100 Shock-absorbers and snubbers gave "complete relaxation." Some
people bought rubber pedal pads, to fit over the standard metal

pedals. (I didn't like these, I remember.) Persons of a suspicious or pugnacious turn of mind bought a rear-view mirror; but most Model T owners weren't worried by what was coming from behind because they would soon enough see it out in front. They 105 rode in a state of cheerful catalepsy. Quite a large mutinous clique among Ford owners went over to a foot accelerator (you could buy one and screw it to the floor board), but there was a certain madness in these people, because the Model T, just as she stood, had a choice of three footpedals to push, and there were 110 plenty of moments when both feet were occupied in the routine performance of duty and when the only way to speed up the engine was with the hand throttle.

9. Gadget bred gadget. Owners not only bought ready-made gadgets, they invented gadgets to meet special needs. I myself 115 drove my car directly from the agency to the blacksmith's, and had the smith affix two enormous iron brackets to the port running board to support an army trunk.

10. People who owned closed models builded along different lines: they bought ball grip handles for opening doors, window 120 anti-rattlers, and de-luxe flower vases of the cut-glass anti-splash type. People with delicate sensibilities garnished their car with a device called the Donna Lee Automobile Disseminator—a porous vase guaranteed, according to Sears, to fill the car with a "faint clean odor of lavender." The gap between open cars and closed 125 cars was not as great then as it is now: for $11.95, Sears Roebuck converted your touring car into a sedan and you went forth renewed. One agreeable quality of the old Fords was that they had no bumpers, and their fenders softened and wilted with the years and permitted the driver to squeeze in and out of tight 130 places.

11. Tires were 30 x 3½, cost about twelve dollars, and punctured readily. Everybody carried a Jiffy patching set, with a nutmeg grater to roughen the tube before the goo was spread on. Everybody was capable of putting on a patch, expected to have to, and 135 did have to.

12. During my association with Model T's, self-starters were not a prevalent accessory. They were expensive and under suspicion. Your car came equipped with a serviceable crank, and the

140 first thing you learned was how to Get Results. It was a special
trick, and until you learned it (usually from another Ford owner,
but sometimes by a period of appalling experimentation) you
might as well have been winding up an awning. The trick was to
leave the ignition switch off, proceed to the animal's head, pull
145 the choke (which was a little wire protruding through the radiator) and give the crank two or three nonchalant upward lifts.
Then, whistling as though thinking about something else, you
would saunter back to the driver's cabin, turn the ignition on,
return to the crank, and this time, catching it on the down stroke,
150 give it a quick spin with plenty of That. If this procedure was
followed, the engine almost always responded—first with a few
scattered explosions, then with a tumultuous gunfire, which you
checked by racing around to the driver's seat and retarding the
throttle. Often, if the emergency brake hadn't been pulled all the
155 way back, the car advanced on you the instant the first explosion
occurred and you would hold it back by leaning your weight
against it. I can still feel my old Ford nuzzling me at the curb,
as though looking for an apple in my pocket.

13. In zero weather, ordinary cranking became an impossi-
160 bility, except for giants. The oil thickened, and it became necessary to jack up the rear wheels, which, for some planetary reason,
eased the throw.

14. The lore and legend that governed the Ford were boundless. Owners had their own theories about everything; they dis-
165 cussed mutual problems in that wise, infinitely resourceful way
old women discuss rheumatism. Exact knowledge was pretty
scarce, and often proved less effective than superstition. Drop-
ping a camphor ball into the gas tank was a popular expedient;
it seemed to have a tonic effect on both man and machine. There
170 wasn't much to base exact knowledge on. The Ford driver flew
blind. He didn't know the temperature of his engine, the speed of
his car, the amount of his fuel, or the pressure of his oil (the old
Ford lubricated itself by what was amiably described as the
"splash system"). A speedometer cost money and was an extra,
175 like a windshield-wiper. The dashboard of the early models was
bare save for an ignition key; later models, grown effete, boasted
an ammeter which pulsated alarmingly with the throbbing of the

car. Under the dash was a box of coils, with vibrators which you adjusted, or thought you adjusted. Whatever the driver learned of his motor, he learned not through instruments but through sudden developments. I remember that the timer was one of the vital organs about which there was ample doctrine. When everything else had been checked, you "had a look" at the timer. It was an extravagantly odd little device, simple in construction, mysterious in function. It contained a roller, held by a spring, and there were four contact points on the inside of the case against which, many people believed, the roller rolled. I have had a timer apart on a sick Ford many times. But I never really knew what I was up to—I was just showing off before God. There were almost as many schools of thought as there were timers. Some people, when things went wrong, just clenched their teeth and gave the timer a smart crack with a wrench. Other people opened it up and blew on it. There was a school that held that the timer needed large amounts of oil; they fixed it by frequent baptism. And there was a school that was positive it was meant to run dry as a bone; these people were continually taking it off and wiping it. I remember once spitting into a timer; not in anger, but in a spirit of research. You see, the Model T driver moved in the realm of metaphysics. He believed his car could be hexed.

15. One reason the Ford anatomy was never reduced to an exact science was that, having "fixed" it, the owner couldn't honestly claim that the treatment had brought about the cure. There were too many authenticated cases of Fords fixing themselves— restored naturally to health after a short rest. Farmers soon discovered this, and it fitted nicely with their draft-horse philosophy: "Let 'er cool off and she'll snap into it again."

16. A Ford owner had Number One Bearing constantly in mind. This bearing, being at the front end of the motor, was the one that always burned out, because the oil didn't reach it when the car was climbing hills. (That's what I was always told, anyway.) The oil used to recede and leave Number One dry as a clam flat; you had to watch that bearing like a hawk. It was like a weak heart—you could hear it start knocking, and that was when you stopped to let her cool off. Try as you would to keep the oil supply right, in the end Number One always went out.

"Number One Bearing burned out on me and I had to have her replaced," you would say, wisely; and your companions always had a lot to tell about how to protect and pamper Number One to keep her alive.

220   17. Sprinkled not too liberally among the millions of amateur witch doctors who drove Fords and applied their own abominable cures were the heaven-sent mechanics who could really make the car talk. These professionals turned up in undreamed-of spots. One time, on the banks of the Columbia River in Wash-
225   ington, I heard the rear end go out of my Model T when I was trying to whip it up a steep incline onto the deck of a ferry. Something snapped; the car slid backward into the mud. It seemed to me like the end of the trail. But the captain of the ferry, observing the withered remnant, spoke up.

230   18. "What's got her?" he asked.

19. "I guess it's the rear end," I replied, listlessly. The captain leaned over the rail and stared. Then I saw that there was a hunger in his eyes that set him off from other men.

20. "Tell you what," he said, carelessly, trying to cover up his
235   eagerness, "let's pull the son of a bitch up onto the boat, and I'll help you fix her while we're going back and forth on the river."

21. We did just this. All that day I plied between the town of Pasco and Kennewick, while the skipper (who had once worked in a Ford garage) directed the amazing work of resetting the
240   bones of my car.

22. Springtime in the heyday of the Model T was a delirious season. Owning a car was still a major excitement, roads were still wonderful and bad. The Fords were obviously conceived in madness: any car which was capable of going from forward into
245   reverse without any perceptible mechanical hiatus was bound to be a mighty challenging thing to the human imagination. Boys used to veer them off the highway into a level pasture and run wild with them, as though they were cutting up with a girl. Most everybody used the reverse pedal quite as much as the regular
250   foot brake—it distributed the wear over the bands and wore them all down evenly. That was the big trick, to wear all the bands down evenly, so that the final chattering would be total and the whole unit scream for renewal.

23. The days were golden, the nights were dim and strange. I still recall with trembling those loud, nocturnal crises when you drew up to a signpost and raced the engine so the lights would be bright enough to read destinations by. I have never been really planetary since. I suppose it's time to say goodbye. Farewell, my lovely!

255

※※※※※※※※※※

Before writing an essay on any subject, one must decide how to handle the subject—what to say for what audience, what not to say, what tone to use, what to suggest or imply. The problem of scale is a serious one for any writer, but probably most serious for the beginner. Too often students try to put everything they know about a subject into one essay; too often the essay thus handled is badly organized, ponderous, and boring; and too often the writer himself, tired with all the detail he has included in his half-finished essay, tries to finish up quickly and skips over or merely hints at points that he should have covered more fully.

Lee Strout White's essay *Farewell, My Lovely!* is an example of how a good writer handles the problem of scale. White hasn't tried to tell us everything he knows about the Model T. Instead he has decided to pay a light-hearted tribute to the old car and has selected and controlled his details to suit his purpose. The special quirk to this piece is that it is almost certainly written for people who knew and owned a Model T, because the explanations are not really explanations but reveries, reminiscences, and love-songs.

1. Paragraphs 1 and 2 serve as White's introduction. Yet he gives us a great deal of information in these paragraphs, and he introduces ideas and words that he develops later in the essay. See if you can identify them.

2. White also establishes in this introduction the mood and tone that are sustained throughout the piece. What are they? Define the tone of "The great days have faded, the end is in sight," (3–4), "gaudy, irretrievable" (18). Why eschew the "sob" of line 21? Does White stand by the promise he makes here?

3. Where in the first two paragraphs is White's "statement of purpose"—that is, where does he specifically tell us what he is going to talk about in the rest of the essay?

4.   White plays with the word "planetary" (introduced in line 24) all through the essay. Look it up in a good dictionary. What does the phrase "in its epicyclic sense" (26) mean? Notice, now, how this meaning of "planetary" and the second meaning ("wandering, erratic") are juxtaposed in the sentences in lines 28–33. In what sense is it used in line 161? In line 258? Write a short essay on the games White plays with the word. Some of the twists and turns require very close attention.

5.   White says that the Model T was "hardworking" and "commonplace" (16). Indeed, throughout the essay, he emphasizes the simple wholesomeness of the car. Go through it marking words and passages that suggest this attitude. What figures and metaphors in the essay also indicate the car's wholesomeness?

6.   Much of the charm of this essay is due to White's description of the Model T as a unique mixture of machine and animal. Often he refers specifically to a steel machine with parts that need oil and repair, yet often he speaks of the car as a living, throbbing organism—stubborn, whimsical, and ailing. Study Par. 12. What words does he use to describe each of these aspects of the car? Why must the owner whistle "as though thinking about something else"? What is the effect of words like "association" (137) and "nuzzling" (157)? Go through the entire essay marking passages that describe the Model T as an animal. What qualities of an animal are used *metaphorically* to describe it?

7.   What words in the first sentence of Par. 7 establish the identification of the owner with the Model T? Where else in the essay does White deal with the rapport between car and owner?

8.   What is the effect of the capital letters in "Get Results" (140), "That" (150), "Number One Bearing" (207)?

9.   Paragraph 14 moves from generalization to example and back again. What facts support the statement in lines 166–167, "Exact knowledge was pretty scarce, and often proved less effective than superstition." What facts support the metaphorical abstraction, "flew blind" (170–171)?

10.   *Gaudy* (18), *heroic* (16), *glorious* (46), *enthroned* (54), *Pegasus, godlike* (82–83) develop what theme? Are there other words in the same pattern?

11.   Some of White's diction is utterly whimsical, like "brood-

ing" (56), the pun on "unbend" (62), "cheerful catalepsy" (106), "port" (117). How many others of this order can you find? Relate them to the overall tone of the essay.

12. In line 71 "decorative and functional" states a theme. List the concrete details that develop each abstraction thereafter.

13. Mark the passages in the essay that do not seem to be understandable unless one has known a Model T. For instance, line 15, what industries? Or what "peculiar nature" (28)? and why a "fluttering" hood (99)? Can you explain these?

14. Alas, time plays tricks on some writers. In 1961 the meaning of lines 47–50, "The human leg was (and still is) incapable of letting in a clutch with anything like the forthright abandon that used to send Model T on its way," will escape many a young person who has driven only with automatic transmissions, whose take-off would atomize a Model T. But never mind, White knows this; he means to carry his aging reader back to his youth. Where can you identify evidence for this fact? Note the extreme accuracy of "abruptness" (46); is it equivalent to "rapidly"? Explain.

Find words and phases that show that White is using the Model T in order to evoke the image and tone of another way of life.

15. In this atomic age of ours, things are outdated often before they get off the assembly line. Newer, bigger, and better products are constantly replacing "old, reliable" ones. Write a reminiscent essay on something which has gone out of date or out of style. You might recall the old-fashioned soda fountain or grocery store of the days before the supermarket, or the penny candy shelf, or the pre-electric typewriter that always had a sticky "i," or the swell baseball or stickball games before the organized "little league" games, or dolls that didn't walk and didn't have real hair that curled, or long car-rides of discovery before your first plane trip. You might even imagine, in your essay, what the days before the telephone were like. Before the airplane, or electric saw, or electricity. To be interesting, you must have facts, facts, facts.

Dwell on the pleasant aspects of the out-dated thing, how even its faults or flaws were humorous.

Alternately, in a more serious vein, you might write an essay comparing the attack on change-for-the-sake-of-change in *The Post Office Pen* (p. 41) with the very different nostalgia for an old-fashioned thing seen in *Farewell, My Lovely*.

The Sunless Sea

RACHEL L. CARSON

1. Between the sunlit surface waters of the open sea and the hidden hills and valleys of the ocean floor lies the least known region of the sea. These deep, dark waters, with all their mysteries and their unsolved problems, cover a very considerable part of the earth. The whole world ocean extends over about three-fourths of the surface of the globe. If we subtract the shallow areas of the continental shelves and the scattered banks and shoals, where at least the pale ghost of sunlight moves over the underlying bottom, there still remains about half the earth that is covered by miles-deep, lightless water, that has been dark since the world began.

2. This region has withheld its secrets more obstinately than any other. Man, with all his ingenuity, has been able to venture only to its threshold. Wearing a diving helmet, he can walk on the ocean floor about 10 fathoms down. He can descend to an extreme limit of about 500 feet in a complete diving suit, so heavily armored that movement is almost impossible, carrying with him a constant supply of oxygen. Only two men in all the history of the world have had the experience of descending, alive, beyond the range of visible light. These men are William Beebe and Otis Barton. In the bathysphere, they reached a depth of 3028 feet in the open ocean off Bermuda, in the year 1934. Barton alone, in a steel sphere known as the benthoscope, descended to the great depth of 4500 feet off California, in the summer of 1949.

3. Although only a fortunate few can ever visit the deep sea, the precise instruments of the oceanographer, recording light

penetration, pressure, salinity, and temperature, have given us the materials with which to reconstruct in imagination these eerie, forbidding regions. Unlike the surface waters, which are sensitive to every gust of wind, which know day and night, respond to the pull of sun and moon, and change as the seasons change, the deep waters are a place where change comes slowly, if at all. Down beyond the reach of the sun's rays, there is no alternation of light and darkness. There is rather an unending night, as old as the sea itself. For most of its creatures, groping their way endlessly through its black waters, it must be a place of hunger, where food is scarce and hard to find, a shelterless place where there is no sanctuary from ever-present enemies, where one can only move on and on, from birth to death, through an endless night, confined as in a prison to his own particular layer of the sea.

4. They used to say that nothing could live in the deep sea. It was a belief that must have been easy to accept, for without proof to the contrary, how could anyone conceive of life in such a place?

5. A century ago the British biologist Edward Forbes wrote: "As we descend deeper and deeper into this region, the inhabitants become more and more modified, and fewer and fewer, indicating our approach to an abyss where life is either extinguished, or exhibits but a few sparks to mark its lingering presence." Yet Forbes urged further exploration of "this vast deep-sea region" to settle forever the question of the existence of life at great depths.

6. Even then, the evidence was accumulating. Sir John Ross, during his exploration of the arctic seas in 1818, had brought up from a depth of 1000 fathoms mud in which there were worms, thus proving there was animal life in the bed of the ocean notwithstanding the darkness, stillness, silence, and immense pressure produced by more than a mile of superincumbent water.

7. Then from the surveying ship *Bulldog*, examining a proposed northern route for a cable from Faroe to Labrador in 1860, came another report. The *Bulldog's* sounding line, which at one place had been allowed to lie for some time on the bottom at a depth of 1260 fathoms, came up with 13 starfish clinging to it. Through these starfish, the ship's naturalist wrote, "the deep has sent forth the long coveted message." But not all the zoologists

65 of the day were prepared to accept the message. Some doubters
asserted that the starfish had "convulsively embraced" the line
somewhere on the way back to the surface.

8. In the same year, 1860, a cable in the Mediterranean was
raised for repairs from a depth of 1200 fathoms. It was found to
70 be heavily encrusted with corals and other sessile animals that
had attached themselves at an early stage of development and
grown to maturity over a period of months or years. There was
not the slightest chance that they had become entangled in the
cable as it was being raised to the surface.

75 9. Then the *Challenger* set out from Portsmouth in the year
1872 and traced a course around the globe. From bottoms lying
under miles of water, from silent deeps carpeted with red clay
ooze, and from all the lightless intermediate depths, net-haul
after net-haul of strange and fantastic creatures came up and
80 were spilled out on the decks. Poring over the weird beings thus
brought up for the first time into the light of day, beings no man
had ever seen before, the *Challenger* scientists realized that life
existed even on the deepest floor of the abyss.

10. The recent discovery that a living cloud of some unknown
85 creatures is spread over much of the ocean at a depth of several
hundred fathoms below the surface is the most exciting thing that
has been learned about the ocean for many years.

11. When echo sounding was developed to allow ships while
under way to record the depth of the bottom, probably no one
90 suspected that it would also provide a means of learning something about deep-sea life. But operators of the new instruments
soon discovered that the sound waves, directed downward from
the ship like a beam of light, were reflected back from any solid
object they met. Answering echoes were returned from interme-
95 diate depths, presumably from schools of fish, whales, or sub-
marines; then a second echo was received from the bottom.

12. These facts were so well established by the late 1930's that
fishermen had begun to talk about using their fathometers to
search for schools of herring. Then the war brought the whole
100 subject under strict security regulations, and little more was
heard about it. In 1946, however, the United States Navy issued
a significant bulletin. It was reported that several scientists, work-

ing with sonic equipment in deep water off the California coast, had discovered a widespread "layer" of some sort, which gave back an answering echo to the sound waves. This reflecting layer, 105 seemingly suspended between the surface and the floor of the Pacific, was found over an area 300 miles wide. It lay from 1000 to 1500 feet below the surface. The discovery was made by three scientists, Eyring, Christensen, and Raitt, aboard the U.S.S. *Jasper* in 1942, and for a time this mysterious phenomenon, of 110 wholly unknown nature, was called the ECR layer. Then in 1945 Martin W. Johnson, marine biologist of the Scripps Institution of Oceanography, made a further discovery which gave the first clue to the nature of the layer. Working aboard the vessel, *E. W. Scripps,* Johnson found that whatever sent back the echoes moved 115 upward and downward in rhythmic fashion, being found near the surface at night, in deep water during the day. This discovery disposed of speculations that the reflections came from something inanimate, perhaps a mere physical discontinuity in the water, and showed that the layer is composed of living creatures capable 120 of controlled movement.

13. From this time on, discoveries about the sea's "phantom bottom" came rapidly. With widespread use of echo-sounding instruments, it has become clear that the phenomenon is not something peculiar to the coast of California alone. It occurs 125 almost universally in the deep ocean basins—drifting by day at a depth of several hundred fathoms, at night rising to the surface, and again, before sunrise, sinking into the depths.

14. On the passage of the U.S.S. *Henderson* from San Diego to the Antarctic in 1947, the reflecting layer was detected during 130 the greater part of each day, at depths varying from 150 to 450 fathoms, and on a later run from San Diego to Yokosuka, Japan, the *Henderson's* fathometer again recorded the layer every day, suggesting that it exists almost continuously across the Pacific.

15. During July and August 1947, the U.S.S. *Nereus* made a 135 continuous fathogram from Pearl Harbor to the Arctic and found the scattering layer over all deep waters. It did not develop, however, in the shallow Bering and Chuckchee seas. Sometimes the *Nereus* fathogram showed two distinct layers, the second following the first downward in the morning after an interval of about 140

20 minutes, showing that whatever composed it responded differently to the growing illumination in the water.

16. Despite attempts to sample it or photograph it, no one is sure what the layer is, although the discovery may be made any
145 day. There are three principal theories, each of which has its group of supporters. According to these theories, the sea's phantom bottom may consist of small planktonic shrimps, of fishes, or of squids.

✳✳✳✳✳✳✳✳✳✳✳

How does one invest reliable scientific information with an atmosphere of breathless, almost romantic excitement? What at first glance seems a sort of magic performed by Rachel Carson can be traced to her diction, her manner of allowing her reader to make a series of satisfying discoveries with her, and her prose rhythms.

1. In Par. 1 what words and phrases extend and modify and enrich the idea of "least known"? There are at least eight, yet they are woven into an orderly presentation of fact. In addition to the words just mentioned, there are a number which contribute an air of wonder—"the whole world," for example. What others? Mark and explain phrases that express these two ideas—mystery and wonder—throughout the selection.

2. What two words in Par. 2 dramatize the mystery into a contest, and between what contestants? How do the denotations and connotations of "venture" and "threshold" affect this dramatic setting? What does "in all the history of the world" do for it?

3. At first glance there seems to be a contradiction between "fortunate few" (25) and "eerie, forbidding" (28–29), but the effect is actually very much in keeping with the tone of the selection. But what if the two phrases were reversed so that the impact of "eerie, forbidding" came first? How would this alter the effect of the sentence?

4. What theme is introduced by the sequence, "sensitive . . . know . . . respond" (29–30)? And what is the relationship between these words and the ocean depths? Does it, in effect, humanize or dehumanize them?

5. What is the most purely emotional, rather than informative phrase in Par. 3? What words in the paragraph evoke human emotions in the sea depths?—like "grope." How do they do this?

6. A new form of dramatization appears with Par. 4: instead of *informing* us about deep-sea life, Rachel Carson presents the adventure of its discovery in the eyes and thoughts of those who doubted and those who participated. Tell in a sentence or two just how she contrives to make her reader participate emotionally in the debate and discovery.

7. Observe how the drama brings you to such a degree of involvement that you experience a certain triumph in the disclosures of Par. 9. Now, show how her confidence in this involvement permits the writer to introduce strong, imaginative words into the paragraph. Mark them and describe their effects. Are these terms in any way associated with the feelings of the persons involved in the drama, or do they seem to represent primarily the feelings of the author?

8. How does Par. 12 introduce a new scene in the drama? What people are the actors; what opposition or hazards do they combat? We are dealing here with what has become a standard twentieth-century technique of exposition. Besides the dramatic contest, the human involvement, and the sense of being present at the unfolding action, this technique has a further advantage of incorporating its evidence or proof into the story. Paragraphs 10–12 could be written as fact, with the dates and places supplied in footnotes; here such information comes with the unfolding story as part of the action.

9. *Periodicity* is a name for a type of sentence order. A periodic sentence is one in which the culminating, revealing word is withheld till the end—or very near the end. All the digressions, qualifications, modifiers are given before the main clause is completed. Depending on the context, periodicity produces stateliness or suspense. For Rachel Carson it produces suspense. In Sen. 1 the culminating verb, *lies*, is near the end. Sen. 4 (l. 7) has two subordinate clauses before the main clause, and one following it. The sentences beginning at lines 13, 18, 21, 22, 25, 29, and 33—to list only the early examples—all have modifiers and qualifications *before* the main clause. Again and again, the sentence itself is a form of suspense, with the key word withheld as long as possible.

Go through the rest of the selection marking all the verbs of the main clauses, in order to identify the amount of periodicity; and note where the word order creates the effect of suspense or excites the curiosity of the reader. Try to use this device in your next essay.

10.   Write a fairly detailed exposition of a process, procedure, discovery, or experiment, using this method of dramatic involvement. The spectatorship of author-reader can be achieved in several ways. One reliable and standard way is to have the writer interviewing the person who has made the discovery or developed the process, making him recount the stages of his contest with his problem; another is to join a discussion among the people concerned with the problem. Any method you choose must be carefully planned and executed, ironically because this technique conveys the notion of artlessness.

Celestial Navigation by Birds

E. G. F. SAUER

1. In spring and summer the songbirds known as the warblers are familiar residents in the countries throughout Europe. City dwellers know them well, for the small, gray birds find a home to their liking in the shrubs and hedges of gardens and small parks. During the spring breeding season the air is filled with their loud, melodic singing as each male establishes a small territory for himself in noisy battle with a rival. Once the claims are decided, the truculence and the songs subside; the birds proceed to mate and to raise their young. In late summer they feed amicably on elderberries and blackberries and they flit about in peace among the bushes. Then in August the birds begin to grow restless; their migratory instinct stirs. Suddenly, in one night, the whole resident population of one species is off and away. The next morning the bushes are filled with a new lot of warblers that have flown in from more northern areas; they stay for a few days and then they too fly on to the south. Through the weeks of September and October there is a continuous coming and going of hordes of the migrating warblers. Gradually the number passing through diminishes. The species called the garden warblers disappears first, then the whitethroats, after them the lesser whitethroats, and finally the blackcaps.

2. Where do they go? Ornithologists know exactly where the warblers go, for they have banded these birds for many years and followed them to their winter homes. With the exception of some blackcaps, these warblers travel to various parts of Africa. Some of them migrate as far as from Scandinavia to the southern part

of Africa—a distance of seven thousand miles and more. In the spring the birds migrate back to the same place that they left in the fall.

30   3. Most remarkable of all is that each bird finds its own way to its destination! The warblers do not follow a leader or make the journey as a group; they navigate individually. And young birds making their first migration reach their goal as surely as the experienced travelers. Somehow, purely by instinct, the warblers
35 know exactly how to set their course.

4. The navigation powers of birds have fascinated investigators for more than a century. By now there is a large literature of well-documented testimony to their amazing performances. The late Werner Rüppell of Germany, one of the leading experi-
40 menters on bird migration, found that starlings taken from their nests near Berlin and carried away to all points of the compass would find their way back to their nesting places from as far as 1,250 miles away. The Manx Shearwater, a sea bird, has astonished investigators with still more spectacular feats; one shear-
45 water, taken from the west coast of England by G. V. T. Matthews and flown by plane to Boston, was back in its English nest in 12 days, having winged its own way 3,067 miles across the unknown Atlantic. The Pacific golden plover migrates each fall from its breeding grounds along the Bering Sea coast to its winter home
50 in the Hawaiian Islands. This bird, lacking webbed feet, cannot rest on the water as waterfowl do; it must fly on steadily for several days to reach its destination over thousands of miles of ocean. If it wandered only slightly off course, it would become lost and exhausted in the vast Pacific, but it finds its way unerr-
55 ingly to Hawaii.

5. Until recently attempts to explain the incredible navigation feats of birds were almost entirely a matter of speculation. Various theorists proposed that the birds were guided by the earth's magnetic field, by the Coriolis force arising from the earth's rota-
60 tion, by landmarks, and so on. But more and more ornithologists have been driven to the conclusion that birds must rely mainly on celestial navigation—the sun by day, the constellations by night.

6. The idea that birds are guided by the sun was suggested as long as half a century ago, but it was not taken seriously until the

early 1950's, when experimenters began to turn up some interest- 65
ing evidence. Gustav Kramer in Germany and G. V. T. Matthews
in England discovered independently that homing pigeons and
wild birds can use the sun as a compass and that they possess a
"time sense" which allows them to take account of the sun's
motion across the sky. Other zoologists have confirmed these 70
findings. It has now been proved, in fact, that our warblers can
orient themselves by the sun.

7. But the warblers fly mainly at night. What sort of system do
they use to steer their course in their nocturnal migrations nearly
halfway around the globe? Several years ago the author and his 75
wife started a systematic laboratory study of this question by
means of specially designed cages in our aviary at Freiburg.

8. We had already seen laboratory proof of the stirring of the
migratory instinct in these small world-travelers and of a seasonal
time sense that governed this urge. We had hatched and raised 80
warblers in completely closed, sound-proof chambers where they
lived in the illusion of eternal summer, year in and year out. Yet,
although they seemed to have no outward cues of the yearly
rhythm of nature, in the autumn the birds would begin to flit
restlessly from branch to branch or flutter continually over their 85
perches, night after wakeful night. They kept this up for many
weeks—about the length of time it would have taken them to fly
to Africa. Then they went back to sleeping again at night. In the
spring, about the time that warblers migrate back from Africa to
their European homes, our birds again had a spell of restless, 90
wakeful nights. It was as if they had an inner clock which told
them when the time had come to take wing for distant parts.

9. To explore the orientation question we now placed warblers
in a cage with a glass opening at the top, so that they could see
part of the sky (but nothing else of their surroundings). At the 95
season of migration the birds would begin to flutter and, peculiarly enough, each would take up a position pointing in a particular geographic direction, like the needle of a compass. Even
when we tried to turn the birds away by rotating their ring-
shaped perch, they stubbornly turned back to the preferred direc- 100
tion. The direction in each case was characteristic of the species:
the garden warblers, the whitethroats, and the blackcaps all

pointed toward the southwest, the lesser whitethroats toward the southeast (that is, in the fall; in the spring these directions were
105 reversed). Now these are precisely the directions in which the respective species start their migrations from central Europe to Africa! The lesser whitethroats start southeastward, flying across the Balkans, and then turn south up the Nile Valley; the other species all take off southwestward and fly to Africa by way of
110 Spain and Gibraltar.

10. Experienced or inexperienced, the birds invariably took up the appropriate direction of flight in the cage. How did they know the direction? Seemingly the only clue available to them was the starry night sky overhead. To explore this theory further we now
115 put them through a series of tests. We found that when the stars were hidden by thick clouds, the birds became completely disoriented. They were likewise confused when only diffuse and strongly polarized light came through their skylight. To adopt and keep to a definite direction they needed a look at the starry
120 sky. Indeed, the birds watched the sky so intently that shooting stars made them change their direction for a short time.

11. For still more rigidly controlled experiments we proceeded to test the birds in a cage placed in a planetarium: that is, with a dome showing an artificial replica of the natural starry sky. Again,
125 when the dome was merely illuminated with diffuse light (showing no stars), the warblers were unable to choose a preferred direction. But when the planetarium sky matched the local night sky, the birds took up the proper direction just as if they were seeing the natural sky, but now adjusted to the artificial plane-
130 tarium directions.

12. Now our artificial dome permitted us to shift the stars and constellations about. By changing the north-south declination (height) of the stars we could change the apparent geographical latitude, making the birds believe that they were farther south or
135 north than they actually were. Similarly by shifting the sky in the east-west direction we might mislead the birds about their position in longitude. How would they behave under these circumstances?

13. To illustrate the results I shall describe some experiments
140 with a lesser whitethroat warbler. Recall that the lesser white-

throat normally first travels southeastward across the Balkans and then turns due south, flying along the Nile to its winter home in the region of the Nile headwaters. In our experiments it turned out that as long as the planetarium sky was adjusted to the latitudes of 50 to 40 degrees north, this bird took up the expected 145 flight position facing southeast. But as we shifted the sky, simulating more southerly latitudes, the bird tended to turn more and more toward the southern direction, until, at the latitude of 15 degrees, it set its course due south!

14. In other words, this lesser whitethroat, which had spent all 150 its life in a cage and never traveled under a natural sky, let alone migrated to Africa, still displayed an inborn ability to use the guidance of the stars to follow the usual route of its species, adjusting its direction nicely at each given latitude. Earlier investigators had supposed that these birds used landmarks to find 155 their route: for example, that the coastline at the eastern end of the Mediterranean was the cue which told them to turn south. But our experiments proved that the birds are able to do it only by the stars.

15. Now let us see what happened when we shifted the plane- 160 tarium sky to change the longitude, or, corresponding to it, the time. One night, while the lesser whitethroat was flapping its wings and heading in the southeast direction, we suddenly presented the bird with a sky shifted to the configuration five hours and 10 minutes ahead of the local time; in other words, the 165 apparent geographical position of the cage then corresponded to a point 77.5 degrees eastward in longitude at this particular time. The bird at once showed that it was deeply disturbed. It looked excitedly at the unfamiliar sky and for almost a full minute stood irresolutely. Then it suddenly turned and took wing in the west- 170 ward direction. According to the sky, its position at the moment corresponded to a point near Lake Balkhash in Siberia; the bird, to correct its displacement, was heading directly toward the usual migration starting point in Europe.

16. As we reduced its displacement, the bird shifted its head- 175 ing more and more from due west toward the south. When the displacement was only an hour, corresponding to a position near Vienna, the lesser whitethroat headed south; when the canopy

of stars was restored to the correct configuration at our locality
180 for the season and time of night, the bird took up the normal
heading toward the southeast.

17. The behavior of this individual, confirmed by experiments
with other birds, leaves no doubt that the warblers have a remarkable hereditary mechanism for orienting themselves by the stars
185 —a detailed image of the starry configuration of the sky coupled
with a precise time sense which relates the heavenly canopy to
the geography of the earth at every time and season. At their very
first glimpse of the sky the birds automatically know the right
direction. Without benefit of previous experience, with no cue
190 except the stars, the birds are able to locate themselves in time
and space and to find their way to their destined homes.

18. To be sure, the warblers do not have to rely solely on the
constellations. In daytime they can guide themselves by the position of the sun. On cloudy nights they get some guidance from
195 mountain ranges, coastlines, and river courses gleaming in the
pale night shine. Only in almost total darkness, when thick clouds
utterly hide the sky, are the birds in trouble: they circle help-
lessly and often are drawn to lighthouses.

19. We are going on to study the warblers' orientation system
200 in more detail, systematically removing constellations or stars
from our planetarium sky one by one to see if we can reduce the
guidance cues to a basic pattern. One very interesting puzzle is
the fact that the birds must somehow be able to make adjustments to astronomical evolution, for in the course of time the
205 pattern of constellations in the sky is slowly but constantly changing. Even more difficult to explain is the mystery of how the birds
ever came to rely on celestial navigation and to develop their
skill in the first place. We know that the warblers are not the only
creatures possessing this gift: other birds, fish, insects, crabs, and
210 spiders have been found by experiment to be capable of guiding
themselves by the sun. But there are many other guidance mech-
anisms and signposts available on earth. What evolutionary process was it that endowed these animals with the highly sophisticated ability to read the stars?

215 20. Whatever the answer, we cannot help marveling at the
wondrous celestial instinct of the warblers. When fall comes, the

little garden warbler, weighing barely three quarters of an ounce, sets off one night on an unbelievable journey. All alone, never in the collective security of a flock, it wings its solitary way south-westward over Germany, France, and Spain, and then swings 220 south to its distant goal in southern Africa. It flies on unerringly, covering a hundred miles and more in a single night, never once stopping in its course, certain of its goal. When drifted by heavy sidewinds, the bird navigates back to its primary course in the next calm night. In the spring it takes off again and northward 225 retraces its path to its nesting place in a European thicket—there to give birth to a new generation of little warblers which will grow up, without being taught, with the self-same capacity to follow the same route across the continents and oceans by the map of the stars. 230

****

E. G. F. Sauer's essay is similar to Rachel Carson's in that both are informative and scientific, and both authors are plainly fasci-nated by their subjects. Yet there are differences in approach in the two essays. Carson's explanations are more lengthy, more poetic, though she leaves no doubt that her explanations are accurate. She describes the findings of other people, but without going into intricate detail. We don't, for example, learn how the sounding instruments work or what the benthoscope is like.

1. Turn back to Rachel Carson's essay (p. 130). Note the very general terms: "sonic equipment" (103), "widespread layer of some sort" (104), "echo-sounding instruments" (123–4), and "worms" (54). They give the least information possible. Is this to maintain the scale and pace of Carson's dramatic narrative? Does it heighten the mystery? Does the information become more detailed as we come to the major discoveries or disclosures? Or is it merely a question of purpose—that she is dealing more with the adventure of discovery than with the facts discovered? Note, in this connection, the comments in question 13 below.

2. Sauer gives us a more detailed, first-hand account of his own experiments. His subject seems just as exciting to him, but he is less romantic, less breathless. Notice, now, the sort of details

Sauer gives in describing the cage (94–95), the perch (99–100), and the planetarium (Par. 11). How do they differ from Carson's?

3. Consider the audience that each writer is aiming at. Do you think that one is aiming at a larger, less scientific audience than the other? Is this matter of scale (questions 1 and 2) related to the kind of audience expected? This question may lead to a debate over which essay *is* more "popular," if either.

4. How does the difference in point of view (first-person point of view in Sauer as opposed to third-person in Carson) affect what, how, and how much the author says? Does this difference affect the tone of the essay? That is, does one have to be more objective in one case than the other? Trace through the essay the means by which Sauer produces an effect of modesty-through-objectivity; compare with Carson's somewhat more intense and emotional effect.

5. The first paragraph of Sauer's essay is descriptive and expository. While the author poses no questions directly, his simple expository prose leads the reader to question Why? and Where? No doubt this is why we are immediately satisfied when Sauer himself asks the question in the first sentence of Par. 2. Note where else in the essay Sauer uses this device—setting up a problem by merely stating facts, and then asking a question that he subsequently answers. In each case is the device effective?

6. Suppose Sauer had started his essay with Par. 4. Would it be as interesting? Why? What does he accomplish in the first three paragraphs? Compare Sauer's introduction with Carson's: what ideas, emotions, expectations does each evoke?

7. Sauer continually uses words that express marvel at this migratory instinct in birds. List the words that express this idea.

8. Let us examine more closely the method of this exposition. What are the ideas, and how are they set forth? In Par. 6 we move from older theories to the statement that birds are now known to have both a *direction* and a *time* sense (or instinct), for solar navigation. Paragraph 7 asks a question about night flight and announces that the author and his wife "started" a systematic study of the question. Why did he not say "have conducted," instead of the simple past, "started"? How does the verb used create suspense?

9. The "started" here is accounted for by the "had . . . seen" of line 78; this verb places the reader in the *middle* of an action and then takes him back to look at what had gone before: the proof of the migratory instinct. In this proof does the evidence come before or after the conclusion?

10. With Par. 9, we join the action. What *aspect* of the migratory instinct is explored? Underline in red the sentences (or parts of sentences) that describe actual events, in black those that generalize. The phrase "characteristic of the species" (101) is *exemplified* with increasing concreteness to the end of the paragraph. Is the phrase necessary, or is it there as a mechanism of transition from "perch" to "direction"?

11. What is the function of the first sentence in Par. 10? In the examples that follow, are we in an action as in Par. 9 or hearing a report of an action?

12. Write an explanation of what was proved with the planetarium that could not have been proved otherwise. How do you justify the fact that the exposition becomes increasingly dense—and therefore difficult—from Par. 13 through Par. 16? Would the reader become bored with too full an exposition? Can he understand the evidence even without the geographical knowledge to follow it? Thereafter we return to generalization which sets forth the conclusions proved in the dense paragraphs. Does the writer here fail to manage the problem of *scale* effectively? What statement in Par. 18 seems questionable?

13. A scientific subject does not have to be treated coldly, unemotionally, and unpoetically, as we see from this essay and Rachel Carson's. In Par. 1, for example, Sauer uses words like *truculence, amicably, flit, hordes.* Make a study of the colorful words that Sauer has used. For example, in Par. 1 the warblers are humanized with what words and phrases? Now what happens when a "resident population" (13) becomes a "horde" (18)? Examine the connotations of the word *horde* and decide whether a better word could replace it. Note, by the way, that the warblers become "experienced travelers" presently (33) and "small world-travelers" a bit later. Now examine and evaluate other colorful words: *incredible* (56), *nocturnal* (74), *wakeful* (91), *stubbornly* (100), *amazing* (38), *spectacular* (44).

By now you will be able to evaluate the diction of this piece, detecting its flaws as well as its virtues.

14.   The maintenance of proper and consistent *tense* is one of the most difficult tasks for the writer of expository prose that contains any amount of narrative. This is so because facts are more or less timeless, whereas events happen (or happened) at particular times, and relating the two may trap or disorient the unwary. Note that Sauer, dealing with facts, begins with the present tense, which he maintains till line 23, where "have banded" is *present perfect;* that is, it describes an action beginning in the past and continuing up to the present, and so is oriented to the present tense. What tense is "followed" (24)? Careful!

The first *past* tense (40) is oriented to the present by the word *late* (39). *Would find* (42) represents the present of Werner Rüppell's experiment, and *has astonished* (43), *present perfect* again, maintains the reference to the present.

Now, with Par. 6, we find a necessary shift to the past tense as we come to *events* in the past. But note that the *facts* discovered in the past are presented with the *present* tense in lines 68 and 69. This device keeps us with the author. In Par. 7 the author takes himself into the past with a careful time-transition. What is it? This new orientation requires him to use the *past perfect* tense in line 78, when he refers to events in the past prior to the fixed past of "the author and his wife *started*" (76). The past perfect relates to the past exactly as the present perfect relates to the present.

Go through the rest of the essay—or as far as your instructor suggests—underlining all the verbs; then analyze the management of tenses.

15.   An investigation is required to explain the first point made in Par. 19. You will have to find how fast the relative positions of the "fixed" stars change: how much, that is, has the "pattern of constellations" (205) altered during the last thousand or million years? Next, how old are these species of warblers? Correlating and interpreting these facts will make an interesting and valuable paper which you can write in the dramatic reporting manner of Carson or Sauer. Another project is to investigate the celestial navigation of "other birds, insects, crabs, and spiders . . ."

Lenses

DONALD CULROSS PEATTIE

1. The storm is gone, and here in the country a mild sun has bit by bit argued the cold and snow away. There is the upheaval of a final thaw in the March lawns that are the color of old straw, and in the ponderous black velvet loam, this Illinois sod without a pea-sized pebble 5 in it. Across the roll and dip of the great plain I saw, as I went walking with my blackthorn, the distant woods as blueblack, rainy-looking islands upon the immense watery prairie, and near at hand the young yellow of the willow whips, first brilliance of the year. Now this was a scene a midlander could love, but I 10 went thinking, thinking, wagging that human tail my cane, how all that I saw came to me thus only because of a specified convexity in the cornea of my eye.

2. My sense of proportion, to say nothing of esthetics, is really superbly egotistic. Matter, to regard it more exactly than humanly, 15 is full of holes. The solidest thing is as a net; the space between the electronic particles is like unto the spaces between the sun and the planets. The trouble with our human concepts is that we are so pitifully small when it comes to the great, and so unbearably gross when it comes to the small. We occupy a position 20 in the scale of things that is somewhat on the trivial side of total mediocrity. Little wonder if our ideas are mediocre too.

3. A bee, the first of the year, went by with that direct flight of hers—the most practical people in the world, bees, having no eye for scenery and hence no temptation either to wander or to won- 25 der. A hawk cut a great circular glide through the pale blue air

above me, balanced, it seemed, upon the tip of one wing, the other wing pointing almost to the zenith. He takes the opposite view of things. He sees all, for miles about, is curious about all, 30 and much of the time appears simply to be enjoying his perspective, save when emotions incomprehensible to me suddenly shake him, and set up a windy metallic clamor.

4. I cannot ever share the bee's-eye view or the hawk's-eye view. Whatever their God-given lenses showed them of reality, I 35 would never know what it was. I saw the scene in my human way—the roll and dip of the great plain, the black-silver lakes of snow water seeking out unsuspected dimples, the cottonwood stands, very white of bark as they always are at winter's end, looking at a distance lofty and thoughtful, but turning out—like liter- 40 ary lions on closer acquaintance—to be talkative and flimsy.

5. My swinging cane struck something soft, was delayed in some yielding yet persistent medium. And I knew, even through the blackthorn, that it was living tissue. There is something about almost any living thing that is plasmic, resilient, and in a way 45 alarming. We say, "I touched something—and it was *alive!*" There is no such shock in touching that which has never lived. The mineral world is vast, it is mighty, rigid and brittle. But the hand that touches vital matter infallibly recognizes the feel of life and recoils in excitement.

50 6. What I had struck was nothing but a big, soggy fungus, a giant puffball persistent from autumn. From the wound I had made in it there was still curling on the airs a smoke of mustard-green powder. I struck it again deliberately, and like a staked snake teased into spewing venom, it coughed forth another belch 55 of spores.

7. I unscrewed the crystal of my watch, caught a little of the living dust in it, screwed the watch face down upon the upturned glass, and pocketed the whole. At home, at least, I had a pair of eyes that would deprive the infinitely little of half its mystery. 60 Eyes such as neither hawk nor bee possesses, eyes for probing into the nature of Nature, that man has made for himself with monstrous patience, intricate invention piled upon invention.

8. At my desk, I draw the microscope out of its case, and though it is heavy, it slides out to me, when I grasp it by its middle, with

an ease like a greeting. It is a matter of a moment to whisk the 65
fungus spores on a glass slide, a moment more to find them in the
lower magnification, and then with a triumphant click to swing
the intense myopic gaze of the tinier lens upon them.

9. From a speck as fine as a particle of wandering cigarette
smoke, a spore leaps suddenly up at my eyes as a sphere of gold 70
meshed with vitreous green bands that cut up this tiny world, this
planetesimal of sealed-up life, into latitude and longitude. Here
a living plant has put its substance into minutest compass and
launched it upon the air, where only the most wildly improbable
chances, really an unbroken series of lucky one-in-a-thousand 75
hazards, would ever see it grow to a puffball. Here was the whole
of heredity, here the past and future of a chain of lives. Intricate,
formed to a pattern and plan by the stresses within it, organized
by the very fact that it had specific form, this frail and tiny speck
of life differed, I saw, from the atom of cigarette smoke precisely 80
as the cry of the hawk differed from the squeal of a rusty hinge
which it so much resembled.

10. I would be at a loss to show the difference between the
sound made by a living thing and an inorganic noise. But the lens
takes soundings for us in the depths of optical dimensions. There 85
is no shock, for the young mind with a bent for science, like the
first look through a microscope. I am not likely to forget the
moment when I saw the green world of the algae come alive—
delicate twisted bands of color in the glassy cell walls, diatoms
like bits of carven glass, desmids like a trembling green lace, the 90
hexagonal meshes of the water-net like the work of bobbins, and
Oscillatoria, that plant that swims with a slow eel-like motion.
Under the lens I witnessed life's crucial event, when I saw the
whip-tailed male cells escape from the sack of a sea kelp and
assault the great, inert egg cell, like meteors raining upon a 95
ponderous planet. Under that purposeful attack the planet cell
began to roll, with a great, a gentle but irresistible momentum,
until one dart, predestined, broke through the surface tensions,
dropped to the nuclear core like a solid thing descending through
a gas, and then the conquered planet ceased its rolling and the 100
rejected meteors dropped away. Life had begun again.

11. By a coincidence which has no meaning—or perhaps it has

every meaning—human fertilization is startlingly like that in the big red seaweed, and who has seen this latter has in effect looked 105 into the very bottom of the well of self.

12. Because the lens has left scant privacy to Nature, it is difficult for the modern mind to recall what battles were once waged over the subject of fertilization, the sexuality of plants, the structure of the cell. Men without the weapon of the lens tussled then 110 in bootless speculation as the Trojans and Greeks pulled the body of Patroclus this way and that.

13. One comes at last to feel that the invention of the microscope by Janssen of Holland in the seventeenth century was the beginning of modern natural history, for the lens added a new 115 dimension to our eyes and enabled us literally to see to the heart of many a problem. The sentence I have just written sounds good enough to pass unchallenged. But it sounds better than it is, for it seems to assert that one man invented the microscope, and it leaves us to infer that, once it was invented, men, peering through 120 it, saw truth at last. In fact, however, having seventeenth century minds, they did not in the least make of what they saw what we would. Except for a few larger minds, the early microscopists were largely engaged in watching the antics of fleas.

14. And the revolution in biological thought consequent on the 125 use of the microscope did not take place in the seventeenth century but in the unfinished century, 1850 to our times. It is the modern technical improvements, coupled with the forward march of allied sciences, that have created the merciful triumphs of bacteriology, carried us into a deep perspective of atomic struc- 130 ture and brought light into the dark mystery of protoplasm itself. The seventeenth century microscopy was necessarily limited by the imperfections of the early instruments, and still more by the state of the allied sciences at the time. But it was, none the less, an era of high adventure in natural history, for the lens, however 135 faulty, gave to all greatly inquisitive minds the first rapturous look at the wonderworld of structure.

※※※※※※※※※※

1. Note all the visual observations in Pars. 1, 3, and 4. How do

these observations made during a walk in the country eventually lead to a discussion of the microscope? What theme, in short, unifies the two?

2. We notice in Par. 1 that observation leads to speculation. Examine the entire essay, indicating sections of observation of fact and sections of speculation and commentary upon it. How does one lead to the other? This is a technique that you can use yourself.

3. In Par. 1 Peattie mentions the "roll and dip of the great plain," and he repeats the phrase exactly in Par. 4. What effect does this repetition have on the observation-speculation sequence? What does it *do* to the material between the original statement and its repetition?

4. Figurative language is not only arresting, but also economical. "The solidest thing is as a net" (16) is enormously economical, even though it involves at least two inaccuracies in "net." [Can the net's two dimensionality be properly used as a symbol of molecular structure? Is its rectangular regularity accurate for the fact presented?]

5. In Par. 2 we are carried from a question of pure physical scale—the essential point being *perspective*—to words dealing with the same point but strongly colored—one in its connotation, one in its present denotation—with unpleasant or unfavorable judgments: "gross," "trivial," "mediocre." What *proper* part do these words play in what, though personal, is also a technical discourse?

6. What effect does the author achieve in Par. 5 by not identifying the "something" touched?

7. Paragraphs 8–10 are filled with the excitement of scientific discovery. What words and phrases lend this air of excitement? Note especially the lively verbs and the many metaphors and similes. What branch of science is Peattie discussing? What words in this paragraph (and in the entire passage) indicate this?

8. Throughout the essay Peattie plays with scale and perspective. He juxtaposes thing infinitely larger and infinitely smaller than man, often relating them to man.

In a piece about the microscopic world of a spore, one might think it out of order to refer to the vast cosmos of sun and planets as often as Peattie does (see 17, 72, 96–101). But there is a reason for this reference. What is it? What, in short, does it suggest about perspective?

9.   Is the purpose of Par. 11 to reduce man to a mere organism like red seaweed or to suggest that science, a creation of man's mind, has penetrated toward ultimate philosophical revelations? This is worth a paragraph or two of careful exposition. Indeed, the extremes suggested may be traced through the whole essay.

10.   Throughout the essay Peattie describes natural phenomena in human terms. Thus he mentions the "forward *march*" of science (127), the "talkative and flimsy" cottonwood trees (40), and the sun that has "*argued* the cold and snow away" (2). Make a list of the humanizing words in the selection. When you do you will be able to write a paragraph explaining how Peattie gives the selection its life and vigor.

11.   Examine the way the theme of perspective—of lenses and eyes and sight—is carried throughout the essay. Where is the theme first mentioned? Make a list of words drawn from this theme and indicate where they are used literally and where figuratively. "Seeing" is so generally synonymous with "knowing" that we may use "see" figuratively without realizing we do.

12.   Peattie refers to the eyes of the bee and the hawk as "God-given *lenses*" (34) and to the microscope as a "pair of eyes" (58). What is the effect of this reversal? How does it serve to develop the theme?

13.   In Par. 13 the author appears to be telling us how he writes, or at least commenting on his writing. Can you show that this is actually only a slightly different form of what he has been doing all the way through the essay, in going from observation to speculation?

14.   Check meaning and etymology of these words: *loam* (5), *blackthorn* (7), *egotistic* (15), *resilient* (44), *spewing* (54), *vitreous* (71), *bootless* (110).

The Line

HERMAN MELVILLE

1. With reference to the whaling scene shortly to be described, as well as for the better understanding of all similar scenes elsewhere presented, I have here to speak of the magical, sometimes horrible whale-line.

2. The line originally used in the fishery was of the best hemp, slightly vapored with tar, not impregnated with it, as in the case of ordinary ropes; for while tar, as ordinarily used, makes the hemp more pliable to the rope-maker, and also renders the rope itself more convenient to the sailor for common ship use; yet, not only would the ordinary quantity too much stiffen the whale-line for the close coiling to which it must be subjected; but as most seamen are beginning to learn, tar in general by no means adds to the rope's durability or strength, however much it may give it compactness and gloss.

3. Of late years the Manilla rope has in the American fishery almost entirely superseded hemp as a material for whale-lines; for, though not so durable as hemp, it is stronger, and far more soft and elastic; and I will add (since there is an æsthetics in all things), is much more handsome and becoming to the boat, than hemp. Hemp is a dusky, dark fellow, a sort of Indian; but Manilla is as a golden-haired Circassian to behold.

4. The whale-line is only two thirds of an inch in thickness. At first sight, you would not think it so strong as it really is. By experiment its one and fifty yarns will each suspend a weight of one hundred and twenty pounds; so that the whole rope will bear a strain nearly equal to three tons. In length, the common Sperm Whale-line measures something over two hundred fathoms.

From *Moby Dick*.

Towards the stern of the boat it is spirally coiled away in the tub,
not like the worm-pipe of a still though, but so as to form one
30 round, cheese-shaped mass of densely bedded "sheaves," or layers
of concentric spiralizations, without any hollow but the "heart,"
or minute vertical tube formed at the axis of the cheese. As the
least tangle or kink in the coiling would, in running out, infallibly
take somebody's arm, leg, or entire body off, the utmost precau-
35 tion is used in stowing the line in its tub. Some harpooners will
consume almost an entire morning in this business, carrying the
line high aloft and then reeving it downwards through a block
towards the tub, so as in the act of coiling to free it from all possible wrinkles and twists.

40   5. In the English boats two tubs are used instead of one; the
same line being continuously coiled in both tubs. There is some
advantage in this; because these twin-tubs being so small they fit
more readily into the boat, and do not strain it so much; whereas,
the American tub, nearly three feet in diameter and of proportion-
45 ate depth, makes a rather bulky freight for a craft whose planks
are but one half-inch in thickness; for the bottom of the whale-
boat is like critical ice, which will bear up a considerable distributed weight, but not very much of a concentrated one. When
the painted canvas cover is clapped on the American line-tub, the
50 boat looks as if it were pulling off with a prodigious great wed-
ding-cake to present to the whales.

6. Both ends of the line are exposed; the lower end terminating
in an eye-splice or loop coming up from the bottom against the
side of the tub, and hanging over its edge completely disengaged
55 from everything. This arrangement of the lower end is necessary
on two accounts. First: In order to facilitate the fastening to it of
an additional line from a neighboring boat, in case the stricken
whale should sound so deep as to threaten to carry off the entire line originally attached to the harpoon. In these instances,
60 the whale of course is shifted like a mug of ale, as it were, from
the one boat to the other; though the first boat always hovers at
hand to assist its consort. Second: This arrangement is indispensable for common safety's sake; for were the lower end of the
line in any way attached to the boat, and were the whale then to

run the line out to the end almost in a single, smoking minute 65
as he sometimes does, he would not stop there, for the doomed
boat would infallibly be dragged down after him into the profundity of the sea; and in that case no town-crier would ever find
her again.

7. Before lowering the boat for the chase, the upper end of the 70
line is taken aft from the tub, and passing round the loggerhead
there, is again carried forward the entire length of the boat, resting crosswise upon the loom or handle of every man's oar, so that
it jogs against his wrist in rowing; and also passing between the
men, as they alternately sit at the opposite gunwales, to the 75
leaded chocks or grooves in the extreme pointed prow of the boat,
where a wooden pin or skewer the size of a common quill, prevents it from slipping out. From the chocks it hangs in a slight
festoon over the bows, and is then passed inside the boat again;
and some ten or twenty fathoms (called box-line) being coiled 80
upon the box in the bows, it continues its way to the gunwale
still a little further aft, and is then attached to the short-warp—
the rope which is immediately connected with the harpoon; but
previous to that connexion, the short-warp goes through sundry
mystifications too tedious to detail.   85

8. Thus the whale-line folds the whole boat in its complicated
coils, twisting and writhing around it in almost every direction.
All the oarsmen are involved in its perilous contortions; so that to
the timid eye of the landsman, they seem as Indian jugglers, with
the deadliest snakes sportively festooning their limbs. Nor can any 90
son of mortal woman, for the first time, seat himself amid those
hempen intricacies, and while straining his utmost at the oar,
bethink him that at any unknown instant the harpoon may be
darted, and all these horrible contortions be put in play like
ringed lightnings; he cannot be thus circumstanced without a 95
shudder that makes the very marrow in his bones to quiver in
him like a shaken jelly. Yet habit—strange thing! what cannot
habit accomplish?—Gayer sallies, more merry mirth, better jokes,
and brighter repartees, you never heard over your mahogany,
than you will hear over the half-inch white cedar of the whale- 100
boat, when thus hung in hangman's nooses; and, like the six

burghers of Calais before King Edward, the six men composing
the crew pull into the jaws of death, with a halter around every
neck, as you may say.

105   9. Perhaps a very little thought will now enable you to account
for those repeated whaling disasters—some few of which are casu-
ally chronicled—of this man or that man being taken out of the
boat by the line, and lost. For, when the line is darting out, to
be seated then in the boat, is like being seated in the midst of the
110   manifold whizzings of a steam-engine in full play, when every flying beam, and shaft, and wheel, is grazing you. It is worse; for
you cannot sit motionless in the heart of these perils, because the
boat is rocking like a cradle, and you are pitched one way and the
other, without the slightest warning; and only by a certain self-
115   adjusting buoyancy and simultaneousness of volition and action,
can you escape being made a Mazeppa of, and run away with
where the all-seeing sun himself could never pierce you out.

      10. Again: as the profound calm which only apparently pre-
cedes and prophesies of the storm, is perhaps more awful than
120   the storm itself; for, indeed, the calm is but the wrapper and en-
velope of the storm; and contains it in itself, as the seemingly
harmless rifle holds the fatal powder, and the ball, and the explosion; so the graceful repose of the line, as it silently serpentines
about the oarsmen before being brought into actual play—this is
125   a thing which carries more of true terror than any other aspect of
this dangerous affair. But why say more? All men live enveloped
in whale-lines. All are born with halters round their necks; but
it is only when caught in the swift, sudden turn of death, that
mortals realize the silent, subtle, everpresent perils of life. And
130   if you be a philosopher, though seated in the whale-boat, you
would not at heart feel one whit more of terror, than though seated
before your evening fire with a poker, and not a harpoon, by your
side.

✳✳✳✳✳✳✳✳✳✳

      The problem here is a special one of scale and selection, for the
writer is involved with a threefold task: He must tell enough
to give us more than a general impression, because he has earlier

avowed his intention of describing the whale fishery in comprehensive detail, and the complexity of the facts could easily bring the reader's attention to a standstill. Second, he must convey an impression of the extreme danger and emotional flavor of being in a small whale-boat on the chase. And he must work up to a *symbolic* expansion and penetration of his subject, at the end, that will add one further touch to his enterprise—sustained through the long narrative—of making whaling a symbol of life.

The whale-line runs from its tub, which sits aft of the last oarsman on the bottom of the whale-boat, around a low fat snubbing-post (here called the loggerhead) at the after point of the boat, forward through the chock in the prow, thence to the box-line, thence to the short-warps, and thence to the harpoons. Some hundreds of feet must be coiled loosely after the line has passed through the chocks, so that the harpoons can be thrown freely.

These are the facts. The author's problem of spacing these facts, of spreading them out so that the reader can take them in, becomes the means by which he introduces color, drama, and—finally—symbolic dimensions into his account. Read the selection aloud.

1. List the progression of qualities of the line enumerated in the first four paragraphs. Put the abstract in one column, the concrete in a second, and the figurative in a third.

2. Note the method used, lines 29–32, to convey a visual image of the line in its tub. How would the "worm-pipe of a still" look? At what point do you discover that this comparison is humorous? Look up: *stow, impregnate, concentric, reeve, facilitate, stricken, sound* (vb), *profundity, chock, festoon, sundry, sally, repartee, burgher, halter,* and *volition.*

3. Look up "sheaf." Can you find a sense that fits here? What phrase of Melville's defines it? What do the quotation marks in lines 30 and 31 indicate? Define axis as used here.

4. What purpose does the mention of English boats (40) serve, other than as information? The reference to Mazeppa (116) will disclose an extraordinary meaning if you explore it carefully.

5. Does the speculation in the last paragraph soften the terrors of the alien sea—or does it bring these terrors to the quiet hearth?

This tricky (perhaps unanswerable) question is complicated by the intrusion of various homely and landlubbing details into the earlier description,—such as "wedding cake," "mug of ale," and "consort." Mark other words and phrases of this class and see whether you can explain how the humor they carry enables the author to raise the tricky and ambiguous question referred to above. Observe that such homely terms become more than images in the last paragraph.

6. Without aspiring to Melville's range or intensity, you may try a description of a process or device, to which you bring an extra dimension of tone, symbol, or idea, for example: digging for clams, tuning a carburetor, bull fighting, mountain climbing, skiing.

A Caddy's Diary

RING LARDNER

Wed. Apr. 12

1. I am 16 of age and
am a caddy at the Pleasant View Golf Club but only temporary
as I expect to soon land a job some wheres as asst pro as my game
is good enough now to be a pro but to young looking. My pal
Joe Bean also says I have not got enough swell head to make a 5
good pro but suppose that will come in time, Joe is a wise cracker.

2. But first will put down how I come to be writeing this diary,
we have got a member name Mr Colby who writes articles in the
newspapers and I hope for his sakes that he is a better writer then
he plays golf but any way I cadded for him a good many times 10
last yr and today he was out for the first time this yr and I cadded
for him and we got talking about this in that and something was
mentioned in regards to the golf articles by Alex Laird that comes
out every Sun in the paper Mr Colby writes his articles for so I
asked Mr Colby did he know how much Laird got paid for the 15
articles and he said he did not know but supposed that Laird had
to split 50–50 with who ever wrote the articles for him. So I said
don't he write the articles himself and Mr Colby said why no he
guessed not. Laird may be a master mind in regards to golf he
said, but that is no sign he can write about it as very few men can 20
write decent let alone a pro. Writeing is a nag.

3. How do you learn it I asked him.

4. Well he said read what other people writes and study them and write things yourself, and maybe you will get on to the nag and maybe you wont.

5. Well Mr Colby I said do you think I could get on to it?

6. Why he said smileing I did not know that was your ambition to be a writer.

7. Not exactly was my reply, but I am going to be a golf pro myself and maybe some day I will get good enough so as the papers will want I should write them articles and if I can learn to write them myself why I will not have to hire another writer and split with them.

8. Well said Mr Colby smileing you have certainly got the right temperament for a pro, they are all big hearted fellows.

9. But listen Mr Colby I said if I want to learn it would not do me no good to copy down what other writers have wrote, what I would have to do would be write things out of my own head.

10. That is true said Mr Colby.

11. Well I said what could I write about?

12. Well said Mr Colby why dont you keep a diary and every night after your supper set down and write what happened that day and write who you cadded for and what they done only leave me out of it. And you can write down what people say and what you think and etc., it will be the best kind of practice for you, and once in a wile you can bring me your writeings and I will tell you the truth if they are good or rotten.

13. So that is how I come to be writeing this diary is so as I can get some practice writeing and maybe if I keep at it long enough I can get on to the nag.

Sat. Apr. 29

14. Today they had the first club tournament of the yr and they have a monthly tournament every month and today was the first one, it is a handicap tournament and everybody plays in it and they have prizes for low net score and low gross score and etc. I cadded for Mr Thomas today and will tell what happened.

15. They played a 4 some and besides Mr Thomas we had Mr Blake and Mr Carter and Mr Dunham. Mr Dunham is the worst

man player in the club and the other men would not play with
him a specialy on a Saturday only him and Mr Blake is partners 60
together in business. Mr Dunham has got the highest handicap
in the club which is 50 but it would have to be 150 for him to win
a prize. Mr Blake and Mr Carter has got a handicap of about 15
a piece I think and Mr Thomas is 30, the first prize for the low net
score for the day was a dozen golf balls and the second low 65
score a ½ dozen golf balls and etc.

16. Well we had a great battle and Mr Colby ought to been
along to write it up or some good writer. Mr Carter and Mr Dunham played partners against Mr Thomas and Mr Blake which
ment that Mr Carter was playing Thomas and Blakes best ball, 70
well Mr Dunham took the honor and the first ball he hit went
strate off to the right and over the fence outside of the grounds,
well he done the same thing 3 times. Well when he finely did hit
one in the course why Mr Carter said why not let us not count
them 3 first shots of Mr Dunham as they was just practice. Like 75
H we wont count them said Mr Thomas we must count every shot
and keep our scores correct for the tournament.

17. All right said Mr Carter.

18. Well we got down to the green and Mr Dunham had about
11 and Mr Carter sunk a long putt for a par 5, Mr Blake all ready 80
had 5 strokes and so did Mr Thomas and when Mr Carter sunk
his putt why Mr Thomas picked his ball up and said Carter wins
the hole and I and Blake will take 6s. Like H you will said Mr
Carter, this is a tournament and we must play every hole out
and keep our scores correct. So Mr Dunham putted and went 85
down in 13 and Mr Blake got a 6 and Mr Thomas missed 2 easy
putts and took a 8 and maybe he was not boiling.

19. Well it was still their honor and Mr Dunham had one of his
dizzy spells on the 2d tee and he missed the ball twice before he
hit it and then Mr Carter drove the green which is only a midiron 90
shot and then Mr Thomas stepped up and missed the ball just
like Mr Dunham. He was wild and yelled at Mr Dunham no man
could play golf playing with a man like you, you would spoil
anybodys game.

20. Your game was all ready spoiled said Mr Dunham, it 95
turned sour on the 1st green.

21. You would turn anybody sour said Mr Thomas.

22. Well Mr Thomas finely took a 8 for the hole which is a par 3 and it certainly looked bad for him winning a prize when he 100 started out with 2 8s, and he and Mr Dunham had another terrible time on No 3 and wile they was messing things up a 2 some come up behind us and hollered fore and we left them go through tho it was Mr Clayton and Mr Joyce and as Joe Bean said they was probly dissapointed when we left them go through as they 105 are the kind that feels like the day is lost if they cant write to some committee and preffer charges.

23. Well Mr Thomas got a 7 on the 3d and he said well it is no wonder I am off of my game today as I was up ½ the night with my teeth.

110 24. Well said Mr Carter if I had your money why on the night before a big tournament like this I would hire somebody else to set up with my teeth.

25. Well I wished I could remember all that was said and done but any way Mr Thomas kept getting sore and sore and we got 115 to the 7th tee and he had not made a decent tee shot all day so Mr Blake said to him why dont you try the wood as you cant do no worse?

26. By Geo I beleive I will said Mr. Thomas and took his driver out of the bag which he had not used it for 3 yrs.

120 27. Well he swang and zowie away went the ball pretty near 8 inchs distants wile the head of the club broke off clean and saled 50 yds down the course. Well I have got a hold on myself so as I dont never laugh out loud and I beleive the other men was scarred to laugh or he would of killed them so we all stood there in silents 125 waiting for what would happen.

28. Well without saying a word he come to where I was standing and took his other 4 wood clubs out of the bag and took them to a tree which stands a little ways from the tee box and one by one he swang them with all his strength against the trunk of the 130 tree and smashed them to H and gone, all right gentlemen that is over he said.

29. Well to cut it short Mr Thomas score for the first 9 was a even 60 and then we started out on the 2d 9 and you would not think it was the same man playing, on the first 3 holes he made 2

4s and a 5 and beat Mr Carter even and followed up with a 6 and 135
a 5, and that is how he kept going up to the 17th hole.

30. What has got in to you Thomas said Mr Carter.

31. Nothing said Mr Thomas only I broke my hoodoo when I broke them 5 wood clubs.

32. Yes I said to myself and if you had broke them 5 wood 140 clubs 3 yrs ago I would not of broke my back lugging them around.

33. Well we come to the 18th tee and Mr Thomas had a 39 which give him a 99 for 17 holes, well everybody drove off and as we was following along why Mr Klabor come walking down the 145 course from the club house on his way to the 17th green to join some friends and Mr Thomas asked him what had he made and he said he had turned in a 93 but his handicap is only 12 so that give him a 81.

34. That wont get me no wheres he said as Charley Crane 150 made a 75.

35. Well said Mr Thomas I can tie Crane for low net if I get a 6 on this hole.

36. Well it come his turn to make his 2d and zowie he hit the ball pretty good but they was a hook on it and away she went in 155 to the woods on the left, the ball laid in behind a tree so as they was only one thing to do and that was waste a shot getting it back on the fair so that is what Mr Thomas done and it took him 2 more to reach the green.

37. How many have you had Thomas said Mr Carter when we 160 was all on the green.

38. Let me see said Mr. Thomas and then turned to me, how many have I had caddy?

39. I dont know I said.

40. Well it is either 4 or 5 said Mr. Thomas.   165

41. I think it is 5 said Mr. Carter.

42. I think it is 4 said Mr Thomas and turned to me again and said how many have I had caddy?

43. So I said 4.

44. Well said Mr Thomas personly I was not sure myself but 170 my caddy says 4 and I guess he is right.

45. Well the other men looked at each other and I and Joe

Bean looked at each other but Mr Thomas went ahead and putted and was down in 2 putts.

175   46. Well he said I certainly come to life on them last 9 holes.

47. So he turned in his score as 105 and with his handicap of 30 why that give him a net of 75 which was the same as Mr. Crane so instead of Mr Crane getting 1 dozen golf balls and Mr Thomas getting ½ a dozen golf balls why they will split the 1st and 2d
180   prize makeing 9 golf balls a piece.

Fri. May 5

48. Well I never thought we would have so much excitement in the club and so much to write down in my diary but I guess I better get busy writeing it down as here it is Friday and it was Wed. a.m. when the excitement broke loose and I was getting
185   ready to play around when Harry Lear the caddy master come running out with the paper in his hand and showed it to me on the first page.

49. It told how Chas Crane our club champion had went south with $8000 which he had stole out of Mr Thomas bank and a
190   swell looking dame that was a stenographer in the bank had elloped with him and they had her picture in the paper and I will say she is a pip but who would of thought a nice quiet young man like Mr Crane was going to prove himself a gay Romeo and a specialy as he was engaged to Miss Rennie tho she now says she
195   broke their engagement a month ago but any way the whole affair has certainly give everybody something to talk about and one of the caddys Lou Crowell busted Fat Brunner in the nose because Fat claimed to of been the last one that cadded for Crane. Lou was really the last one and cadded for him last Sun-
200   day which was the last time Crane was at the club.

50. Well everybody was thinking how sore Mr Thomas would be and they would better not mention the affair around him and etc. but who should show up to play yesterday but Mr Thomas himself and he played with Mr Blake and all they talked about
205   the whole p.m. was Crane and what he had pulled.

51. Well Thomas said Mr Blake I am curious to know if the thing come as a surprise to you or if you ever had a hunch that he was libel to do a thing like this.

52. Well Blake said Mr Thomas I will admit that the whole thing come as a complete surprise to me as Crane was all most 210 like my son you might say and I was going to see that he got along all right and that is what makes me sore is not only that he has proved himself dishonest but that he could be such a sucker as to give up a bright future for a sum of money like $8000 and a doll face girl that cant be no good or she would not of let him do 215 it. When you think how young he was and the carreer he might of had why it certainly seems like he sold his soul pretty cheap.

53. That is what Mr Thomas had to say or at lease part of it as I cant remember a ½ of all he said but any way this p.m. I cadded 220 for Mrs Thomas and Mrs Doane and that is all they talked about to, and Mrs Thomas talked along the same lines like her husband and said she had always thought Crane was to smart a young man to pull a thing like that and ruin his whole future.

54. He was geting $4000 a yr said Mrs Thomas and everybody 225 liked him and said he was bound to get ahead so that is what makes it such a silly thing for him to of done, sell his soul for $8000 and a pretty face.

55. Yes indeed said Mrs Doane.

56. Well all the time I was listening to Mr Thomas and Mr 230 Blake and Mrs Thomas and Mrs Doane why I was thinking about something which I wanted to say to them but it would of ment me looseing my job so I kept it to myself but I sprung it on my pal Joe Bean on the way home tonight.

57. Joe I said what do these people mean when they talk about 235 Crane selling his soul?

58. Why you know what they mean said Joe, they mean that a person that does something dishonest for a bunch of money or a gal or any kind of a reward why the person that does it is selling his soul.   240

59. All right I said and it dont make no differents does it if the reward is big or little?

60. Why no said Joe only the bigger it is the less of a sucker the person is that goes after it.

61. Well I said here is Mr Thomas who is vice president of a 245 big bank and worth a bbl of money and it is just a few days ago

when he lied about his golf score in order so as he would win 9 golf balls instead of a ½ a dozen.

62. Sure said Joe.

250   63. And how about his wife Mrs Thomas I said, who plays for 2 bits a hole and when her ball dont lie good why she picks it up and pretends to look at it to see if it is hers and then puts it back in a good lie where she can sock it.

64. And how about my friend Mrs Doane that made me move
255 her ball out of a rut to help her beat Miss Rennie out of a party dress.

65. Well said Joe what of it?

66. Well I said it seems to me like these people have got a lot of nerve to pan Mr Crane and call him a sucker for doing what
260 he done, it seems to me like $8000 and a swell dame is a pretty fair reward compared with what some of these other people sells their soul for, and I would like to tell them about it.

67. Well said Joe go ahead and tell them but maybe they will tell you something right back.

265   68. What will they tell me?

69. Well said Joe they might tell you this, that when Mr Thomas asks you how many shots he has had and you say 4 when you know he has had 5, why you are selling your soul for a $1.00 tip. And when you move Mrs Doanes ball out of a rut and give it
270 a good lie, what are you selling your soul for? Just a smile.

70. O keep your mouth shut I said to him.

71. I am going to said Joe and would advice you to do the same.

※※※※※※※※※※※

Our problem with this selection is to consider the virtues and the limitations of its very special method.

1.   This selection has been placed toward the middle of this volume because it requires more knowledge of composition to enjoy it than many of the earlier selections. How can this be so? Write a paragraph or two explaining and demonstrating exactly how and where the humor depends on the reader's mastery of the rules and forms of good writing. This assignment is a test of your

powers of analysis, selection, and exposition. You may even find yourself forced to explore some of the theories of humor or "laughter." George Meredith, Max Eastman, and others have written on the subject. So have many psychologists.

2.   Next—and here we come on to thin and slippery ice—see whether you can write a description of some of the personal characteristics of the diarist that do not depend on his relative illiteracy. It has been said that "The style is the man." Argue whether or not the diarist's "style" does him justice as a human being. This is not a contrived issue but a very serious problem. Is man man without language, the garment and the substance of thought? Is there a "self" not expressed by the man's style? Or would another "self" come into existence if the style were changed by education and culture?

3.   Then see whether you can identify and discuss some merits in the caddy's writing quite apart from his errors. You may do this by copying out the first two or three paragraphs in the second entry with correct spelling and punctuation. Then you will still have a style to explain; and you may be able to phrase some firm opinions on the quality of mind and spirit revealed merely by the order in which he sets down his ideas.

4.   Ring Lardner is famous for his ability to make a speaking character reveal facts of which he is not himself aware. This is, indeed, his special talent. Examine the selection for this element. See whether you can locate and explain some spots where it happens and so explain how the discrepancy between the character's and the reader's sense of the facts is established. You may also thus identify limitations in the caddy's self-knowledge. Where?

5.   As you come to the end of the third entry you find a change of tone that will, in its full impact, astonish you. What light does the ending throw upon the caddy's earlier more-or-less unspoken attitudes toward the people who employ him?

6.   Using a dictionary or perhaps a glossary of literary terms, explain how, as we come to the end of the third entry, we move from humor to satire. If the change of tone has struck you forcibly, you may be able to describe, in a paragraph or two, how it is achieved, how the humor of the writing itself becomes less important at the end.

7.   Two exercises in literary method are suggested by this piece: You may try to rewrite one entry in another style but developing the same ideas. Or you may take the material and write a different anecdote about it—something that gives a different emphasis and brings out a different central idea or impression.

The Industrial Magnate

D. H. LAWRENCE

1. Without bothering
to *think* to a conclusion, Gerald jumped to a conclusion. He abandoned the whole democratic-equality problem as a problem of
silliness. What mattered was the great social productive machine.
Let that work perfectly, let it produce a sufficiency of everything, 5
let every man be given a rational portion, greater or less according to his functional degree or magnitude, and then, provision
made, let the devil supervene, let every man look after his own
amusements and appetites, so long as he interfered with nobody.

2. So Gerald set himself to work, to put the great industry in 10
order. In his travels, and in his accompanying readings, he had
come to the conclusion that the essential secret of life was harmony. He did not define to himself at all clearly what harmony
was. The word pleased him, he felt he had come to his own conclusions. And he proceeded to put his philosophy into practice by 15
forcing order into the established world, translating the mystic
word harmony into the practical word organization.

3. Immediately he *saw* the firm, he realized what he could do.
He had a fight to fight with Matter, with the earth and the coal it
enclosed. This was the sole idea, to turn upon the inanimate mat- 20
ter of the underground, and reduce it to his will. And for this fight
with Matter, one must have perfect instruments in perfect organization, a mechanism so subtle and harmonious in its workings
that it represents the single mind of man, and by its relentless
repetition of given movement will accomplish a purpose irre- 25
sistibly, inhumanly. It was this inhuman principle in the mecha-

nism he wanted to construct that inspired Gerald with an almost
religious exaltation. He, the man, could interpose a perfect,
changeless, godlike medium between himself and the Matter he
30 had to subjugate. There were two opposites, his will and the resistant Matter of the earth. And between these he could establish
the very expression of his will, the incarnation of his power, a
great and perfect machine, a system, an activity of pure order,
pure mechanical repetition, repetition ad infinitum, hence eternal
35 and infinite. He found his eternal and his infinite in the pure
machine-principle of perfect co-ordination into one pure, complex, infinitely repeated motion, like the spinning of a wheel; but
a productive spinning, as the revolving of the universe may be
called a productive spinning, a productive repetition through
40 eternity, to infinity. And this is the God-motion, this productive
repetition ad infinitum. And Gerald was the God of the machine,
Deus ex Machina. And the whole productive will of man was the
Godhead.

4. He had his life-work now, to extend over the earth a great
45 and perfect system in which the will of man ran smooth and
unthwarted, timeless, a Godhead in process. He had to begin with
the mines. The terms were given: first the resistant Matter of the
underground; then the instruments of its subjugation, instruments
human and metallic; and finally his own pure will, his own mind.
50 It would need a marvellous adjustment of myriad instruments,
human, animal, metallic, kinetic, dynamic, a marvellous casting
of myriad tiny wholes into one great perfect entirety. And then,
in this case there was perfection attained, the will of the highest
was perfectly fulfilled, the will of mankind was perfectly enacted;
55 for was not mankind mystically contra-distinguished against inanimate Matter, was not the history of mankind just the history of
the conquest of the one by the other?

5. The miners were overreached. While they were still in the
toils of divine equality of man, Gerald had passed on, granted
60 essentially their case, and proceeded in his quality of human
being to fulfil the will of mankind as a whole. He merely represented the miners in a higher sense when he perceived that the
only way to fulfil perfectly the will of man was to establish the
perfect, inhuman machine. But he represented them very essen-

tially, they were far behind, out of date, squabbling for their 65
material equality. The desire had already transmuted into this
new and greater desire, for a perfect intervening mechanism between man and Matter, the desire to translate the Godhead into
pure mechanism.

6. As soon as Gerald entered the firm, the convulsion of death 70
ran through the old system. He had all his life been tortured by a
furious and destructive demon, which possessed him sometimes
like an insanity. This temper now entered like a virus into the
firm, and there were cruel eruptions. Terrible and inhuman were
his examinations into every detail; there was no privacy he would 75
spare, no old sentiment but he would turn it over. The old grey
managers, the old grey clerks, the doddering old pensioners, he
looked at them, and removed them as so much lumber. The whole
concern seemed like a hospital of invalid employees. He had no
emotional qualms. He arranged what pensions were necessary, he 80
looked for efficient substitutes, and when these were found, he
substituted them for the old hands.

7. "I've a pitiful letter here from Letherington," his father
would say, in a tone of deprecation and appeal. "Don't you think
the poor fellow might keep on a little longer? I always fancied he 85
did very well."

8. "I've got a man in his place now, father. He'll be happier out
of it, believe me. You think his allowance is plenty, don't you?"

9. "It's not the allowance that he wants, poor man. He feels it
very much that he is superannuated. Says he thought he had 90
twenty more years of work in him yet."

10. "Not of this kind of work I want. He doesn't understand."

※※※※※※※※※※

This selection from *Women in Love*, perhaps the best novel by
one of the greatest English novelists, is included here so that we
may examine some odd and individual qualities of Lawrence's
style. The passage should be read aloud more than once, with
special attention to the *rhythms* and *repetitions*. An unusual voice
is speaking, and a voice is to be heard.

1. Look up *magnitude* (7), *supervene* (8), *mystic* (16),

exaltation (28), *interpose* (28), *incarnation* (32), *subjugation* (48), *kinetic* (51), *myriad* (52), *transmute* (66), *superannuated* (90), *deprecation* (84)—and note that it is not *depreciation*.

2.   The selection deals with two opposing *principles*—the living organic, and the lifeless mechanical. These principles stand for life and death to Lawrence, in so far as they determine the texture of society or of personal relations. List six or more terms in Par. 1 that indicate Gerald's values. Is he on the side of the organic or the mechanical? What tone is introduced by *silliness*? Explain what part of man's activities is controlled by the devil, in Gerald's view.

3.   Now, if we consider thought and emotion as opposing principles, we have terms for them in the first sentence. What are they? Why is emotion *not* on the side of the life principle? In what circumstances—according to this paragraph and indeed to the whole selection—are the emotions untrustworthy?

4.   It looks as if Deus ex Machina (42) means God of the machine. Does it? Explain Lawrence's use of the Latin phrase.

5.   In Pars. 2 and 3 underline or list the terms indicating the mechanical principle. Begin with *work, order, forcing,* and so on; there are an extraordinary number of them in Par. 3.

6.   What prevents Gerald's "religious exaltation" (28) from being on the side of life? Your answer to Question 3 should be, substantially, the answer to this question. In this connection, does Gerald endow the Deity with the attributes of life or death—of the organic or the mechanical?

7.   Explain how, in the middle of Par. 3, *matter* moves over on to the side of life. It is a question of what is ranged against it.

8.   In the phrase "productive repetition ad infinitum," (40) what word is most strongly identified with Lawrence's notion of the death principle? You can answer this question easily if you look back over the paragraph and mark the many spots where either the word or its meaning is repeated or demonstrated or suggested. Mark all the words that participate in this effect. What aspect of the *machine* illustrates the key word of the phrase?

9.   The words *perfect* and *pure* ring through Pars. 3 and 4. What quality is built into the rhythm of the prose by these repeti-

tions? Is the tone produced soft, gentle, harsh, jangling, derisive, indignant, mocking, or what? If you read the paragraphs aloud you will feel the tone (for definition of tone see questions after James selection) and express it. Write a paragraph in which you describe this tone and tell how it is produced. You should deal with vocabulary, rhythm, and repetition, for they are the main ingredients of this tone.

10.   Paragraph 5 is full of irony—or, rather, sarcasm, for sarcasm is stronger than irony. It begins with *toils,* goes on to *quality of human being,* and *in a higher sense;* trace it to the end of the paragraph.

11.   What exactly is the "perfect *intervening* mechanism" (67)? You can find the answer by determining *in whom* the desire is *transmuted* (66).

12.   In lines 79–80 Lawrence seems to slip into an inconsistency when he identifies emotion with, perhaps, conscience, or with a sense or instinct for right. How do you reconcile this passage with what appears in the first sentence of the selection? If it cannot be reconciled, can you explain the source of the inconsistency? What qualities are traditionally attributed to the emotions in our world?

13.   If you are of an analytical turn of mind, conduct a bit of an investigation into people's opinions and give an account of the relative status of thought and emotion in our society.

Sounds

HENRY DAVID THOREAU

1. Now that the [railroad] cars are gone by and all the restless world with them, and the fishes in the pond no longer feel their rumbling, I am more alone than ever. For the rest of the long afternoon, perhaps, my
5 meditations are interrupted only by the faint rattle of a carriage or team along the distant highway.

2. Sometimes, on Sundays, I heard the bells, the Lincoln, Acton, Bedford, or Concord bell, when the wind was favorable, a faint, sweet, and, as it were, natural melody, worth importing
10 into the wilderness. At a sufficient distance over the woods this sound acquires a certain vibratory hum, as if the pine needles in the horizon were the strings of a harp which it swept. All sound heard at the greatest possible distance produces one and the same effect, a vibration of the universal lyre, just as the intervening
15 atmosphere makes a distant ridge of earth interesting to our eyes by the azure tint it imparts to it. There came to me in this case a melody which the air had strained, and which had conversed with every leaf and needle of the wood, that portion of the sound which the elements had taken up and modulated and echoed
20 from vale to vale. The echo is, to some extent, an original sound, and therein is the magic and charm of it. It is not merely a repetition of what was worth repeating in the bell, but partly the voice of the wood, the same trivial words and notes sung by a wood-nymph.

25 3. At evening, the distant lowing of some cow in the horizon beyond the woods sounded sweet and melodious, and at first I would mistake it for the voices of certain minstrels by whom I

From *Walden.*

174

was sometimes serenaded, who might be straying over hill and dale; but soon I was not unpleasantly disappointed when it was prolonged into the cheap and natural music of the cow. I do not mean to be satirical, but to express my appreciation of those youths' singing, when I state that I perceived clearly that it was akin to the music of the cow, and they were at length one articulation of Nature.

4. Regularly at half past seven, in one part of the summer, after the evening train had gone by, the whippoorwills chanted their vespers for half an hour, sitting on a stump by my door, or upon the ridge-pole of the house. They would begin to sing almost with as much precision as a clock, within five minutes of a particular time, referred to the setting of the sun, every evening. I had a rare opportunity to become acquainted with their habits. Sometimes I heard four or five at once in different parts of the wood, by accident one a bar behind another, and so near me that I distinguished not only the cluck after each note, but often that singular buzzing sound like a fly in a spider's web, only proportionally louder. Sometimes one would circle round and round me in the woods a few feet distant as if tethered by a string, when probably I was near its eggs. They sang at intervals throughout the night, and were again as musical as ever just before and about dawn.

5. When other birds are still the screech owls take up the strain, like mourning women their ancient u-lu-lu. Their dismal scream is truly Ben Jonsonian. Wise midnight hags! It is no honest and blunt tu-whit tu-who of the poets, but, without jesting, a most solemn graveyard ditty, the mutual consolations of suicide lovers remembering the pangs and the delights of supernal love in the infernal groves. Yet I love to hear their wailing, their doleful responses, trilled along the woodside; reminding me sometimes of music and singing birds; as if it were the dark and tearful side of music, the regrets and sighs that would fain be sung. They are the spirits, the low spirits and melancholy forebodings, of fallen souls that once in human shape night-walked the earth and did the deeds of darkness, now expiating their sins with their wailing hymns or threnodies in the scenery of their transgressions. They give me a new sense of the variety and capacity of that nature

which is our common dwelling. *Oh-o-o-o-o that I never had been bor-r-r-r-n!* sighs one on this side of the pond, and circles with the restlessness of despair to some new perch on the gray oaks. Then *—that I never had been bor-r-r-r-n!* echoes another on the farther
70 side with tremulous sincerity, and*—bor-r-r-r-n!* comes faintly from far in the Lincoln woods.

6. I was also serenaded by a hooting owl. Near at hand you could fancy it the most melancholy sound in Nature, as if she meant by this to stereotype and make permanent in her choir the
75 dying moans of a human being,—some poor weak relic of mortality who has left hope behind, and howls like an animal, yet with human sobs, on entering the dark valley, made more awful by a certain gurgling melodiousness,—I find myself beginning with the letters gl when I try to imitate it,—expressive of a mind
80 which has reached the gelatinous mildewy stage in the mortification of all healthy and courageous thought. It reminded me of ghouls and idiots and insane howlings. But now one answers from far woods in a strain made really melodious by distance,—*Hoo hoo hoo, hoorer hoo;* and indeed for the most part it suggested
85 only pleasing associations, whether heard by day or night, summer or winter.

7. I rejoice that there are owls. Let them do the idiotic and maniacal hooting for men. It is a sound admirably suited to swamps and twilight woods which no day illustrates, suggesting
90 a vast and undeveloped nature which men have not recognized. They represent the stark twilight and unsatisfied thoughts which all have. All day the sun has shone on the surface of some savage swamp, where the single spruce stands hung with usnea lichens, and small hawks circulate above, and the chickadee lisps amid
95 the evergreens, and the partridge and rabbit skulk beneath; but now a more dismal and fitting day dawns, and a different race of creatures awakes to express the meaning of Nature there.

8. Late in the evening I heard the distant rumbling of wagons over bridges,—a sound heard farther than almost any other at
100 night,—the baying of dogs, and sometimes again the lowing of some disconsolate cow in a distant barn-yard. In the mean while all the shore rang with the trump of bullfrogs, the sturdy spirits of ancient winebibbers and wassailers, still unrepentant, trying to

sing a catch in their Stygian lake,—if the Walden nymphs will
pardon the comparison, for though there are almost no weeds, 105
there are frogs there,—who would fain keep up the hilarious rules
of their old festal tables, though their voices have waxed hoarse
and solemnly grave, mocking at mirth, and the wine has lost its
flavor, and become only liquor to distend their paunches, and
sweet intoxication never comes to drown the memory of the past, 110
but mere saturation and waterloggedness and distention. The
most aldermanic, with his chin upon a heart-leaf, which serves for
a napkin to his drooling chaps, under this northern shore quaffs a
deep draught of the once scorned water, and passes round the
cup with the ejaculation *tr-r-r-oonk, tr-r-r-oonk, tr-r-r-oonk!* and 115
straightway comes over the water from some distant cove the
same password repeated, where the next in seniority and girth
has gulped down to his mark; and when this observance has
made the circuit of the shores, then ejaculates the master of ceremonies, with satisfaction, *tr-r-r-oonk!* and each in his turn repeats 120
the same down to the least distended, leakiest, and flabbiest
paunched, that there be no mistake; and then the bowl goes
round again and again, until the sun disperses the morning mist,
and only the patriarch is not under the pond, but vainly bellow-
ing *troonk* from time to time, and pausing for a reply. 125

9. I am not sure that I ever heard the sound of cock-crowing
from my clearing, and I thought that it might be worth the while
to keep a cockerel for his music merely, as a singing bird. The
note of this once wild Indian pheasant is certainly the most remarkable of any bird's, and if they could be naturalized without 130
being domesticated, it would soon become the most famous
sound in our woods, surpassing the clangor of the goose and the
hooting of the owl; and then imagine the cackling of the hens to
fill the pauses when their lords' clarions rested! No wonder that
man added this bird to his tame stock,—to say nothing of the eggs 135
and drumsticks. To walk in a winter morning in a wood where
these birds abounded, their native woods, and hear the wild
cockerels crow on the trees, clear and shrill for miles over the re-
sounding earth, drowning the feebler notes of other birds,—think
of it! It would put nations on the alert. Who would not be early 140
to rise, and rise earlier and earlier every successive day of his life,

till he became unspeakably healthy, wealth, and wise? This foreign bird's note is celebrated by the poets of all countries along
with the notes of their native songsters. All climates agree with
145 brave Chanticleer. He is more indigenous even than the natives.
His health is ever good, his lungs are sound, his spirits never flag.
Even the sailor on the Atlantic and Pacific is awakened by his
voice; but its shrill sound never roused me from my slumbers. I
kept neither dog, cat, cow, pig, nor hens, so that you would have
150 said there was a deficiency of domestic sounds; neither the churn,
nor the spinning-wheel, nor even the singing of the kettle, nor the
hissing of the urn, nor children crying, to comfort one. An old-
fashioned man would have lost his senses or died of ennui before
this. Not even rats in the wall, for they were starved out, or rather
155 were never baited in,—only squirrels on the roof and under the
floor, a whippoorwill on the ridge-pole, a blue-jay screaming beneath the window, a hare or woodchuck under the house, a
screech-owl or a cat-owl behind it, a flock of wild geese or a laugh-
ing loon on the pond, and a fox to bark in the night. Not even a
160 lark or an oriole, those mild plantation birds, ever visited my
clearing. No cockerels to crow nor hens to cackle in the yard. No
yard! but unfenced Nature reaching up to your very sills. A young
forest growing up under your windows, and wild sumachs and
blackberry vines breaking through into your cellar; sturdy pitch-
165 pines rubbing and creaking against the shingles for want of room,
their roots reaching quite under the house. Instead of a scuttle or
a blind blown off in the gale,—a pine tree snapped off or torn up
by the roots behind your house for fuel. Instead of no path to the
front-yard gate in the Great Snow,—no gate—no front-yard,—and
170 no path to the civilized world.

✳✳✳✳✳✳✳✳✳✳✳

Here is prose that you can only wonder at, for it is among the
finest writing that our country has produced. *Walden*, from which
this and the other selection by Thoreau in this volume were taken,
was rewritten five times—to produce an effect of ease and natural-
ness and forthright vigor that we should be happy to see as the

spontaneous utterance of a perfect Natural Man. But alas it is not so. Such writing is the end product of years of self-discipline, education, and practice.

Situated for two years in a small cabin by Walden Pond, Thoreau lived virtually on nature while be observed, studied, thought, and wrote—demonstrating that it would cost incredibly little trouble and money to obtain one's necessary food, clothing, and shelter, even in this latitude. "It is not necessary that a man should earn his living by the sweat of his brow, unless he sweats easier than I do," Thoreau wrote, and a million or more Americans since his day have wondered, increasingly, whether there may not be better ways to spend their lives than caring for the labor-saving gadgets that consume the spare time in their lives today.

This passage is from the second of a series of three chapters, "Reading," "Sounds," and "Solitude," which are placed in this order to show a progressively more *direct* and *profound* approach to Reality. Books take us to other minds and to the experience of mankind, but the medium of print is also an artifice and a veil. Ultimate Reality is *embodied* and *expressed* in the physical world which is a form of Spirit or Thought. Sounds are Nature's direct, immediate voice, speaking to the receptive mind directly through the senses. In Solitude the contemplative, intuitive powers are called into play, and one may experience Reality without artifice or even a sensory medium. In "Sounds," however, Thoreau is exploring Reality in its physical and sensory manifestations—but always with the intent of finding its essence. The meanings that Thoreau reaches in his descriptions of sounds are, we believe, essentially products of the symbolizing power of language. We shall attempt to see them in this light.

As this passage opens, Thoreau brings us to the scene of his meditations.

1. From what point in Sen. 1 does Sen. 2 take off? By what means does Thoreau in Par. 1 make it appear that he is *attuned* to the country about him? What sensory experiences unite the two sentences in Par. 1? List, in Pars. 1 and 2, the *sound* words.

2. In Par. 2, "vibratory hum" picks up a theme introduced in Par. 1. What is it? Trace it through *rumbling, rattle, hum,* and *harp.* How does a harp relate to a lyre? There is a basic difference

between what *modulates* and what *echoes,* yet Thoreau has related both to a human and a natural force. Describe and explain each.

3. It may appear, on careful study, that Thoreau has developed a *dialogue* between his sounds and the natural objects which "strain" them. Find two or three other places where Thoreau repeats the idea of "strained" in some form. What total idea or notion do they express? Compare the two uses of "strain" (17 and 51) and explore their etymologies carefully. Does one use of the word affect the other in the passage?

4. What does "original" (20) mean? Explain the effect of "trivial" in line 23.

5. In Par. 3 Thoreau expresses quite specifically his ideas of man's relation to nature. Why is it almost a compliment to the young singers to say that their music is like the "natural music of the cow?" "Not unpleasantly disappointed" (29) uses a double negative which establishes a certain order; in this instance it may be considered a version of anti-climax. Why? Relate the anti-climax to "satirical" in the next sentence. What is the antecedent of "they" (33)?

6. Paragraph 4 is factual and restrained. Mark the *exact* impressions of sounds, their timing, and their relation to the author. Is the "particular time" (39–40) before or after sunset? Why is the information not included? In the sentence,

> Sometimes I heard four or five at once in different parts of the wood, by accident one a bar behind another, and so near me that I distinguished not only the cluck after each note, but often that singular buzzing sound like a fly in a spider's web, only proportionally louder.

something is omitted—the effect of the sounds. What is suggested by "one a bar behind another?"

7. Having inserted the skeptical "by accident" (43), Thoreau launches on a wholly fanciful flight in Par. 5. This paragraph cannot be read aloud often enough or carefully enough; it is a symphony of assonance and rhythm. Identify Ben Jonson; we can only guess at the work referred to; but we can identify several Elizabethan phrases. (The *Oxford English Dictionary,* ten volumes, in your library, is the proper reference work for this.)

What are they? Why does "groves" (57) introduce a Classical note?

8. When he says that the owls' screech reminds him "of music and singing birds," has Thoreau forgotten that owls are birds, or has he some other discernible intention here? "Would fain" (60) is a difficult phrase; it refers to the essence or spirit of music, as if it had a life of its own. Define the pun on "spirits" (61).

9. Thoreau's feeling of oneness with nature is stated in Par. 5:

> They give me a new sense of the variety and capacity of that nature which is our common dwelling.

What does the word "our" refer to?

10. Mark the words in Par. 6 that indicate some aspect of *decay*. Why is the paragraph more amusing than horrifying, even with its ghastly image of "gelatinous mildewy" (80)? In short, can you define what the language adds to the mere *subject* under discussion?

11. To Thoreau, nature is a symbol, a metaphor, an embodiment of the human spirit—and every natural manifestation therefore represents some quality of man. With this key you can write a brief essay—perhaps only a paragraph or two, but perhaps it will require more—explaining the rather odd combination in Pars. 6 and 7, especially the latter, of humor and astute, personal introspection, which conveys, in turn, insights into the human condition. Give close attention to "more dismal and fitting day dawns." (96).

12. Now you come to the most extraordinary passage. Here the Classical theme that has just been touched in "infernal groves," (57) "threnodies," (64) and "dark valley" (77) bursts forth in many voices. Beginning with "ancient" (103), mark and explain every word that has a Classical reference. "Sweet intoxication" (110) is straight out of Homer. You will have to use a dictionary with some care to find them all.

13. The clue, "napkin" (113), tells us that "pond" (124) stands for what piece of furniture? You have often been told, no doubt, that it is important to maintain a certain "level of diction," that is, to keep your discourse consistently proper to its subject and audience. Yet here Thoreau mixes Classical reference

and modern slang in a sort of pun. What is the level of his diction?

14. Where is the "mark" (118)? If girth determines seniority, what, here, does seniority determine?

15. When Thoreau says, "An old-fashioned man would have lost his senses or died of ennui before this," (152–153) what kind of man is he implying *he* is? Specifically, what is "new-fashioned" about forgoing the tokens of domesticity? Think carefully about the root-meaning of "fashioned." Here then is a subtle pun on it.

16. The speculation on un-domesticating the cockerel (rooster) in the last paragraph may seem a trifle elaborate until you realize that it is an extended metaphor which is modulated into a more nearly literal statement beginning with line 161. What *personal* (that is, for the author) meaning and purpose are involved in the elimination of *all* domestic and civilized paraphernalia—even paths and gates? (Ques. 11 may give the clue to your answer.) The American Dream of human perfection finds its highest expression in these insights. You may trace its outlines in a hundred myths and notions, still current, about the Common Man, simple horse sense, Back to Nature, Natural Man, The Good Old Days, Equality, and so on.

Smile, Smile, Smile

MARYA MANNES

1. We are, as everyone knows, a very friendly people. Even the Russians concede this. Foreign visitors are overwhelmed with our kindliness and informality, and even Americans returning from abroad feel a wave of warmth rushing out from the continent to greet them. 5 The hearty welcome, the easy smile are among our most endearing traits. But they can be overdone.

2. The Rheingold Girls smile too much, people in television commercials smile too much, families in magazine ads smile too much, and government leaders smile too much. The American 10 flag is one large grin. Everyone wants to be liked.

3. This obsessive need to be liked, rather than respected, has become the soft core of our state and our state of mind; as common to the White House as it is to a Coca-Cola ad. In a society of selling you cannot afford to offend the customers. You must try, 15 therefore, to please all.

4. So this friendliness, this American quality to be cherished, has now been packaged into a product trademarked with a smile and claiming three ingredients: prosperity, piety, and equality. An American who can make money, invoke God, and be no better 20 than his neighbor, has nothing to fear but truth itself. It is better to be liked than brave or free.

5. There are times, of course, when gravity is not only permissible but required. The stern face may be worn when God is mentioned and the stock market falls; when dignity is assaulted, hon- 25 esty is impugned, and other nations chastised. Otherwise our

teeth, which owe their whiteness and regularity to American dentistry, are to be bared whenever possible as a sign of the good nature for which we are justly famous.

30 6. Yet it is doubtful whether Washington or Jefferson or Lincoln ever had to prove their humanity in this manner, and it is difficult to visualize their faces split by a chronic grin. Our greatest president had a profoundly sad face; even his smile must have wrenched the beholder's heart.

35 7. But now good-fellowship, unflagging, is the prime requisite for success in our society, and the man or woman who smiles only for reasons of humor or pleasure is a deviate: a prey—and therefore antisocial—to sinister forces. The passport photographer says: "How about a little smile?" The lover, seeing a grave face, says 40 "What's wrong?" A President unsmiling means bad news. To be serious is not to be loved, and that is unbearable.

8. Now there is clearly nothing wrong with a smile. It can illumine and often make beautiful features dimmed by passivity or grooved by sadness. But the smile I am speaking of, and which so 45 many wear so much, is less an expression of joy than the muscular reflex of popularity. No better, or more horrible, example of this exists than the smile of television masters of ceremonies or the sellers of products: a smile directed at all and therefore at no one, a mass ingratiation wholly devoid of feeling. This kind of promiscuity—for it is exactly that—robs a man both of his dignity and his 50 virility. Poets, dreamers, lovers, fighters and saints—the men who conquer the imagination either through the power of their spirit or the force of their sex have features more often composed by inner disciplines than fragmented by easy grins. They are not 55 popular here.

※※※※※※※※※※

America has been a puzzle, a target, and a concern for Europe since 1492. In the early nineteenth century, British travelers made us so angry that we delighted in satires on them, to which they responded in kind. Several books have been written on versions of the America Through Foreign Eyes topic. In the twentieth century we have come in for our share of reasonable and unrea-

sonable criticism from natives, newcomers, one-shot visitors, and
many who have never set foot on these shores. We have responded with every variety of attitude, from abject humility to
bumptious contempt. Today the matter is no longer funny, because, as Simone de Beauvoir says, "America is one of the world's
pivotal points: the future of man is at stake here . . . one can
only be stirred by the struggle she carries on within herself, a
struggle whose stakes are beyond measure."

And yet the European's image of America is as confused as our
own image of ourselves. This selection is one of a number following that deal with the issue. Miss Mannes builds a case on a single
glowing word; let us look at it to see how the structure is put together.

1.   Paragraph 1 has how many words that obviously refer to the
title?

2.   Paragraph 2 funnels all these notions into the word "smile"
and *then* concludes with a generalization which is obviously the
theme of the first two paragraphs. The writer could have begun
with the thesis and gone on to illustrate it; the order she has
chosen has a certain surprise effect. Why? Is the thesis the only
possible explanation of the facts already given in Pars. 1 and 2?

3.   Paragraph 3 gives a specific and practical reason why we
"want to be liked." Now, how does this reason fit with the idea of
"obsessive" (12)? In short, identify two contradictory motives
offered to us in Par. 3.

4.   Does the "now" of line 18 indicate that the friendliness *began*
for a reason different from the desire to sell things? Exactly what
is the "product" of line 18? Par. 4 quickly becomes very sarcastic:
". . . nothing to fear but truth itself" is a reflection of Franklin D.
Roosevelt's famous rallying cry when the United States was at the
bottom of the Great Depression: "We have nothing to fear but
fear itself." Comment on the tone, and on the justice of the last
sentence.

5.   The distance from God to the stock market (24–25) makes
for a classic example of *anti-climax*. Does the same rhetorical
device appear in the following clause?

6.   Evaluate the effect and the relevance of the reference to
American dentistry (27–28).

7.   Decide whether the last two paragraphs add new ideas or merely embellish those already presented. Determine the precise force of words like *packaged* (18), *trademarked* (18), *no better than his neighbor* (20–21), *split* (32), *deviate* (37), *sinister* (38), *grooved* (44), *reflex of popularity* (46; is this phrase perfectly accurate?), *mass ingratiation* (49), and *fragmented* (54).

8.   Write a paragraph or a short essay characterizing a person or group with a single dominating figure like the "smile" of this selection. Be as fair or as unfair as you choose.

Selling America Abroad

WILLIAM H. WHYTE, JR.

1. The communication
job we face abroad—"selling America," as it is so often put—seems
far removed from our immediate communication problems at
home. It is remarkable, however, how very parallel they are. The
analogy between them, of course, should not be too closely 5
drawn; there is quite a difference between persuading Americans
of something and persuading *New Statesman and Nation* readers
of it, and the difference is more considerable than a sales-minded
nation likes to believe. Nevertheless, on the basic points the lessons we are learning with such pain abroad have much more 10
pertinence to our domestic misunderstandings than might appear.

2. They have a pertinence for more reasons than comparison;
indeed, it can be argued that unless we attend better to the overseas job our domestic ones will become somewhat academic. For
it one day might very well be written that the free world de- 15
stroyed itself because of a myth. It would not be the Big Lie of
the Russians; only the fools believed that. It would be something
much more inexplicable; the myth that for all our bathtubs and
our cars and our skyscrapers we are without moral purpose; that
we are the New Carthage—all money no spirit; that we are, in 20
short, a country without a soul.

3. Already this myth has sapped the will of our allies, made
those who benefited from the ECA cynical of its purpose; and
each month it grows more in virulence, ready to attack at each
crisis. But even more terrible has been the effect on us. For when 25
we hear it played back to us, we grow petulant and dismayed,

From *Is Anybody Listening?*, by William H. Whyte, Jr. Published by
Simon and Schuster, Inc. Courtesy of Fortune Magazine; © 1951 Time Inc.

and in our anger many of us can think of nothing but to pull
down the pillars on a world that does not understand.

4. Yet the West is desperately eager to listen. That it tragically
30 misunderstands us is not easily explained by the accusations that
come so readily to American minds. Nor is it simply a matter of
slicker gimmicks or extra kilowatts or more pamphlets. We have
sold the world many things—sold them so well half Europe would
pack up and come over if it could. We have left unsold the ideas
35 that would destroy the myth.

5. We talk of "A Campaign of Truth." This, certainly, is in
order. But what is "the truth"? Speeches? Statistics? A day in the
life of a Wisconsin farmer? Our congenital dislike of abstract
thought has at last come home to roost. *We have failed to deter-*
40 *mine what it is we wish to communicate.*

6. Once we knew very well what we were and what we wanted
to be, and we thought it out into some of the most contagious
prose of all time. But we went on to become the great pragmatists,
so eager to be on with the job, so impatient of theory and reflec-
45 tion, that we worked ourselves into a moral isolationism. Why
analyze America? It worked, didn't it?

7. Curiously, by keeping our philosophy so tacit, we have managed to show ourselves to the world as little different from the
Marxists—seeming, like them, to believe that material prosperity
50 is an end that in itself will bring all the other qualities. Instinctively we know better, but we have never bothered to articulate
for ourselves what we take for granted, much less convey it to
others. And so we have talked of the manifestations of our success
rather than the causes. Not for us woolly-headed theories or im-
55 practical idealism; instead, down-to-earth, hard-rock facts: the
miles of cement, the telephones, the cars laid end to end—all the
things, in short, our friends have envied and our enemies have
conceded.

8. But what made the telephones and the cars possible? When
60 we have tried to explain, it has been in a lazy man's shorthand
that has obscured our national character rather than illuminated
it. Thus have we talked to foreigners of our "individualism," when
we have achieved the most horizontal, cooperative of all societies;
of "competition" and "incentive economy," when we have

achieved the kind of security that socialists everywhere hunger 65
for. And we wonder why the audience is confused.

9. And not only have we failed to define *what* we are to say;
we have failed to define *why* we want to say it. Of all the many
aims of our propaganda, which is to be primary? Interestingly,
almost every private organization that has thought of an overseas 70
propaganda program of its own has stumbled on precisely this
question. More to the point, so has the government.

10. What is the aim? Friendship? To many Americans this is
the end-all. And nothing has done us more grievous harm—for we
are offended terribly when love is not forthcoming from others. 75

11. It's quite impossible anyway. We have only to look at India;
since their departure, the British, who never gave a damn
whether anyone liked them or not, have become increasingly
popular, while we, who did our best to expedite that departure,
are becoming increasingly unpopular. The fruits of leadership do 80
not necessarily include love, and we would do well to take the
fact in our stride.

12. To Americanize people? No one ever puts it quite this
baldly, but there lurks deep in some American breasts the feeling
that there is a mystically beneficent quality in certain of our 85
folkways, and that if only they could be exported, the chasm in
understanding would be bridged. Again, we have a failure to
isolate the particulars from the principles. After all, what was so
Japanese as baseball?

13. To refute Communist lies? Obviously, this is an important 90
part of any propaganda program, but as the primary aim it is a
defensive course that would foredoom us to a constant shellack-
ing. They'll always be a lie ahead. Furthermore, we must recognize that anti-Communism does not fill vacuums, nor is it necessarily pro-U.S.; indeed, our biggest problem lies in those people 95
who think we are *as bad as* the Russians. . . .

14. The obstacles to success may seem appalling. For even
when we have articulated our philosophy we have the task of
projecting it over the tremendous gap in attitudes and environment that separates us from other people. And it is a gap, unfor- 100
tunately, that we do not readily appreciate.

15. We have been so unaware of basic differences that we have

persisted in talking to the Europeans in terms for which there is
no foreign equivalent: *participation, community relations, incen-*
105 *tive, public relations, productivity, man-in-the-street, public opin-*
ion—the very listing itself produces a syllabus of the American
philosophy. And a glossary of misunderstanding.

16. Taking the evocative power of these words for granted, we
have assumed that "hard facts" will do the job—and that, in a sort
110 of question-and-answer fashion, we can use prepackaged nuggets
of truth to beat down each fallacy we come across. It won't work.
Like the hydra, the myth is proof against piecemeal attack.
Americans are barbarians. The U.S. is a dehumanizing tech-
nocracy. Here are the two chief elements in the myth—yet both
115 are so mutually supporting that to refute either we must trace
them back to their common source.

17. Europe today presents an odd paradox. While "neutralism"
has been reduced politically—in the words of one observer—to a
"hard core of jerks," emotionally it has never been more powerful.
120 Its underpinnings go something like this: since there is no spiritual
base to the U.S., it is as culturally barren as the U.S.S.R.; its
people are barbarians, and any who must accept succor from
them should hate themselves for it. To spell this out essayists have
a whole new lexicon of psychiatric and anthropological terms for
125 the job, and they have been using it with increasing frequency to
demonstrate that the jukebox, the milk shake, or some such thing
is the universal clue to America's "infantilism," "reverted uncle
complex," "*Kino-Weltschmerz*," etc.

✳✳✳✳✳✳✳✳✳✳✳

The previous chapter of the book from which this selection was
taken deals with the current interest, in business circles, in "plain
talk"—short, brisk, folksy, concrete sentences devoid of long abstract words or complex thoughts. "Plain talk" has been recom-
mended as the businessman's best medium for selling himself and
his product. W. H. Whyte makes the point that true "plain talk"
is the hard-won reward of intellectual discipline, courage, and
simplicity; whereas this contrived plain talk is pure fraud, an instrument of persuasion and deception,—actually double-talk to
conceal the real facts.

1.   Now he turns to the job we face of "selling America" abroad. What sentence states the theme of Par. 1? The "difference" (6) depends, obviously, on what ability of the British readers of *New Statesman and Nation*? What two words in the last sentence of Par. 1 are transitional in that they indicate matters to be dealt with later? Mark the transitional devices throughout the selection. What word carries us into Par. 2?

2.   "Comparison" (12) refers to the similarity between what two matters in Par. 1?

3.   Explain "academic" (14); is it an understatement or an overstatement?

4.   Whose "myth" (16)—our or our Allies'? But first you may study the word *myth* and determine which of its many uses applies here. Whether a myth is true is not so essential as *what*?

5.   Review the metaphorical underpinning of Par. 3. It goes *sapped . . . virulence . . . attack . . . played back*. Is it a consistent image? Who (27) "pulled down the pillars"? Would our action have motives similar to his?

6.   The "accusations that come so readily to American minds" (30–31) are our answers to Europe's acceptance of the Myth. Does Whyte suggest that they are adequate or inadequate answers? What are these accusations? Some you have heard; others you can guess.

7.   At the climax of the preliminary definition, we come, in line 38, to a use of "abstract" that seems, in the context, exactly opposite to Simone de Beauvoir's use of the term to explain America (p. 201, l. 68). Write an explanation of the matter, defining the contradiction or showing that it is only apparent.

8.   The "contagious prose" was written by such men as Franklin, Jefferson, Emerson, and Thoreau. Pragmatism came later; lines 44–45 define it in part. You will have to look further to discover how pragmatism, although impatient of abstractions, was initially a program for realizing the ideals of that contagious prose. Show how "tacit" (47) summarizes Par. 6. It should be one of the transitional words you have marked for Ques. 1.

9.   In the discussion of our pragmatism, "what we wanted to be" (41–42) is opposed to "be on with the job" (44). How do

"manifestations" and "causes" (53–54) line up with these positions? Why, in terms of the Myth, have our enemies *conceded* what our friends have *envied?*

10.   Paragraph 8 indicates some profound confusions that have sprung up along the path from nineteenth-century idealism to twentieth-century materialism. An added confusion is the fact that great wealth and special privilege seem to be growing in Russia, whereas they are disappearing in America; yet we continue to sell capitalism and attack socialism abroad. To what extent are the confusions dependent upon the sort of words that are in quotation marks in this paragraph?

11.   In considering *what* we are and *why* we want to say it, Whyte moves through friendship, folkways, truth, etc.

Explain the point about Japanese baseball in terms of "particulars" and "principles" (88).

What are the "vacuums" of 94? Is it possible that there is no such thing?

Why is *as bad as* (96) italicized?

12.   How are gaps in attitudes and environment (99–100) illustrated by the italicized terms in the next paragraph?

13.   The American version of the European accusation is set forth in Par. 17. The refutation has been seen in Par. 6. Write an essay comparing this case with the arguments on the very same subject found in Simone de Beauvoir (pp. 195 and 199).

14.   That Whyte's essay is, itself, a version of the "shorthand" he attributes to American propaganda is shown by the number of explanatory comments and questions we have formulated. Can you find more spots where clarification is needed? This is probably a serious defect of the writing. An interesting commentary on this point is the fact that Whyte expanded this material into a larger, more concrete, and much more successful book, *The Organization Man.* You may undertake a close analysis of parallel passages from the two books.

Good Humor of Americans

SIMONE DE BEAUVOIR

1. What makes daily
life so agreeable in America is the cordial good humor of the
Americans. Of course, these qualities have their ugly side. I
loathe those imperious invitations "to look at the best side of life,"
repeated in phrases and pictures as long as the day itself. On 5
posters, for instance, what displays of shining white teeth before
Coca-Cola, Lucky Strikes and dishes of Quaker Oats; a smile like
lockjaw. The constipated young woman smiles lovingly at the
lemonade which eases her stomach. In the subway, in the street,
on magazine pages, these smiles pursue me like obsessions. In a 10
drugstore I read on a showcard, "Not to grin is a sin." You sense
instructions and discipline. Cheer up! Take it easy! Optimism is
necessary for the peace of society and the prosperity of the country. If a banker has generously lent fifty dollars without security
to a young foreigner in difficulties, if my hotel manager has taken 15
the risk of cashing my checks, it is because this trust is ordained
and implied by an economy based on credit and spending.

2. Kindness, too, is planned. This afternoon I went to cash a
check. As soon as I entered the bank a uniformed employee advanced towards me and offered his services: I almost thought he 20
was expecting me. He took me into a kind of hall where desks
were arranged in rows; on each desk was a card with the name
of a functionary. I sat down, showed my papers to a Mr. John
Smith: he was not an anonymous cog in a machine, nor I an
anonymous client, and he showed me courtesy addressed to me 25
personally. He marked my check, and the cashier immediately

From *America Day By Day*, by Simone de Beauvoir (trans. by Patrick
Dudley). Reprinted by permission of Grove Press, Inc. and Librairie Gallimard.

paid me the money. At home my papers would have been verified
on the other side of the counter, without consultation with me,
and no doubt harshly; and I should have been treated as a mere
30 number. I am not easily duped, and I know that this respect
shown to individuals is quite formal; the polite smile which marks
David Brown as an individual is also gratifying to the individual
John Williams; nothing is more general than this singular trait
which they all take so seriously. You sense a hoax, but it does not
35 prevent the fact that, owing to this personal consideration, the
American does not have to be stuck-up to feel his dignity; busi-
nesslike perhaps, but the friendliness of salesmen, employees,
waiters and porters is, though not disinterested, nonetheless never
servile; they are neither sour nor stiff, and their pleasantness is
40 real. We held the German soldiers responsible for the way in
which they carried out cruel orders. Indeed, man is never passive;
in his obedience he sets limits to his liberty, and in submitting to
evil accepts it; as a rule, this acceptance is carried out through
invention and initiative which reveal the responsibility of the indi-
45 vidual. And, in the same way, Americans do not submit passively
to the propaganda of smiles; in an atmosphere in which optimism
is obligatory they gladly become cordial, trusting and generous;
a man's pleasant manner becomes less suspect the less interested
he personally is in the success of the system; he is more hoaxed
50 than hoaxer.

3. Whatever my view of American ideologies, I shall always
have a warm feeling for the taxi drivers, the newspapermen, shoeshine boys and all those people who suggest by their daily acts
that men can be friends. For they create an atmosphere of trust,
55 friendship and gaiety. The man beside you is not *a priori* your
enemy; even if he is wrong, he is not immediately guilty; with us,
goodwill such as this has become uncommon. I am a foreigner;
they found no fault with that, nor did it strike them as eccentric;
they did not laugh at my accent, which was shocking; rather, they
60 tried to understand me. If I had no change with which to pay the
taxi, the driver did not question my honesty; he helped me to
find some: indeed, he would generously let me off a few cents. In
any case, I was especially fond of taxi drivers. They talked
throughout the entire ride, and it was often difficult to understand

them. New Yorkers themselves are at times put out by their 65
accent. Many of them had been in France during the war, and
we talked of Paris; each time I thought with emotion: here, then,
was one of the men whom we had greeted so joyously, one whose
uniform and steel helmet signified our deliverance. It was strange
to find them again, each with his name and his private occupa- 70
tion—anonymous soldiers who came to my country from an inaccessible world, a world separated from all our misery by barriers
of fire and steel. Their feeling for Paris was a little condescending,
like the customs man who greeted me with the words, "You are
coming from a beautiful country to a country which is even more 75
beautiful." Their cordiality irritated me after I caught a cold; the
fault lay with the New York climate, which changes without
warning from hot to cold; but as they saw it, I was going around
with one of those wretched complaints of old Europe. They asked
severely, "You have a cold?" They seemed disturbed. A good 80
American is never ill, and it is not polite for a stranger in New
York to catch cold. They suggested remedies, and some even produced pillboxes from their pockets and offered them to me.

✳✳✳✳✳✳✳✳✳✳

The author of this passage is a distinguished French novelist,
philosopher, and feminist. Marya Mannes' parents are Europeans;
the French Simone de Beauvoir traveled to America to observe
and comment. Both see the ubiquitous good humor of America.

1. Identify the first word by which the writer indicates her
approval of American good humor. To what extent does the thesis
of Par. 1 repeat that of Marya Mannes' essay?

2. Paragraph 2 adds a branch to the tree of the smile with
"kindness," which is elaborated as "courtesy." For some reason,
"the American does not have to be stuck-up to feel his dignity."
(36). Evaluate the explanation given in the paragraph. Be
sure to find the correct meaning of *disinterested* (38). Observe
how it relates to *interested* in 48. Your explanation should also
take rather careful account of the play on *hoax, hoaxed* from line
34 to line 49.

3. The transitional phrase that takes us into Par. 3 is difficult. What part does *ideology* play in Par. 2, and how do the concrete details in Par. 3 grow from this abstract introduction?

4. You have as good grounds as anybody for judging the justice of the motives identified in lines 79–82. Do so.

The Attraction of America

SIMONE DE BEAUVOIR

1. It would be difficult to tear myself away from these splendid visions of hope; and yet I knew their wiles. In America, life also ebbs away in the effort to survive. "I've been out since 10 A.M.," a taxi driver told me at 10 P.M. "You bet I want to get home!" I remembered how people rushed to the ferryboat that took them across to New Jersey. All my friends had told me how hard the working days were in this city of distances, especially for women who have a job and a home to run at the same time; they are exhausted when night comes: I have often seen them too tired to accept an invitation to go out. I have come to understand that if people drink so much it is not because they have a mania; they need a spur at the end of the afternoon.

2. That is not all. One has a premonition that anything might happen. But what is actually happening? What do they do with their time and the money they earn? No doubt, I did not get to know the ruling class, those who invent, study and speculate; but they make up only a small minority. Americans, for the most part, are like those with whom I rubbed shoulders; they let their lives go around in circles. They have neither a liking for, nor the sense of, collective life; nor have they any concern for their own personal destinies. This is the source of the sadness that I often felt when with them. This world full of generous promise crushes them; and its splendor soon appears barren, for no one controls it.

3. Each civilization offers in the "banality of everyday life" a means of escape, but what strikes one here is the point to which

From *America Day By Day,* by Simone de Beauvoir (trans. by Patrick Dudley). Reprinted by permission of Grove Press, Inc. and Librairie Gallimard.

this escapism is organized. Neither his education nor the atmosphere in which he develops are designed to shed light on the inner self of the individual. He is aware of himself not only as a
30 human body but also as an organism protected and prolonged by a whole arsenal of devices; he goes from floor to floor by elevator, travels by subway, speaks into the telephone, typewrites, and sweeps the floor with a vacuum cleaner. Between his stomach and the food he eats there is a world of canned food factories, refrig-
35 erators, electric cookers. Between his sexual desires and their fulfilment there is the paraphernalia of moral precepts and hygienic practices. He is hemmed in by society from childhood. He searches outside himself, among other people, for his models for conduct; hence what is called American conformism: Actually,
40 individuals are just as different and just as isolated one from another in the new world as in the old, but here they find easier means of escape from their individuality and the feeling of "forlornness"; or perhaps they do not find them, but then, at least, they seek them more stubbornly. Like everyone else, they know
45 dissatisfaction, boredom and doubt, but they try to rationalize their own confusion by posing "problems": instead of drawing strength from solitude, or overcoming it by plumbing its depths, they cling to the given facts; they see the source of values and of truth in things, not in themselves.
50   4. Their own existences are things of chance to which they attach no importance. That is why they are interested in net results, and not in the spirit that engenders them. In much the same way, they think they can isolate the part from the whole, as witnessed in the call for specialization that one finds in the
55 sciences, technology and education. To use Hegelian terms, one can say that the very negation of the subject leads to the triumph of understanding over the spirit, that is to say, the triumph of abstraction. And that is why in this country, which seems to turn so decidedly toward the concrete world, the word abstraction so
60 often came to my lips; the object set up as an idol loses its human values and becomes abstract, for concrete reality is that which actually envelops object and subject simultaneously. That is the paradox of all positivisms, all pseudo-realisms which forsake humanity to proclaim the importance of things; they are lacking

in the object itself, and never attain to anything more than 65
concepts.

5. I often felt, while listening to American jazz or talking to
Americans, that the very time in which they lived was abstract.
They respect the past, but only insofar as it is a thing embalmed;
the idea of a living past, integrated with the present, is foreign to 70
them. They only want to recognize a present cut by the course of
time, and the future they visualize is that which can be deduced
mechanically, not one whose ripening, or whose sudden explosion, implies unforeseeable risks. They believe in the future of a
bridge, for instance, or of an economic plan, but not in the future 75
of an art or of a revolution. Their time is "the physicist's time,"
an exterior concept which doubles that of space.

6. Because they refuse to accept the durability of things, they
also refuse to recognize their quality; it is not only for economic
reasons that "craftsmanship" does not exist in the States. Even in 80
leisured occupations qualitative success is never sought for: food
is cooked, just as fruit is ripened, as fast as possible; in every walk
of life one must always hurry, lest the result be already outdated
by the time it is achieved. Cut off from the past and from the
future, the present has no weight. Nothing is more foreign to 85
Americans than the idea of regarding the passing moment as a
repetition of time, a mirror of eternity, and of anchoring oneself
to it to grasp truths or values that are in themselves timeless. To
them, the content of the passing moment is as fragile as the
moment itself. Because they will not admit that truths and values 90
become, they do not know how to conserve them in the movement that leaves them behind: they just deny them.

※※※※※※※※※

1. The use of "collective life" (21) seems to contradict head-on
a cliché about America—that we are so herd-minded as to have
lost the ability to be alone. Find where Mlle. de Beauvoir makes
this latter charge herself. Is she guilty of contradiction, or is she
using the phrase in another sense? How does it relate to the
"banality of everyday life" (25)?

2. Trace the argument from "personal destinies" through "gen-

erous promises" to "controls" by making the statement in different words, using a clear literal word in place of the image, "crushes." Does "barren" go with "crushes" effectively, as a figure?

3. "They find easier means of escape . . ." (41–42). This sentence contradicts, "This world full of generous promise crushes them"—and no sooner has the contradicting sentence been written than it is contradicted. What rhetorical or expository value, if any, is attained by the inclusion of a statement that must immediately be denied?

4. With the word *things* in line 49, we are brought squarely up against the old charge of materialism. Note the materialistic objects and activities listed earlier in the paragraph, that prepare for the charge. But here the charge is *not* simply materialism but something more complex. You may define it in a paragraph.

5. Paragraph 4 is difficult, but it becomes plainer with every sentence. The "subject" is the person or self. The "object" of course refers to things other than the self. Now relate "existence," "results," "understanding," and other key terms of the Par. by placing them in two columns under Subject and Object. Finally, explain how concrete, as opposed to abstract, reality "actually envelops object and subject simultaneously" (62).

6. How does *object* (65) relate to *time* (68)? Explain the proportion: object : concept = time : abstract. To what word in Par. 4 does *integrate* (70) correspond? Explore the Latin etymology to discover the concrete source of the two terms and decide how well they serve as figures for indicating proper attitudes toward *time* and *objects*.

7. The somewhat mystical union between a proper relation to time and a proper relation to things produces the concept of "craftsmanship." How do these relations flower in craftsmanship? The point is worth close attention and careful thought.

8. Compare the writer's "never" (81) with comments on the same point elsewhere in this group of selections (pp. 190, 192, etc.).

9. To say that "truths and values *become*" (91) is to assert that such absolutes, as they are called, come into being as they are lived. They do not, that is, exist apart from man in some realm

of perfect Essences—but in living experience and process. You may write an essay on one of several aspects of this subject: morals and values as you see them in *practice;* how some of your own beliefs and values have been born in your living rather than learned abstractly; what America professes contrasted with what she does; how your friends or associates think they behave and how they actually do; the eternal problem, in short, of the ideal and the actual. It will take effective form only in so far as you observe a definite area closely.

You may also find material for a very effective essay in the attempt to illustrate (or disprove) the charge made against American life in the last two paragraphs—which is summed up in a later passage: ". . . these people about me are lonely; because they flee in terror their essential solitude, because they run away from themselves, they have no real self-possession." It has been argued (and persuasively) that these charges apply to the metropolitan areas of the United States but not to the more essential America of town and country. If you are from town or country you may write effectively about the quality of life there as contrasted with what you know of the big cities.

An American Writer Abroad

JAMES BALDWIN

1. The story of what can happen to an American Negro writer in Europe simply illustrates, in some relief, what can happen to any American writer there. It is not meant, of course, to imply that it happens to them
5 all, for Europe can be very crippling, too; and, anyway, a writer, when he has made his first breakthrough, has simply won a crucial skirmish in a dangerous, unending, and unpredictable battle. Still, the breakthrough is important, and the point is that an American writer, in order to achieve it, very often has to leave
10 this country.

2. The American writer, in Europe, is released, first of all, from the necessity of apologizing for himself. It is not until he is released from the habit of flexing his muscles and proving that he is just a "regular guy" that he realizes how crippling this habit
15 has been. It is not necessary for him, there, to pretend to be something he is not, for the artist does not encounter in Europe the same suspicion he encounters here. Whatever the Europeans may actually think of artists, they have killed enough of them off by now to know that they are as real—and as persistent—as rain,
20 snow, taxes, or businessmen.

3. Of course, the reason for Europe's comparative clarity concerning the different functions of men in society is that European society has always been divided into classes in a way that American society never has been. A European writer considers himself
25 to be part of an old and honorable tradition—of intellectual activ-

ity, of letters—and his choice of a vocation does not cause him any uneasy wonder as to whether or not it will cost him all his friends. But this tradition does not exist in America.

4. On the contrary, we have a very deep-seated distrust of real intellectual effort (probably because we suspect that it will 30 destroy, as I hope it does, that myth of America to which we cling so desperately). An American writer fights his way to one of the lowest rungs on the American social ladder by means of pure bull-headedness and an indescribable series of odd jobs. He probably *has* been a "regular fellow" for much of his adult life, 35 and it is not easy for him to step out of that lukewarm bath.

5. We must, however, consider a rather serious paradox: though American society is more mobile than Europe's, it is easier to cut across social and occupational lines there than it is here. This has something to do, I think, with the problem of status in American 40 life. Where everyone has status, it is also perfectly possible, after all, that no one has. It seems inevitable, in any case, that a man may become uneasy as to just what his status is.

6. But Europeans have lived with the idea of status for a long time. A man can be as proud of being a good waiter as of being 45 a good actor, and, in neither case, feel threatened. And this means that the actor and the waiter can have a freer and more genuinely friendly relationship in Europe than they are likely to have here. The waiter does not feel, with obscure resentment, that the actor has "made it," and the actor is not tormented by the fear 50 that he may find himself, tomorrow, once again, a waiter.

7. This lack of what may roughly be called social paranoia causes the American writer in Europe to feel—almost certainly for the first time in his life—that he can reach out to everyone, that he is accessible to everyone and open to everything. This is an 55 extraordinary feeling. He feels, so to speak, his own weight, his own value.

8. It is as though he suddenly came out of a dark tunnel and found himself beneath the open sky. And, in fact, in Paris, I began to see the sky for what seemed to be the first time. It was borne in 60 on me—and it did not make me feel melancholy—that this sky had been there before I was born and would be there when I was

dead. And it was up to me, therefore, to make of my brief opportunity the most that could be made.

※※※※※※※※※※※

This short excerpt has been introduced merely for its exposition
of a single point—a question of class and status in relation to art,
mixed with a serious personal problem. Our problem is to analyze
these elements and discover how the ideas about art relate to the
ideas about the artist, and in turn how they relate to questions of
the American myth and its effect on Europe.

1.   Explain the idea of "breakthrough"; it is the key to Par. 1,
one of a number of military words (mark them); here does it
refer to a social or a psychological gain? It also implies, very
clearly, something about the part that art plays in the life of the
artist. Try to define it.

2.   In Par. 2 "breakthrough" becomes "release" from pretending
"to be something he is not." What does he have to pretend to be?
Mark the words that give substance to this pretense, in the paragraph. What kind of suspicion does the artist encounter in America? What has the European killing of artists to do with all this?

3.   Has the subject, "comparative clarity concerning the different
functions of men in society," been prepared for? If not, what is
the function of the "Of course" that opens the paragraph?

4.   Does the American youth who declares his intention to be
an artist run the risk, in your experience, of losing all his friends?

5.   The important statement in Par. 4 is probably the parenthesis. Now, what is the myth referred to in the parenthesis? Is
it the same myth that W. H. Whyte discusses (pp. 189, 192)?
How does it reconcile the lukewarm bath and the life of odd jobs,
since both are apparently essential to the myth?

6.   Paragraph 5 may contain a significant ambiguity: is "cut
across" to be understood figuratively or literally, that is, in terms
of communication or actual movement? Write a paragraph explaining the "paradox."

7.   By exactly what does a person "feel threatened" in a society
where his status is dubious? (Par. 6) If the waiter does not feel

"resentment," is his emotion pride or, in fact, resignation? That is, is the American expatriate's gain a version of the European's loss?

8. "I began to see the sky for what seemed to be the first time"; what does the sky symbolize in this sentence?

9. William Whyte and Simone de Beauvoir have dealt with the idea that America is somehow confused between its idea of coöperation and its idea of individualism. Write an explanation of the *form* that these ideas take in the present essay. What is it that makes the European content with his status and therefore able to communicate across status lines without unhappiness? Why does special talent carry a stigma in America, if it does? Upon what grounds do we feel superior and inferior to Europe? This selection is, like Whyte's, elliptical, and must be read carefully.

10. Since you have been continually reminded of the importance of concreteness, you will discover a challenging topic by comparing the concrete metaphors in this selection (since all metaphor is more or less concrete) with the ideas they convey. For example, we have "crippling," and the military figures (see Ques. 1) in Par. 1; "rungs" and "ladder" and a "bath" in Par. 4; and on through "paranoia" and "weight" and the "sky." If you study the manner in which the metaphors embody or seem to embody the abstract ideas, you will be able to demonstrate something about writing.

Conversation and Manners

1. In private life, the counterpart of public debate is conversation. The word sounds old-fashioned and its meaning is blurred, because in the years since conversation was given a name and made an ideal, its
5 nature has changed as much as that of public debate—and for the same reasons. Yet whether we use the word to mean all forms of verbal exchange or, more narrowly, the sociable sifting of opinion for pleasure, conversation is the testing ground of manners. This is so because manners are minor morals which facilitate the rela-
10 tions of men, chiefly through words. When those verbal relations are deliberately staged, for no other purpose than pleasure, men find themselves engaged in an intellectual exercise that is one of the delights of life. Manners, therefore, are not solely a clue to the deeper moral assumptions of an age, they are also a strong or
15 weak guardian of Intellect at its most exposed.

2. Conversation being difficult, the reality of it has always been inferior to the ideal. We can nevertheless deduce almost as much from the ideal—or the lack of it—as from the audible reality. The reader will have noticed that I did not speak of sociable
20 conversation as the *exchange*, but as the *sifting* of opinion. The "exchange" view is a nearly correct description of modern practice: A delivers an opinion while B thinks of the one he will inject as soon as he decently can. It is an exchange in the same sense that we "exchange" greetings: we offer a formula and are offered
25 another, but generally go off with our own.

3. In this rudimentary game Intellect plays a small role. It

From *The House of Intellect* by Jacques Barzun. Copyright © 1959 by
Jacques Barzun. Reprinted by permission of Harper & Brothers.

contents itself with finding words adequate to the belief or impression of the moment, while navigating a passable course among other ideas suspected of being afloat in the vicinity. The genuine exercise or true conversation sifts opinion, that is, tries to develop tenable positions by alternate statements, objections, modifications, examples, arguments, distinctions, expressed with the aid of the rhetorical arts—irony, exaggeration, and the rest— properly muted to the size and privateness of the scene. . . .

4. A German writer, noting recently that in the title of the latest edition of Brockaus, the term *"Konversations-lexicon"* has been dropped, attributes the general decay of conversation to the lack of an idle class, or more simply, of leisure. But leisure is increasing, and enough time, surely, is spent by persons with a college degree in "exchanging" ideas, on social as well as on public occasions. It cannot be our material circumstances alone that hamper us, but rather our manners, that is to say, at bottom, our emotions.

5. For the starting point of conversation is contradiction, and this democratic manners do not tolerate. Contradiction implies that one or another of the conversing group must be wrong, and under modern manners, as I said earlier without trying to explain it, peculiar feelings cling to error. Perhaps science has made small accuracy sacred to all, though everybody thinks that to be caught in a mistake is necessary to prove that one is human. Or again it may be that business and industry lead us to overestimate the interest of facts, about which contradiction is foolish. I think it more likely that the fear of being wrong which prohibits contradiction has in view, not error as an intellectual mishap, but the punishment that follows a breach of group unity. If your hostess says that the latest play by Mr. Kentucky Jones is very fine, and you contradict her, no matter how sweetly, one of you will have the majority in opposition. And this, regardless of who is the odd man out, nobody will enjoy. The reasoning goes: you are one against several = you are wrong = you are a fool. In some companies, the series of inferences would run: perverse = showing off = a snob; and the rejection would be no less complete.

6. In either form, the syllogism is bound to be hard to refute when the first premise of a society is that the voice of the people, ascertained by majority vote, is the voice of God. All the great

65 men since Socrates may have asserted the contrary, but their assertion was evidently self-serving. Virtue in modern politics is against the solitary dissident. It is assumed that he too wants the backing of a majority, and having gained it will enjoy power. This is never allowable in a populist culture. Even in the Soviet
70 Union the "cult of personality" has been denounced, which is comic but indicative.

7. By confining conversation to facts or to the exchange of bland opinions, trouble is avoided. This is elementary self-protection in a system where the absence of fixed place and privilege
75 puts one at the mercy of the group. When we quote what Tocqueville said: "I know of no country in which there is so little independence of mind and real freedom of discussion as in America," we must not ascribe wholly to timidity what is in part sensible self-restraint. Even in the great days of militant liberalism it was
80 decreed that politics and religion should be excluded from general conversation. This is a tribute to the power of words, in that people take them as the signs of instant action, of treason, rape, sacrilege. One does not know whether to wonder more at the imagination of the listener who is so readily hurt and alarmed, or
85 at the skill of the speaker who over a cup of tea can with a few phrases produce flushed faces and the grim ardor of a militia defending hearth and home. However it comes about, the motive of curiosity about ideas, the play of mind, is not accounted a social possibility. But subversion is.

90 8. That is why full democracy has simply extended the no-politics-or-religion rule to any strong opinion. Yeats, moving in circles full of intellectuals and full of ideas could yet long for the conversation of a *society*, for gaiety of mind and the fantasy that prepares matured convictions, for the kind of agreement that
95 comes with, and not instead of, the free play of Intellect. What he found and what we have is the political judgment of dissidence carried into the living room and using the threat of mild or harsh ostracism to prevent even the shadow of conflict.

9. In putting first the political, I do not mean to overlook other
100 impeding emotions. Good conversation, like any game, calls for equals in strength. But in a social system where movement is easy and frequent, one meets mostly strangers, whose equality other

than legal and abstract has to be presumed. To safeguard that presumption, democratic manners prevent a jousting in which somebody might appear stronger, brighter, quicker, or richer of 105 mind. This is not to say that democratic society is without snobbery. But like our public opinion, our accepted snobbery seldom ventures outside the tangible. It relies on differences that are not subject to dispute, such as disinfected wealth or descent from a famous historical event. Otherwise, the assumption of social 110 equality indispensable to our life is preserved by blinking or suppressing all signs of the contrary.

10. This description may suggest that underneath its amiability the democratic group hides ugly sentiments. This is rarely true. Whatever his unconscious fear of Intellect, the democrat's con- 115 scious desire is philanthropic; he wants love to prevail; he wants to add friends to friends and find them friends to one another, as in Euclid; he wants, above all, that everything and everybody should be agreeable, by which he means interchangeable, indistinguishable—like a prefabricated part—until the taste for human 120 encounters is purified and uplifted from the social to the gregarious. The highest merit and pleasure is to love people, to want to be with people, to be "good with people."

11. Only a churlish man could profess insensibility to so much warmth and such regal indifference to the marks, precisely, of 125 difference. For the true-born democrat, origin, education, and intellect matter no more than clothes, speech, and deportment. He no longer sees them, or he feels remorse when the thought of them breaks through his proper manners to his conscious mind.

❊❊❊❊❊❊❊❊❊❊

1. In this selection, Barzun explores two types of "conversation." Obviously he criticizes one as destructive of Intellect and approves of the other as true intellectual stimulation. In the first paragraph he defines the two types and thereafter in the essay develops both ideas. Read aloud, study the entire selection, and list the words that clarify each definition. Then write a short paragraph on each type, showing how, when, and why each, according to Barzun, is practiced. Indicate his attitude toward each type.

2. Barzun uses the word *sociable* (or *society* or *social*) in two senses. Notice how it is used in lines 7, 19, 93, and 121. What idea does the word express in these lines? To what idea is it opposed? Now look at the word as it is used in lines 40, 63, 106, and 110. How does this meaning differ from the first one? Do you think Barzum should have used a different word in the first case? Or do you think the differences are thoroughly apparent and clear in the essay?

3. Throughout the essay Barzun uses words to express definite relationships; some are causal relationships, some contrasting, some equivalent. Define the relationships between the following pairs of words: *public debate* and *conversation; conversation* and *manners; manners* and *morals; manners* and *words; manners* and *emotions; exchange* and *sifting; exercise* and *conversation*.

4. Barzun attacks the type of conversation that democracy breeds. What are his reasons? Do you agree? Why? Is it possible that Barzun is attributing too much to democracy? Consider other or more complicated causes of what he describes.

5. "Manners are minor morals" (9). Begin on this puzzling phrase by finding the etymology of *morals*, for when you have done so you will find that it is a simple, literal statement. How, then, do *morals* "facilitate the relations of men?" Or, to put it more literally, how do *customs* do so? Is there any serious difference between customs of speaking, eating, dressing, or introducing people, in this respect? You might write a paragraph or a short essay showing how morals perform the same function that manners do.

6. "Manners are . . . a clue to the deeper moral assumptions of an age" (13–14). Has this statement been proved or supported in this paragraph? What does it mean? The *therefore* of line 13 seems to connect its sentence with what has been said. Does it? When is Intellect "most exposed?" And how do manners guard it at that point? You will find the answer by following the trail of thought through manners—conversation—Intellect.

7. A key phrase is "deliberately staged" (11). The verb *staged* suggests preparation, rehearsal, formality, performance. Tell, then, what more precise notion is conveyed by *staged* than would have been conveyed by *performed*. How does a *staged* discussion

(i.e. conversation) become the testing ground of manners? Is the *staged* discussion more objective, more intense, more academic, less earnest than, say, a violent argument? What other word or words in the paragraph carry the overtones of *staged*? If you can explain how the *staging* of conversation, with courtesy, formality, objectivity, and earnestness, constitutes a highly *civilized* activity, you will be showing how manners, conversation, and Intellect are closely related—how formality and seriousness are not merely compatible but indeed interdependent.

8.   Paragraph 3 begins with abstract and general statements before it swings into an effective figure. "Rudimentary" (26) does not go very well with the figurative "role," for it too is figurative, although the figure is hidden in its Latin origin. In the following sentence "belief" and "impression" are perhaps unnecessarily vague and general—but then we come to the effective figure. Rewrite lines 26–29 so that the "navigation" image is sustained to the end of the second sentence.

9.   The full definition of *conversation* (29–34) is clear and forceful; but what of the connection between "develop tenable positions," which is highly figurative, and "muted," which is also figurative? Can you show how the metaphorical force (see dictionary) of both would be increased if they were both rooted in the same figure (metaphor)? "Scene" (34), however, keys us back to "role," as does, to some degree, "arts" (33). Could the whole paragraph be rewritten around a single sustained image or figure, or would this become a distraction by calling undue attention to itself? The solution is not to have conflicting metaphors, but perhaps to reduce the amount of obvious imagery. The phrase "obvious imagery" calls for some explanation. Actually every abstract or general word is, at bottom, an image; that is, it takes its meaning from the name of some concrete thing or action. "Modification" (32), for example, means in Latin "to make a limit," but here the figure is quite lost. Study the concrete origins of the meanings of a dozen of the abstract terms on this page; indicate any in which the source is still apparent.

10.   What device of logic and rhetoric does Barzun use in Par. 4?

11.   When Barzun says "our manners, that is to say, at bottom, our emotions" (42), which controls which? What assumption have we made about the role of manners in this respect in

connection with Par. 1? As suggested by the *For* of the next paragraph, you will find Barzun's answer there.

12. What is a *syllogism* (62)? Is Barzun's example a good one? Explain.

13. Irish patriots, among whom Yeats (91) moved, were incited by *passions* for political and cultural independence. In such a society, conversation could not be sufficiently staged and decorous, Barzun implies, to achieve the "free play of Intellect," for everyone *had to agree*. To disagree was to be dissident and ostracized. So Yeats disliked his companions not because of their ideas but because of their manners. Now, explain Barzun's reference to Euclid (118).

14. Note the changes in tone in this selection, especially in Pars. 6, 10, and 11. (Remember, tone is the author's attitude toward his subject.) What is the major tone of the essay? How and for what purpose does Barzun make these shifts? What is the tone of the following phrases: *Mr. Kentucky Jones* (55), *voice of God* (64), *self-serving* (66), *self-protection* (73), *churlish* (124)?

Dress as an Expression
of the Pecuniary Culture

THORSTEIN VEBLEN

1.   The function of
dress as an evidence of ability to pay does not end with simply
showing that the wearer consumes valuable goods in excess of
what is required for physical comfort. Simple conspicuous waste
of goods is effective and gratifying as far as it goes; it is good 5
prima facie evidence of pecuniary success, and consequently
prima facie evidence of social worth. But dress has subtler and
more far-reaching possibilities than this crude, first-hand evidence
cf wasteful consumption only. If, in addition to showing that the
wearer can afford to consume freely and uneconomically, it can 10
also be shown in the same stroke that he or she is not under the
necessity of earning a livelihood, the evidence of social worth is
enhanced in a very considerable degree. Our dress, therefore, in
order to serve its purpose effectually, should not only be expensive, but it should also make plain to all observers that the wearer 15
is not engaged in any kind of productive labor. In the evolutionary process by which our system of dress has been elaborated into
its present admirably perfect adaptation to its purpose, this subsidiary line of evidence has received due attention. A detailed
examination of what passes in popular apprehension for elegant 20
apparel will show that it is contrived at every point to convey the
impression that the wearer does not habitually put forth any
useful effort. It goes without saying that no apparel can be considered elegant, or even decent, if it shows the effect of manual
labor on the part of the wearer, in the way of soil or wear. The 25

From *The Theory of the Leisure Class.*

215

pleasing effect of neat and spotless garments is chiefly, if not altogether, due to their carrying the suggestion of leisure—exemption
from personal contact with industrial processes of any kind.
Much of the charm that invests the patent-leather shoe, the stain-
30 less linen, the lustrous cylindrical hat, and the walking-stick,
which so greatly enhance the native dignity of a gentleman,
comes of their pointedly suggesting that the wearer cannot when
so attired bear a hand in any employment that is directly and
immediately of any human use. Elegant dress serves its purpose
35 of elegance not only in that it is expensive, but also because it is
the insignia of leisure. It not only shows that the wearer is able
to consume a relatively large value, but it argues at the same time
that he consumes without producing.

2. The dress of women goes even farther than that of men in
40 the way of demonstrating the wearer's abstinence from productive employment. It needs no argument to enforce the generali-
sation that the more elegant styles of feminine bonnets go even
farther towards making work impossible than does the man's high
hat. The woman's shoe adds the so-called French heel to the
45 evidence of enforced leisure afforded by its polish; because this
high heel obviously makes any, even the simplest and most necessary manual work extremely difficult. The like is true even in a
higher degree of the skirt and the rest of the drapery which char-
acterises woman's dress. The substantial reason for our tenacious
50 attachment to the skirt is just this: it is expensive and it hampers
the wearer at every turn and incapacitates her for all useful exertion. The like is true of the feminine custom of wearing the hair
excessively long.

3. But the woman's apparel not only goes beyond that of the
55 modern man in the degree in which it argues exemption from
labour; it also adds a peculiar and highly characteristic feature
which differs in kind from anything habitually practised by the
men. This feature is the class of contrivances of which the corset
is the typical example. The corset is, in economic theory, substan-
60 tially a mutilation, undergone for the purpose of lowering the
subject's vitality and rendering her permanently and obviously
unfit for work. It is true, the corset impairs the personal attrac-

tions of the wearer, but the loss suffered on that score is offset by
the gain in reputability which comes of her visibly increased
expensiveness and infirmity. It may broadly be set down that the
womanliness of woman's apparel resolves itself, in point of substantial fact, into the more effective hindrance to useful exertion
offered by the garments peculiar to women. This difference
between masculine and feminine apparel is here simply pointed
out as a characteristic feature. The ground of its occurrence will
be discussed presently.

4. So far, then, we have, as the great and dominant norm of
dress, the broad principle of conspicuous waste. Subsidiary to
this principle, and as a corollary under it, we get as a second
norm the principle of conspicuous leisure. In dress construction
this norm works out in the shape of divers contrivances going to
show that the wearer does not and, as far as it may conveniently
be shown, can not engage in productive labour. Beyond these two
principles there is a third of scarcely less constraining force,
which will occur to any one who reflects at all on the subject.
Dress must not only be conspicuously expensive and inconvenient; it must at the same time be up to date. No explanation at all
satisfactory has hitherto been offered of the phenomenon of
changing fashions. The imperative requirement of dressing in the
latest accredited manner, as well as the fact that this accredited
fashion constantly changes from season to season, is sufficiently
familiar to every one, but the theory of this flux and change has
not been worked out. We may of course say, with perfect con-
sistency and truthfulness, that this principle of novelty is another
corollary under the law of conspicuous waste. Obviously, if each
garment is permitted to serve for but a brief term, and if none of
last season's apparel is carried over and made further use of during the present season, the wasteful expenditure on dress is
greatly increased. This is good as far as it goes, but it is negative
only. Pretty much all that this consideration warrants us in saying
is that the norm of conspicuous waste exercises a controlling sur-
veillance in all matters of dress, so that any change in the fashions
must conform to the requirement of wastefulness; it leaves unan-
swered the question as to the motive for making and accepting a

100 change in the prevailing styles, and it also fails to explain why conformity to a given style at a given time is so imperatively necessary as we know it to be.

5. For a creative principle, capable of serving as motive to invention and innovation in fashions, we shall have to go back to 105 the primitive, non-economic motive with which apparel originated—the motive of adornment. Without going into an extended discussion of how and why this motive asserts itself under the guidance of the law of expensiveness, it may be stated broadly that each successive innovation in the fashions is an effort to 110 reach some form of display which shall be more acceptable to our sense of form and color or of effectiveness, than that which it displaces. The changing styles are the expression of a restless search for something which shall commend itself to our æsthetic sense; but as each innovation is subject to the selective action of the 115 norm of conspicuous waste, the range within which innovation can take place is somewhat restricted. The innovation must not only be more beautiful, or perhaps oftener less offensive, than that which it displaces, but it must also come up to the accepted standard of expensiveness.

120   6. It would seem at first sight that the result of such an unremitting struggle to attain the beautiful in dress should be a gradual approach to artistic perfection. We might naturally expect that the fashions should show a well-marked trend in the direction of some one or more types of apparel eminently becom- 125 ing to the human form; and we might even feel that we have substantial ground for the hope that today, after all the ingenuity and effort which have been spent on dress these many years, the fashions should have achieved a relative perfection and a relative stability, closely approximating to a permanently tenable artistic 130 ideal. But such is not the case. It would be very hazardous indeed to assert that the styles of today are intrinsically more becoming than those of ten years ago, or than those of twenty, or fifty, or one hundred years ago. On the other hand, the assertion freely goes uncontradicted that styles in vogue two thousand years ago 135 are more becoming than the most elaborate and painstaking constructions of today.

7. The explanation of the fashions just offered, then, does not

fully explain, and we shall have to look farther. It is well known that certain relatively stable styles and types of costume have been worked out in various parts of the world; as, for instance, 140 among the Japanese, Chinese, and other Oriental nations; likewise among the Greeks, Romans, and other Eastern peoples of antiquity; so also, in later times, among the peasants of nearly every country of Europe. These national or popular costumes are in most cases adjudged by competent critics to be more becom- 145 ing, more artistic, than the fluctuating styles of modern civilized apparel. At the same time they are also, at least usually, less obviously wasteful; that is to say, other elements than that of a display of expense are more readily detected in their structure.

8. These relatively stable costumes are, commonly, pretty 150 strictly and narrowly localized, and they vary by slight and systematic gradations from place to place. They have in every case been worked out by peoples or classes which are poorer than we, and especially they belong in countries and localities and times where the population, or at least the class to which the costume 155 in question belongs, is relatively homogeneous, stable, and immobile. That is to say, stable costumes which will bear the test of time and perspective are worked out under circumstances where the norm of conspicuous waste asserts itself less imperatively than it does in the large modern civilised cities, whose rela- 160 tively mobile, wealthy population today sets the pace in matters of fashion. The countries and classes which have in this way worked out stable and artistic costumes have been so placed that the pecuniary emulation among them has taken the direction of a competition in conspicuous leisure rather than in conspicuous 165 consumption of goods. So that it will hold true in a general way that fashions are least stable and least becoming in those communities where the principle of a conspicuous waste of goods asserts itself most imperatively, as among ourselves. All this points to an antagonism between expensiveness and artistic 170 apparel. In point of practical fact, the norm of conspicuous waste is incompatible with the requirement that dress should be beautiful or becoming. And this antagonism offers an explanation of that restless change in fashion which neither the canon of expensiveness nor that of beauty alone can account for.   175

9. The standard of reputability requires that dress should show wasteful expenditure; but all wastefulness is offensive to native taste. The psychological law has already been pointed out that all men—and women perhaps even in a higher degree—abhor
180 futility, whether of effort or of expenditure—much as Nature was once said to abhor a vacuum. But the principle of conspicuous waste requires an obviously futile expenditure; and the resulting conspicuous expensiveness of dress is therefore intrinsically ugly. Hence we find that in all innovations in dress, each added or
185 altered detail strives to avoid instant condemnation by showing some ostensible purpose, at the same time that the requirement of conspicuous waste prevents the purposefulness of these innovations from becoming anything more than a somewhat transparent pretence. Even in its freest flights, fashion rarely if ever
190 gets away from a simulation of some ostensible use. The ostensible usefulness of the fashionable details of dress, however, is always so transparent a make-believe, and their substantial futility presently forces itself so baldly upon our attention as to become unbearable, and then we take refuge in a new style. But
195 the new style must conform to the requirement of reputable wastefulness and futility. Its futility presently becomes as odious as that of its predecessor; and the only remedy which the law of waste allows us is to seek relief in some new construction, equally futile and equally untenable. Hence the essential ugliness and
200 the unceasing change of fashionable attire.

10. Having so explained the phenomenon of shifting fashions, the next thing is to make the explanation tally with everyday facts. Among these everyday facts is the well-known liking which all men have for the styles that are in vogue at any given time.
205 A new style comes into vogue and remains in favour for a season, and, at least so long as it is a novelty, people very generally find the new style attractive. The prevailing fashion is felt to be beautiful. This is due partly to the relief it affords in being different from what went before it, partly to its being reputable. As indi-
210 cated in the last chapter, the canon of reputability to some extent shapes our tastes, so that under its guidance anything will be accepted as becoming until its novelty wears off, or until the warrant of reputability is transferred to a new and novel structure

serving the same general purpose. That the alleged beauty, or "loveliness," of the styles in vogue at any given time is transient 215 and spurious only is attested by the fact that none of the many shifting fashions will bear the test of time. When seen in the perspective of half-a-dozen years or more, the best of our fashions strike us as grotesque, if not unsightly. Our transient attachment to whatever happens to be the latest rests on other than æsthetic 220 grounds, and lasts only until our abiding æsthetic sense has had time to assert itself and reject this latest indigestible contrivance.

11. The process of developing an æsthetic nausea takes more or less time; the length of time required in any given case being inversely as the degree of intrinsic odiousness of the style in ques- 225 tion. This time relation between odiousness and instability in fashions affords ground for the inference that the more rapidly the styles succeed and displace one another, the more offensive they are to sound taste. The presumption, therefore, is that the farther the community, especially the wealthy classes of the com- 230 munity, develop in wealth and mobility and in the range of their human contact, the more imperatively will the law of conspicuous waste assert itself in matters of dress, the more will the sense of beauty tend to fall into abeyance or be overborne by the canon of pecuniary reputability, the more rapidly will fashions shift and 235 change, and the more grotesque and intolerable will be the varying styles that successively come into vogue.

✳✳✳✳✳✳✳✳✳✳

Veblen's *Theory of the Leisure Class* (1900) has provided a number of terms that have become widely used in social and economic commentary. He has also developed a point of view toward style and status which is virtually unforgettable. Wherever you come upon them, such terms as "conspicuous waste," "conspicuous consumption," and even "predatory," "exploit," and "invidious" in certain contexts immediately suggest Veblen. To understand the very special ideological system—a pure creation of style and intellect—that Veblen has made, you will have to examine five dimensions or aspects of the work which unite to give it its unique quality. They are 1) its anthropology, 2) its "scientific" manner, 3) its strong moral phrasings, 4) its repeated denial of moral attitude, and 5) its tone.

1.   Veblen ascribes the *values* (i.e. the status-producing customs and practices) of the leisure class to qualities of *prowess* and *exploit* which confer status in primitive society where both survival against enemies and success in the hunt depend upon physical strength and skill. These abilities confer upon the primitive hero two marks of status: 1) trophies of the hunt and battle, and 2) exemption from menial or merely useful labor. From these two areas Veblen derives all modern leisure class values.

A. How does "function" in the first line reveal a concern to relate dress to social values? How does "consumes valuable goods in excess of what is required for physical comfort" (3–4) embody the values we have just attributed to the primitive hero or warrior? You will find several answers throughout the selection. The vital connection is that wealth is the *trophy* of modern prowess. In the same connection, "effective" for what, and why and to whom "gratifying" (5)? Go through the whole selection marking passages that somehow relate styles in dress to the modern leisure-class values that depend upon "prowess": *leisure* and *consumption in excess of need.*

B. This passage,

> In the evolutionary process by which our system of dress has been elaborated into its present admirably perfect adaptation to its purpose, (16–18)

is entirely concerned with the *evolution* of certain ceremonial or status *functions* of dress from tribal times to the present. This is strictly a concern of anthropology. Mark other passages which somehow reveal this anthropological orientation, that is, the tracing of modern values to primitive tribal practices.

C. Mark the first three points where this anthropological approach defines a value which seems *directly opposite* to what is generally accepted as fact today. Look at waste = pecuniary success = social worth.

D. For the leisure-class male we have "exemption" (27) from work; for the female, "enforced" (45) leisure! This is because, in Veblen's system, the woman's consumption is evidence of the male's worth and prowess. Can you find other passages where this idea appears? There are at least four more in the same paragraph. It is the theme of Par. 3.

2. The scientific manner appears in the sustained use of a diction that is both abstract and formal, plus an almost tedious explicitness and fullness of statement. Nothing is hinted or suggested; no imaginative jumps are demanded; every point is made in total literal accuracy.

A. Mark a dozen or two formal words of Latin derivation, which create a scientific tone, i.e. *pecuniary* (6), *subsidiary* (18), and *apprehension* (20).

B. Analyze the first three sentences of Par. 4 as "scientific" recapitulation, definition, ordering, etc.

3. Now, scattered among the rather heavy "scientific" sentences are many words which express powerful moral attitudes towards the values described. They usually move in waves or series from formal and abstract toward the homely concrete. Thus in Par. 1 we move through

> "consumes valuable goods in excess of what is required for physical comfort"

to

> "conspicuous waste"

to

> "not engaged in any kind of productive labor"

and

> "does not . . . put forth any useful effort"

to

> ". . . . of any human use."

The last phrase shocks us because it is a severe condemnation coming, by surprise, at the end of a long formal sentence (29–34).

Again, in Par. 2, we go through

> "abstinence from productive employment"
> "making work impossible"
> "enforced leisure"

to

> "hampers . . . and incapacitates her for all useful exertion."

Set up the sequences in each paragraph (where they appear), with special attention to the strong homely words, like "unfit for work," "less offensive," "futile," "odious," and so on.

4. The "scientific" tone and analytical intention obviously do not allow for moral pronouncements. Veblen takes pains, from time to time, to insist that his "moral" terms are used with a purely

descriptive intention. Various such disclaimers can be found in
this selection. For example, the parenthesis, "in economic theory"
(59), strips "mutilation" of æsthetic or moral meanings. Lines
68–70 tell us that all colored words in the paragraph are "simply"
descriptive of economic motives. Mark the passages in the rest
of the selection that perform these same functions.

5. The tone of the selection must be defined with terms that
include the burlesque of scientific method, the pompous style,
the astonishing conclusions about dress, and the other elements
set forth above. Analyze the sentence in lines 13–16 for its tone
and effect. Mark passages that have similar effects.

6. Explain "selective action of the norm of conspicuous waste"
(114–115). Do one or both of the conditions described in the next
sentence depend on the *range* allowed by this norm?

7. The "restless search for something which shall commend itself to our æsthetic sense" (112–113) is said to be constrained
by the norm of conspicuous waste. Just what determines the
"range within which innovation can take place"? Is it described in
the next sentence?

8. Paragraph 6 returns to what *might* be expected of the "restless search . . ." (112), which is here expressed by what
phrase? Paragraph 7 further extends the idea that innovation of
today does *not* move toward greater beauty, let alone equal that
of antiquity. And Par. 8 elaborates still further on the explanation
that has already been given in lines 112–113 and 116–119. The
elaboration, in elaborate language, may well be a conscious burlesque of the language of pedantry—carried on all the way to the
climactic remark that expensive fashionable clothing must be
intrinsically ugly. (183) Identify passages wherein the author
consciously (apparently) repeats with no variation except in
choice of words. Beware missing his fine points, however.

The selection on Toots Shor (p. 107) may provide you with
material for a theme comparing two more-or-less anthropological
more-or-less hoaxes. Or you may feel constrained to discuss Veblen's own bold anthropology—its premises, its logic, its evidence.
Or Veblen's new key to fashion. Or what do you make of the people who cultivate and care for great expanses of lawn—when,
according to Veblen, the status function of a great lawn is to
demonstrate that the owner can keep all that land in useless grass

AND keep one or two gardeners uselessly employed tending it? If you are of an analytical turn of mind, you might analyze the selection to show how these *three* categories are woven together in its construction: 1) Economic Analysis, 2) Description of the emotional Attitudes of the leisure class, and 3) Moral Comment by Veblen.

Philanthropy

HENRY DAVID THOREAU

1. But all this is very selfish, I have heard some of my townsmen say. I confess that I have hitherto indulged very little in philanthropic enterprises. I have made some sacrifices to a sense of duty, and among others
5 have sacrificed this pleasure also. There are those who have used all their arts to persuade me to undertake the support of some poor family in town; and if I had nothing to do—for the devil finds employment for the idle—I might try my hand at some such pastime as that. However, when I have thought to indulge
10 myself in this respect, and lay their Heaven under an obligation by maintaining certain poor persons in all respects as comfortably as I maintain myself, and have even ventured so far as to make them the offer, they have one and all unhesitatingly preferred to remain poor. While my townsmen and women are devoted in so
15 many ways to the good of their fellows, I trust that one at least may be spared to other and less humane pursuits. You must have a genius for charity as well as for anything else. As for Doing-good, that is one of the professions which are full. Moreover, I have tried fairly, and, strange as it may seem, am satisfied that
20 it does not agree with my constitution. Probably I should not consciously and deliberately forsake my particular calling to do the good which society demands of me, to save the universe from annihilation; and I believe that a like but infinitely greater stead-fastness elsewhere is all that now preserves it. But I would not
25 stand between any man and his genius; and to him who does this work, which I decline, with his whole heart and soul and life, I would say, Persevere, even if the world call it doing evil, as it is most likely they will.

From *Walden.*

2. I am far from supposing that my case is a peculiar one; no
doubt many of my readers would make a similar defence. At
doing something,—I will not engage that my neighbors shall pronounce it good,—I do not hesitate to say that I should be a capital
fellow to hire; but what that is, it is for my employer to find out.
What *good* I do, in the common sense of that word, must be
aside from my main path, and for the most part wholly unintended. Men say, practically, Begin where you are and such as
you are, without aiming mainly to become of more worth, and
with kindness aforethought go about doing good. If I were to
preach at all in this strain, I should say rather, Set about being
good. As if the sun should stop when he had kindled his fires up
to the splendor of a moon or a star of the sixth magnitude, and
go about like a Robin Goodfellow, peeping in at every cottage
window, inspiring lunatics, and tainting meats, and making darkness visible, instead of steadily increasing his genial heat and
beneficence till he is of such brightness that no mortal can look
him in the face, and then, and in the mean while too, going about
the world in his own orbit, doing it good, or rather, as a truer
philosophy has discovered, the world going about him getting
good. When Phaeton, wishing to prove his heavenly birth by his
beneficence, had the sun's chariot but one day, and drove out of
the beaten track, he burned several blocks of houses in the lower
streets of heaven, and scorched the surface of the earth, and dried
up every spring, and made the great desert of Sahara, till at
length Jupiter hurled him headlong to the earth with a thunder-
bolt, and the sun, through grief at his death, did not shine for a
year.

3. There is no odor so bad as that which arises from goodness
tainted. It is human, it is divine, carrion. If I knew for a certainty
that a man was coming to my house with the conscious design
of doing me good, I should run for my life, as from that dry and
parching wind of the African deserts called the simoom, which
fills the mouth and nose and ears and eyes with dust till you are
suffocated, for fear that I should get some of his good done to me,
—some of its virus mingled with my blood. No,—in this case I
would rather suffer evil the natural way. A man is not a good *man*
to me because he will feed me if I should be starving, or warm

me if I should be freezing, or pull me out of a ditch if I should
ever fall into one. I can find you a Newfoundland dog that will
do as much. Philanthropy is not love for one's fellowman in the
70 broadest sense. Howard was no doubt an exceedingly kind and
worthy man in his way, and has his reward; but, comparatively
speaking, what are a hundred Howards to *us,* if their philanthropy
do not help *us* in our best estate, when we are most worthy to be
helped? I never heard of a philanthropic meeting in which it was
75 sincerely proposed to do any good to me, or the like of me.

4. The Jesuits were quite balked by those Indians who, being
burned at the stake, suggested new modes of torture to their tor-
mentors. Being superior to physical suffering, it sometimes
chanced that they were superior to any consolation which the
80 missionaries could offer; and the law to do as you would be done
by fell with less persuasiveness on the ears of those who, for their
part, did not care how they were done by, who loved their enemies after a new fashion, and came very near freely forgiving
them all they did.

85 5. Be sure that you give the poor the aid they most need,
though it be your example which leaves them far behind. If you
give money, spend yourself with it, and do not merely abandon
it to them. We make curious mistakes sometimes. Often the poor
man is not so cold and hungry as he is dirty and ragged and gross.
90 It is partly his taste, and not merely his misfortune. If you give
him money, he will perhaps buy more rags with it. I was wont to
pity the clumsy Irish laborers who cut ice on the pond, in such
mean and ragged clothes, while I shivered in my more tidy and
somewhat more fashionable garments, till, one bitter cold day,
95 one who had slipped into the water came to my house to warm
him, and I saw him strip off three pairs of pants and two pairs of
stockings ere he got down to the skin, though they were dirty
and ragged enough, it is true, and that he could afford to refuse the
extra garments which I offered him, he had so many *intra* ones.
100 This ducking was the very thing he needed. Then I began to pity
myself, and I saw that it would be a greater charity to bestow on
me a flannel shirt than a whole slop-shop on him. There are a
thousand hacking at the branches of evil to one who is striking at
the root, and it may be that he who bestows the largest amount

of time and money on the needy is doing the most by his mode of 105
life to produce that misery which he strives in vain to relieve. It
is the pious slave-breeder devoting the proceeds of every tenth
slave to buy a Sunday's liberty for the rest. Some show their kindness to the poor by employing them in their kitchens. Would they
not be kinder if they employed themselves there? You boast of 110
spending a tenth part of your income in charity; may be you
should spend the nine tenths so, and done with it. Society re-
covers only a tenth part of the property then. Is this owing to the
generosity of him in whose possession it is found, or to the
remissness of the officers of justice?   115

6. Philanthropy is almost the only virtue which is sufficiently
appreciated by mankind. Nay, it is greatly overrated; and it is our
selfishness which overrates it. A robust poor man, one sunny day
here in Concord, praised a fellow-townsman to me, because, as he
said, he was kind to the poor; meaning himself. The kind uncles 120
and aunts of the race are more esteemed than its true spiritual
fathers and mothers. I once heard a reverend lecturer on England,
a man of learning and intelligence, after enumerating her scientific, literary, and political worthies, Shakespeare, Bacon, Cromwell, Milton, Newton, and others, speak next of her Christian 125
heroes, whom, as if his profession required it of him, he elevated
to a place far above all the rest, as the greatest of the great. They
were Penn, Howard, and Mrs. Fry. Every one must feel the false-
hood and cant of this. The last were not England's best men and
women; only, perhaps, her best philanthropists.   130

7. I would not subtract anything from the praise that is due
to philanthropy, but merely demand justice for all who by their
lives and works are a blessing to mankind. I do not value chiefly
a man's uprightness and benevolence, which are, as it were, his
stem and leaves. Those plants of whose greenness withered we 135
make herb tea for the sick serve but a humble use, and are most
employed by quacks. I want the flower and fruit of a man; that
some fragrance be wafted over from him to me, and some ripe-
ness flavor our intercourse. His goodness must not be a partial and
transitory act, but a constant superfluity, which costs him nothing 140
and of which he is unconscious. This is a charity that hides a
multitude of sins. The philanthropist too often surrounds man-

kind with the remembrance of his own cast-off griefs as an atmosphere, and calls it sympathy. We should impart our courage, and
145 not our despair, our health and ease, and not our disease, and take
care that this does not spread by contagion. From what southern
plains comes up the voice of wailing? Under what latitudes re-
side the heathen to whom we would send light? Who is that in-
temperate and brutal man whom we would redeem? If anything
150 ail a man, so that he does not perform his functions, if he have a
pain in his bowels even,—for that is the seat of sympathy,—he
forthwith sets about reforming—the world. Being a microcosm
himself, he discovers—and it is true discovery, and he is the man
to make it—that the world has been eating green apples; to his
155 eyes, in fact, the globe itself is a great green apple, which there
is danger awful to think of that the children of men will nibble
before it is ripe; and straightway his drastic philanthropy seeks
out the Esquimaux and the Patagonian, and embraces the popu-
lous Indian and Chinese villages; and thus, by a few years of
160 philanthropic activity, the powers in the mean while using him
for their own ends, no doubt, he cures himself of his dyspepsia,
the globe acquires a faint blush on one or both of its cheeks, as if
it were beginning to be ripe, and life loses its crudity and is once
more sweet and wholesome to live. I never dreamed of any
165 enormity greater than I have committed. I never knew, and never
shall know, a worse man than myself.

8. I believe that what so saddens the reformer is not his sympathy with his fellows in distress, but, though he be the holiest
son of God, is his private ail. Let this be righted, let the spring
170 come to him, the morning rise over his couch, and he will forsake
his generous companions without apology. My excuse for not
lecturing against the use of tobacco is, that I never chewed it, that
is a penalty which reformed tobacco-chewers have to pay; though
there are things enough I have chewed which I could lecture
175 against. If you should ever be betrayed into any of these philan-
thropies, do not let your left hand know what your right hand
does, for it is not worth knowing. Rescue the drowning and tie
your shoestrings. Take your time, and set about some free labor.

❈❈❈❈❈❈❈❈❈❈❈❈

This passage comes at the end of a long chapter, entitled "Economy," in which Thoreau has been telling how, during his two-year stay at Walden Pond, he supported himself in security, comfort, and freedom with so little labor that it was merely a diversion, using his time for study, writing, and contemplation.

1. Many words in this selection have rich overtones and connotations. After reading it aloud until you feel the flow of the sentences, examine the following, not neglecting their etymologies: *indulged* (3), *their* (10), *satisfied* (19), *Robin Goodfellow* (42), *lunatics* (43), *steadfastness* (23), *mainly* (37), *kindness aforethought* (38), *truer philosophy* (47), *beneficence* (45), *carrion* (58), *philanthropy* (69), *cant* (129), *transitory, superfluity* (140), *microcosm* (152), *drastic* (157), *betrayed* (175).

2. Next, there are phrases which call for scrutiny, such as "lay their heaven under an obligation" (10), "less humane" (16), "my particular calling" (21), "even if the world call it doing evil, as it is most likely they will" (27), the sentence beginning at line 40, to understand which, you will have to discover the meaning of "truer philosophy," "in our best estate" (73), "your example which leaves them far behind" (86), "it is our selfishness which overrates it" (117–118), and "awful to think of" (156).

3. Thoreau is defining an attitude toward philanthropy. In Par. 1, besides saying that one must have a talent or genius for philanthropy, what words and phrases indicate a less favorable attitude toward it? Why do you suppose the "certain poor persons" (11) refused Thoreau's offer of support?

4. Translate the figurative sentence (40–49) into a comment on the thesis of the paragraph, which you will find in lines 34–36. In short, what is the matter with setting out to do good? What does the cosmic range of Thoreau's analogy (or figure) do to the problem? Is it absurdly grand, or does it suggest genuinely vast implications?

5. Thoreau compares the effects of "doing good" with those of "being good." Explain the difference. Which is the more *deliberate* of the two? To which category does Phaeton belong? How is the Phaeton episode related to the subject of the paragraph?

6. From the errant "goodness" of Phaeton, Thoreau turns to

"goodness tainted." Here he develops (Par. 3) what specific further charge against philanthropy?

7.   How does the example of the Indians bear on the argument; that is, what is by implication compared to the torture, and to whom in Thoreau's argument do Jesuits and Indians correspond?

8.   In Par. 1 Thoreau has advocated "steadfastness" in whatever one's genius demands. In Par. 5 he says

> There are a thousand hacking at the branches of evil to one who is striking at the root, and it may be that he who bestows the largest amount of time and money on the needy is doing the most by his mode of life to produce that misery which he strives in vain to relieve.

Here is a set of ideas about modern industry with which you may not agree, for whereas Thoreau suggests that we should divide our wealth before we earn it, on the assumption that a limited amount of wealth is unfairly shared by the owner of a factory with his labor, the modern view is to stress productivity at any cost on the theory that all will thereby have more. Write a paragraph or two telling how the captain of industry should earn his wealth in a manner that will not "produce that misery which he strives in vain to relieve." When we prune a bush or a tree, we make it healthier, presumably strengthening its roots. Does Thoreau's metaphor carry this implication?

9.   The last two sentences of Par. 5 are ambiguous and difficult. Write a paraphrase or a clear summary of each. The puzzle is how does society "recover" a tenth part?

10.   Since Par. 7 is allusive and figurative, you can profitably spell out the literal implications of every sentence. You will find images and figures of plants and apples, health and medicine, geography, religion, races, and philosophy. Identify each and trace the means of progression of thought that carries us from one to the next. Is there a figure or metaphor which binds the rest together?

11.   What is the effect of the absolute literalness of the last two sentences of Par. 7? Could it be argued that the exaggeration there is equivalent to figurative language?—Or is Thoreau, after all, speaking literally?

12.   In the last paragraph, Thoreau says "Rescue the drowning and tie your shoestrings." What exactly does this mean? By saying that we should "rescue the drowning" does Thoreau modify his position on philanthropy? For what class or sort of circumstance does the example stand? What have the shoestrings to do with the matter?

13.   Elsewhere Thoreau says that the "swiftest traveler is he that goes afoot," implying that it must be quicker to walk than to make a complicated machine to carry you, or to earn money to pay another to do so. This thinking has led many modern admirers of Thoreau to affirm that our labor-saving gadgets consume more time (to earn, to house, and to maintain) than they save. This is a question you should try to approach with a perfectly open mind, for there is much to be said on both sides. It will, if you observe and gather evidence carefully, make a topic for a fine essay.

A Free Man's Worship

BERTRAND RUSSELL

1. To Dr. Faustus in
his study Mephistopheles told the history of the Creation, saying:

'The endless praises of the choirs of angels had begun to grow
wearisome; for, after all, did he not deserve their praise? Had he
5   not given them endless joy? Would it not be more amusing to obtain undeserved praise, to be worshipped by beings whom he tortured? He smiled inwardly, and resolved that the great drama
should be performed.

'For countless ages the hot nebula whirled aimlessly through
10   space. At length it began to take shape, the central mass threw off
planets, the planets cooled, boiling seas and burning mountains
heaved and tossed, from black masses of cloud hot sheets of rain
deluged the barely solid crust. And now the first germ of life grew
in the depths of the ocean, and developed rapidly in the fructifying
15   warmth into vast forest trees, huge ferns springing from the damp
mould, sea monsters breeding, fighting, devouring, and passing
away. And from the monsters, as the play unfolded itself, Man was
born, with the power of thought, the knowledge of good and evil,
and the cruel thirst for worship. And Man saw that all is passing in
20   this mad, monstrous world, that all is struggling to snatch, at any
cost, a few brief moments of life before Death's inexorable decree.
And Man said: "There is a hidden purpose, could we but fathom
it, and the purpose is good; for we must reverence something, and
in the visible world there is nothing worthy of reverence." And Man
25   stood aside from the struggle resolving that God intended harmony
to come out of chaos by human efforts. And when he followed the
instincts which God had transmitted to him from his ancestry of
beasts of prey, he called it Sin, and asked God to forgive him. But

From *Mysticism and Logic*, by Bertrand Russell. Reprinted by permission
of George Allen & Unwin Ltd.

he doubted whether he could be justly forgiven, until he invented
a divine Plan by which God's wrath was to have been appeased. 30
And seeing the present was bad, he made it yet worse, that thereby
the future might be better. And he gave God thanks for the strength
that enabled him to forgo even the joys that were possible. And God
smiled; and when he saw that Man had become perfect in renun-
ciation and worship, he sent another sun through the sky, which 35
crashed into Man's sun; and all returned again to nebula.

'"Yes," he murmured, "it was a good play; I will have it performed again."'

2. Such, in outline, but even more purposeless, more void of
meaning, is the world which Science presents for our belief. Amid 40
such a world, if anywhere, our ideals henceforward must find a
home. That Man is the product of causes which had no prevision
of the end they were achieving; that his origin, his growth, his
hopes and fears, his loves and his beliefs, are but the outcome of
accidental collocations of atoms; that no fire, no heroism, no in- 45
tensity of thought and feeling, can preserve an individual life
beyond the grave; that all the labours of the ages, all the devo-
tion, all the inspiration, all the noonday brightness of human
genius, are destined to extinction in the vast death of the solar
system, and that the whole temple of Man's achievement must 50
inevitably be buried beneath the débris of a universe in ruins—
all these things, if not quite beyond dispute, are yet so nearly
certain, that no philosophy which rejects them can hope to stand.
Only within the scaffolding of these truths, only on the firm foundation of unyielding despair, can the soul's habitation henceforth 55
be safely built.

3. How, in such an alien and inhuman world, can so power-
less a creature as Man preserve his aspirations untarnished? A
strange mystery it is that Nature, omnipotent but blind, in the
revolutions of her secular hurryings through the abysses of space, 60
has brought forth at last a child, subject still to her power, but
gifted with sight, with knowledge of good and evil, with the
capacity of judging all the works of his unthinking Mother. In
spite of Death, the mark and seal of the parental control, Man is
yet free, during his brief years, to examine, to criticise, to know, 65
and in imagination to create. To him alone, in the world with

which he is acquainted, this freedom belongs; and in this lies his superiority to the resistless forces that control his outward life.

70 4. The savage, like ourselves, feels the oppression of his impotence before the powers of Nature; but having in himself nothing that he respects more than Power, he is willing to prostrate himself before his gods, without inquiring whether they are worthy of his worship. Pathetic and very terrible is the long history of cruelty and torture, of degradation and human sacrifice,
75 endured in the hope of placating the jealous gods: surely, the trembling believer thinks, when what is most precious had been freely given, their lust for blood must be appeased, and more will not be required. The religion of Moloch—as such creeds may be generically called—is in essence the cringing submission
80 of the slave, who dare not, even in his heart, allow the thought that his master deserves no adulation. Since the independence of ideals is not yet acknowledged, Power may be freely worshipped, and receive an unlimited respect, despite its wanton infliction of pain.

85 5. But gradually, as morality grows bolder, the claim of the ideal world begins to be felt; and worship, if it is not to cease, must be given to gods of another kind than those created by the savage. Some, though they feel the demands of the ideal, will still consciously reject them, still urging that naked Power is
90 worthy of worship. Such is the attitude inculcated in God's answer to Job out of the whirlwind: the divine power and knowledge are paraded, but of the divine goodness there is no hint. Such also is the attitude of those who, in our own day, base their morality upon the struggle for survival, maintaining that the
95 survivors are necessarily the fittest. But others, not content with an answer so repugnant to the moral sense, will adopt the position which we have become accustomed to regard as specially religious, maintaining that, in some hidden manner, the world of fact is really harmonious with the world of ideals. Thus Man
100 creates God, all-powerful and all-good, the mystic unity of what is and what should be.

6. But the world of fact, after all, is not good; and, in submitting our judgment to it, there is an element of slavishness from which our thoughts must be purged. For in all things it is well

to exalt the dignity of Man, by freeing him as far as possible 105
from the tyranny of non-human Power. When we have realised
that Power is largely bad, that man, with his knowledge of good
and evil, is but a helpless atom in a world which has no such
knowledge, the choice is again presented to us: Shall we worship
Force, or shall we worship Goodness? Shall our God exist and be 110
evil, or shall he be recognised as the creation of our own conscience?

7. The answer to this question is very momentous, and affects
profoundly our whole morality. The worship of Force, to which
Carlyle and Nietzsche and the creed of Militarism have accus- 115
tomed us, is the result of failure to maintain our own ideals
against a hostile universe: it is itself a prostrate submission to
evil, a sacrifice of our best to Moloch. If strength indeed is to
be respected, let us respect rather the strength of those who
refuse that false 'recognition of facts' which fails to recognise that 120
facts are often bad. Let us admit that, in the world we know,
here are many things that would be better otherwise, and that
the ideals to which we do and must adhere are not realised in the
realm of matter. Let us preserve our respect for truth, for beauty,
for the ideal of perfection which life does not permit us to attain, 125
though none of these things meet with the approval of the unconscious universe. If Power is bad, as it seems to be, let us reject it from our hearts. In this lies Man's true freedom: in determination to worship only the God created by our own love of
the good, to respect only the heaven which inspires the insight 130
of our best moments. In action, in desire, we must submit per-
petually to the tyranny of outside forces; but in thought, in aspira-
tion, we are free, free from our fellow-men, free from the petty
planet on which our bodies impotently crawl, free even, while
we live, from the tyranny of death. Let us learn, then, that energy 135
of faith which enables us to live constantly in the vision of the
good; and let us descend, in action, into the world of fact, with
that vision always before us.

※※※※※※※※※※※

In an essay in which you intend to present your own opinions or philosophy, it is often useful and effective to start with a quotation from a well-known source. The quotation should be on the same subject as your essay, of course, and you will use it only because of its relevance to your own argument. You may agree with and enlarge upon the original quotation; you may present a logical argument against it; or you may grant some parts of it and take exception to others. In any event, unless you are writing a piece of explication or criticism, you will be careful to subordinate the quotation properly—that is, devote enough space to the presentation and development of your own point so that the quotation does not dominate it. Another point to bear in mind when using a quotation is that readers have a bad habit of skipping quotations of prose. Therefore be very careful to engage your reader's interest somehow so that he will surely read your quotation carefully.

1.   What is the function of the quotation from *Dr. Faustus;* that is, does it provide an analogy or a contrast (or both) to what Russell later says? Indicate where the ideas are similar, where they are different.

2.   Why is *Science* capitalized in line 40? To what in the *Dr. Faustus* quotation is Science compared? What scientific speculation leads Russell to say that all is "destined to extinction in the vast death of the solar system"? Consider the fact that he qualifies his statement in lines 52–53. Is this qualification affected by the word *truths* in line 54? Can you justify Russell's use of the word?

3.   Russell says that our ideals must find a new *home* (42). Discover other words that are related to the metaphorical *home*.

4.   What does the phrase "if anywhere" (41) mean? In short, would the meaning of the sentence be changed if the phrase were omitted?

5.   Through the ages the word *nature* has carried many different meanings. In what sense does Russell use the word in line 59? How is it related to Science? When Russell personifies Nature later in Par. 3, is he acknowledging any other meaning of the word?

6.   What is Russell's definition of Power? How does it relate to religion?

7. Russell says that all men feel impotent before the powers of Nature. He then outlines various attitudes toward this power. Why does he reject them? What attitude does he examine in Pars. 4 and 5?

8. For Russell there are two kinds of truth—the truth of science and the truth of morality or ideals. How does he suggest that man reconcile these two sorts of truth? What is Russell's definition of *freedom?*

9. Write a one-paragraph précis of Russell's philosophy as it is stated in this selection.

10. Even those who disagree with Russell's ideas agree that his literary technique is admirable. His sentences are varied and dramatic, yet precise and clear. His words are carefully chosen and effectively used. And his argument is logical and orderly. Note Russell's mastery of rhetorical effects: Par. 2 starts with two relatively short sentences. The third sentence has a complex parallel structure designed to rise to an impressive peak. Sentence 4 levels off in pitch and makes a quiet but firm statement of belief. Note other details:

a) What word in Sen. 1 relates the quotation to the passage? What does the *such* in Sen. 2 accomplish?

b) The long third sentence is filled with parallel constructions. Locate and mark them all. Remember that words, phrases, or clauses in a parallel construction are grammatically the same and also have the same *use* in the sentence.

c) What is the predicate of Sen. 3?

d) What grammatical function does "all these things" (52) have?

e) Find a parallel construction in Sen. 4.

11. Write an essay in which you make central use of one of the following quotations:

a) I submit to you today that we ought to believe what is true, and that the truth is that we live in a moral universe, that the laws of this country and of any country are invalid and will be in fact inoperative except as they conform to a moral order which is universal in time and space. [Oliver Wendell] Holmes held that what I have just said is untrue, irrelevant, and even dangerous.

b) The broadest and most prevalent error requires the most disinterested virtue to sustain it. The slight reproach to which the virtue of patriotism is commonly liable, the noble are the most likely to incur. Those who, while they disapprove of the character and measures of a government, yield to it their allegiance and support are undoubtedly its most conscientious supporters, and so frequently the most serious obstacles to reform.

c) All voting is a sort of gaming, like checkers or backgammon, with a slight moral tinge to it, a playing with right and wrong, with moral questions; and betting naturally accompanies it. The character of the voters is not staked. I cast my vote, perchance, as I think right; but I am not vitally concerned that that right should prevail. I am willing to leave it to the majority.

d) "Love thy neighbor as thyself" is a positive precept. But in all Christian communities the man who obeys this precept is persecuted, suffering at least poverty, usually imprisonment, and sometimes death. The world is full of injustice, and those who profit by injustice are in a position to administer rewards and punishments. The rewards go to those who invent ingenious justifications for inequality, the punishments to those who try to remedy it. I do not know of any country where a man who has a genuine love for his neighbor can long avoid obloquy.

e) It is remarkable that there are few men so well employed, so much to their minds, but that a little money or fame would commonly buy them off from their present pursuit. I see advertisements for *active* young men, as if activity were the whole of a young man's capital.

f) Freedom is the recognition of necessity.

g) Politics is the art of the possible.

h) When, however, it is clearly seen that another life, to supplement this one, must closely resemble it, does not the magic of immortality altogether vanish? Is such a reduplication of earthly society at all credible? And the prospect of awakening again among houses and trees, among children and dotards, among wars and rumors of wars, still fettered to one personality and one accidental past, still uncertain of the future, is not this prospect wearisome and deeply repulsive?

12.   Students with a philosophical turn of mind will be able to write an interesting research paper on the problem of *Freedom and Fate*. They could compare the philosophy of Russell, Ralph Waldo Emerson, the Roman stoics, Calvin, Nietzsche, Jonathan

Edwards, and even Bergson. Is man free according to each philosophy? In what respects? If he is fated, to what extent is he free? One could use original writings as well as secondary sources. The first and perhaps largest problem would be to define and limit the project so that it is manageable.

The Method of Tragedy

HERBERT J. MULLER

1. What, then, does St. Sophia have to tell us? I should not restrict its meaning to the few implications I have chosen to stress from the drama of fourteen hundred years. I should insist only that there is no one simple
5 meaning, and that we must realize the profound incongruities of the drama if we hope to rise on stepping stones of our dead selves to higher things. St. Sophia remains an inspiring monument, glorious and vainglorious. It is a symbol of humility and pride, of holiness and worldliness, of the power of faith and the limitations
10 of faith. It is an everlasting triumph, of a society that failed. It may epitomize all the great societies and golden ages of the past, which also failed and still inspire. It calls for reverence, and for irony.

2. For most contemporaries the plainest need is more rever-
15 ence, or simply a decent interest in the past. An American lady who paid ten cents to visit St. Sophia was so disappointed that she wanted her money back. "They call it a museum," she said in disgust, "and there's nothing in it." So there is nothing in the past for too many Americans, except some blurry notions of their own
20 brief history as a chosen people; and so they cannot really know who they are or where they are. Others are likely to desecrate St. Sophia by regarding it as merely a museum, finding it picturesque; for nothing is more undignified than a past become quaint. But it is we, of course, who really suffer from such impiety. The
25 naive, uncritical faith in material progress that has made Americans feel so superior to the past is still a menace to a hope of

any kind of progress. It is also liable to as naive a despair. Once infatuated with our unprecedented achievements, men are now appalled by the realization that history is big enough to swallow them up too.

3. For this reason, however, more sensitive spirits have been tending to the opposite extreme, the ancient habit of overrating the past. Literary men are always apt to get sentimental about the past for much the same reason that simple men get sentimental about their happy, carefree childhood days, which in fact were full of childish cares. Looking back, they see the great monuments, the enduring records of the highest aspirations. They do not see all the trivial, paltry, vulgar, foolish ends of the unheroic dead—the mean stuff of daily existence that by its nature is perishable, and perishes with little trace. They forget the constant complaint of great men about the mediocrity of their age; or they remember only the nobly expressed complaint, not the mediocrity. We must indeed be grateful for the enchantment of the past, its magical power to lift us above the sordid, petty, nagging concerns of everyday life, and at worst to leave us brooding over the tragic dignity of man's life instead of the indignities of the cost of living. Yet we cannot afford to spare the past its troubles. Such enchantment makes the present seem only more unintelligible, and more intolerable, unless we appreciate as well the value of disenchantment—of an awareness that all the generations whom death has made stately in stillness once strutted and fretted even as we. Too many writers have the habit of representing the loftiest ideal of some former age as its essence, and then contrasting it with the meanest actualities of the present. So the thirteenth century is celebrated as if it were summed up by St. Thomas Aquinas, Dante, and the Virgin of Chartres, while the twentieth century is reduced to Hitler, Hearst, and the sex queens of Hollywood.

4. As it is now easy to be ironical about our vaunted progress, so it is easy to fail in decent respect for the living. A steadfast reverence—a reverence for the human spirit, not merely a few selected dead—itself calls for a more robust, catholic irony. And here St. Sophia may symbolize a wisdom holier than its builders knew, in the sense in which holiness is akin to wholeness, hale-

65 ness, and healing. Its paradoxical history comes down to an age-
old story, as familiar as fantastic. It is the story of a "rational animal" who thereby lacks the sureness of instinct, is a prey to
irrational desires, and of all animals leads the least sensible life;
who alone is free to choose and aspire, and so is forever torn by
70 doubt and discontent, from which spring at once his loftiest
values and his ugliest hates and fears; who alone can know truth
and virtue, and by the same token is prone to error and evil,
capable of a folly and brutality unknown to dumb brutes. In a
time of troubles, it is the story of how the best is apt to become
75 the worst, as high, fixed principles lead to the use of unprincipled
means, and an uncompromising sincerity ends as the terrible
falsity that inspired the old proverb, May God deliver us from
the lies of honest men. At all times it is the story of the ines-
capable hazards that man brought upon himself when he took to
80 playing with fire and then, without forethought, set out on the
extraordinarily bold adventure of making over his world; while
ever since he began to reflect he has been seeking a repose that
he can find only in the death he fears.

5. Our theme, in short, is high Tragedy. We start with the ab-
85 surd incongruities that are the main theme of Comedy too: "O
Lord, what fools these mortals be!" But Tragedy heightens the
incongruities by invoking the emotions of pity and awe, adding
that man is the most wretched and sublime of fools. In its supreme
manifestations, such as the tragedies of Sophocles and Shake-
90 speare, it is an all-inclusive experience, embracing the extremes
of good and evil. It takes on the most awful possibilities of
human life, to display the most splendid possibilities of the
human spirit. It goes through the worst, and by going all the
way through it earns an honorable peace, which is more secure
95 because it is peace without victory. It may therefore afford a
deeper pleasure than the happy endings of Comedy, or even a
more exhilarating pleasure than "calm of mind, all passion spent."
And the principle of its paradoxical success—its resolute com-
plication of its issues, in a spirit at once ironic, compassionate,
100 and reverential—may be broadened into a principle of historical
analysis: a way of viewing history that might not be precise,
rigorous, or decisive enough to be dignified as a logical or scien-

tific method, but that can be comprehensive, consistent, disciplined, roughly systematic, generally incisive, and always pertinent.

6. In historical terms, the incongruities inherent in the nature of man are as naturally heightened by social order and social change. An order requires institutions, officials, routines, conventions, habits; and this indispensable bureaucracy, in thought as in administrative affairs, is always a threat to social health. An order is necessarily a selection from diverse possibilities, and as such it requires the suppression of other possibilities, has the defects of its virtues, and tends to overemphases—as William James said, without too much we cannot have enough, of anything. Social change as necessarily brings further conflict and contradiction, through cultural lag. All creative achievements are disruptive, and create new problems. All victorious creeds and policies have unintended by-products, which may defeat their purposes. All social movements that have the force to go far enough are apt to go too far and so to call out counter-movements, the pendulum swings of history.

7. The "tragic view," accordingly, may not only comprehend but anticipate the technical analyses of sociologists and historians. Without prejudice to science, it may help us to realize the value that Lionel Trilling attributes to literature, as "the human activity that takes the fullest and most precise account of variousness, possibility, complexity, and difficulty." By systematically complicating all issues, stressing the defects and the excesses of all values, insisting on tension, imbalance, uncertainty, and contradiction as the essential conditions of civilization, and the source of both its glory and its tragedy—by ironically qualifying the great triumphs, and reverently qualifying the great failures, we may get both a richer appreciation of the poetry and drama of history and a clearer understanding of the fact, the "reality" that concerns social science. We may hope to be at once more humane and more realistic, more generous in our sympathies and more sober in our judgments.

8. For this reason I have been discounting the obviously wholesome morals, in particular Toynbee's moral that the root evil in human history is pride. *Hubris,* or the insolence of pride,

was indeed the main theme of the Greek poets who originated
Tragedy. Historically it was the nemesis of Athens itself, as of
the Great Kings of Persia, the Pharaohs of Egypt, the Caliphs of
Bagdad, the Autokrators of Byzantium, the Popes of medieval
145 Rome. Yet the tragic poets have not seen a clear justice in man's
fate, nor a shining hope in the gods; and history hardly bears
out such hopes. Toynbee's own study shows that when religious
belief was strongest it bred the worldly pride from which it is
supposed to deliver us, and was most deeply involved in the moral
150 failures of both Eastern and Western Christendom. The "universal nemesis of idolatry" is so universal that, like "nature," it
explains nothing. Pride in man's own creations is common to all
societies, including the longest-lived, and perhaps most common
in their vigorous youth and prime. It may be considered the main-
155 spring of civilization.

9. Here again St. Sophia gives the clue to a basic ambiguity.
Pride goeth before a fall—but first it lifts men to real heights.
Without pride the tragic hero would not be a hero; without it
there would be no tragedy in history because no civilization at
160 all. And without it there would be no higher religions. It was
pride that built St. Sophia. It was still pride that led thousands
to pray in St. Sophia in the miserable last days of Byzantium; for
in their abjectness they were still assuming that the Almighty
took such a keen personal interest in the inhabitants of one small
165 region of this planet that he would perform a miracle to lay low
the inhabitants of other regions. Even the loftiest manifestations
of the religious spirit may be described as overweening pride.
Nothing is prouder than the humility of the ascetic or other-
worldly spirit that proclaims itself superior to the whole natural
170 world, or than the mysticism that renounces the self only to commune with God himself.

10. In short, we are all proud of one thing or another, if we
have any self-respect or any faith in anything at all. Since we can
all recognize the dangers of pride in others, our apparent task is
175 to define and ground our faith, in an awareness of the limitations
and the excesses of all faiths. And for this purpose, finally, I draw
a specific, positive lesson from the history of St. Sophia. The root
evil of Byzantine civilization was not simply its worldly pride—

it was blind faith, a basic unreason. It was exemplified in the tyranny of convention but most concretely in the tyranny of the church-state. Both Church and State claimed absolute authority, without enlisting the free consent of their subjects or permitting free criticism of the principles of their authority. Both were hostile to the life of reason.

11. Another object of this book will be to define and ground the pride or faith implicit in this judgment. It is a liberal, rationalistic, humanistic faith, rooted in the Greek heritage that Byzantium unthinkingly preserved and betrayed. One of its basic tenets is the dictum of Pascal: "Thought makes the whole dignity of man; therefore endeavor to think well—that is the only morality." I assume that thought is most dignified and moral when it recognizes its own limitations, and the hazards it inevitably introduces into the life of man. In confronting history, it must at least begin with the tragic view. It must acknowledge that no civilized society ever has had or can have the stability and security of the far more ancient ant and bee societies, which are regulated by the more efficient, economical mechanism of instinct. Today it must acknowledge that the rationalistic faith that has built the modern Western world is implicated in the frightful state of this world. Nevertheless I continue to believe, in pride, that our only possible hope lies not in prayer but in more thought, and in more earnest, responsible endeavor. The plainest lesson I get from the history of St. Sophia is that men cannot count on miracles.

✳✳✳✳✳✳✳✳✳✳✳

Hagia Sophia—the "Holy Wisdom"—is the great cathedral in Byzantium (at other times Troy, Constantinople, Istanbul) built under the Emperor Justinian toward the middle of the sixth century A.D. After the fall of Byzantium, it was for centuries a Moslem mosque. Today, under a secular Turkish regime, it is a museum. Herbert Muller, in this selection, explores it as a symbol of the force and meaning of religion in history.

1. Look up *implications, incongruity, epitome, desecrate, paltry, catholic, aspire, pertinent, nemesis, rationalistic, humanistic, im-*

plicit, exemplify, infatuated, unprecedented, disenchantment, vaunt, rigorous, and *inherent.*

2. Some literary references: whence comes "strut and fret" (51)? "Playing with fire" (80) is a rich fusion of modern colloquial and the myth of Prometheus; explain. How are "wholeness, haleness, and healing" (64–65) akin? "Calm of mind, all passion spent," from Milton's *Samson Agonistes,* describes the emotions that follow the tragic spectacle. Is Muller here commenting on the effect of Milton's verse drama or Milton's interpretation of it in "Calm of mind, all passion spent"?

3. The commas in lines 10 and 12 are very dramatic, precisely because they are unexpected; tell why. Consider, in the same perspective, the commas in lines 114, 117, 149, and 175.

4. Formal usage demands the insertion of an *also* in line 123. Where?

5. Muller's style is notable for its consistent use of *balance,* in modifiers, phrases, clauses. Like Gibbon and Macaulay, he invests his treatment of history with the formality and the dignity that come with long sentences carefully wrought.

The sentence in Par. 1, lines 8–10, is an outstanding example; consider also lines 10–13, 24–27, 27–30, 43–47, and 48–52. Point out the kind of balance that obtains in each of these sentences. Then look for and analyze some more notable examples in the rest of the selection. Is Muller's use of parallelism more, or less, frequent and studied than Gibbon's? Macaulay's? Oral reading of a paragraph for each will tell you.

6. *Desecrate* (21) is a violent word. Consider its aptness here in terms of its etymology.

7. Are *who* and *where* (21) literal or figurative? Explain your answer. "Nothing in the past for too many Americans" (18–19) also involves a relation of literal and figurative that is probably meant to startle you. What idea is established by the sentence?

8. The last sentence in Par. 2 is, perhaps, meretricious: the step from *infatuated* to *appalled* is made too fast, so that the strength of such powerful words is lost.

Consider the beginnings of the last two long sentences in Par. 2:

The naive, uncritical faith in material progress

and

Once infatuated with our unprecedented achievements.

The similarity of the thought and the parallelism of their positions introducing the two sentences suggests some larger parallelism in the development of the thought. Does it appear? If it does not, the apparent parallelism will be a distraction or a confusion. If the first passage points to our blindness or stupidity, to what does the second point?

9. Paragraph 3 introduces a startling counter-movement. At what point does Par. 3 become *concrete?* Does its effectiveness rise at this point? Is Par. 2 more or less concrete than 3? Divide each paragraph into its concrete and abstract parts and consider the order of these segments of each. Which order seems more effective? Dare one generalize about this?

10. The transition from Par. 3 to Par. 4 is not easy to formulate. You can define it, perhaps, if you can pin down "a more robust, catholic irony." Irony is the recognition of opposites in a situation. The opposites here are the qualities of man that distinguish and torment him because they keep him drawn tight between extremes—extremes of situation, character, and value. Write an essay explaining why the tendency to under- or over-value either the past or the present is an *expression* of the extremes which make human history what it has been.

11. What aspect of the definition of tragedy provides a program for the writing of history—its drama, its seriousness, its violent deaths, its willingness to see man in his utmost complexity, its use of poetic justice, its recognition of the evil in man, or its observation of the unities of time and action?

12. Now explain briefly how Pars. 4, 5, and 6 are connected by what might be termed *descriptive, literary,* and *sociological* approaches to the materials of tragedy. What is the nature of the connection and how does it serve as an expository device?

13. What definition in Par. 7 corresponds to what definition in Par. 5? Show how the correspondence advances the thesis of this latter passage.

14. Paragraph 8 introduces the issue for which the concept of tragedy was, it appears, developed. Our author proposes to chal-

lenge the theory of history advanced in the final volume of Arnold Toynbee's monumental *A Study of History* (1934–1954), a theory which he represents fairly enough in his allusions to it. You can hardly be expected to criticize these theories here; you may, however, be asked by your instructor to write an essay setting forth and discussing the differences in their *assumptions*.

The next selection is a passage from Toynbee's *Civilization on Trial* (1948), from which you may draw evidence. In identifying and defining assumptions, you will be looking for ideas which are not proved or analyzed but assumed as true and reasoned *from*. The significant assumptions about history are:

    a. What constitutes progress?
    b. Has there been progress in human history?
    c. Does progress depend upon individuals or institutions?
    d. What is the force that directs human history?
    e. What part is played by man's reason in the historical process?

Christianity and Civilization

ARNOLD J. TOYNBEE

1. . . . The human
soul that is truly seeking to save itself is as fully social a being
as the ant-like Spartan or the bee-like Communist. Only, the
Christian soul on Earth is a member of a very different society
from Sparta or Leviathan. He is a citizen of the Kingdom of God, 5
and therefore his paramount and all-embracing aim is to attain
the highest degree of communion with, and likeness to, God
Himself; his relations with his fellow men are consequences of,
and corollaries to, his relations with God; and his way of loving
his neighbour as himself will be to try to help his neighbour to win 10
what he is seeking for himself—that is, to come into closer communion with God and to become more godlike.

2. If this is a soul's recognized aim for itself and for its fellow
souls in the Christian Church Militant on Earth, then it is obvious
that under a Christian dispensation God's will *will* be done in 15
Earth as it is in Heaven to an immeasurably greater degree than
in a secular mundane society. It is also evident that, in the
Church Militant on Earth, the good social aims of the mundane
societies will incidentally be achieved very much more success-
fully than they ever have been or can be achieved in a mundane 20
society which aims at these objects direct, and at nothing higher.
In other words, the spiritual progress of individual souls in this
life will in fact bring with it much more social progress than
could be attained in any other way. It is a paradoxical but profoundly true and important principle of life that the most likely 25
way to reach a goal is to be aiming not at that goal itself but at

some more ambitious goal beyond it. This is the meaning of the fable in the Old Testament of Solomon's Choice and of the saying in the New Testament about losing one's life and saving it.

30   3. Therefore, while the replacement of the mundane civilizations by the world-wide and enduring reign of the Church Militant on Earth would certainly produce what to-day would seem a miraculous improvement in those mundane social conditions which the civilizations have been seeking to improve during the
35   last six thousand years, the aim, and test, of progress under a truly Christian dispensation on Earth would not lie in the field of mundane social life; the field would be the spiritual life of individual souls in their passages through this earthly life from birth into this world to death out of it.

40   4. But if spiritual progress in time in this world means progress achieved by individual human souls during their passages through this world to the other world, in what sense can there be any spiritual progress over a time-span far longer than that of individual lives on Earth, and running into thousands of years, such
45   as that of the historical development of the higher religions from the rise of Tammuz-worship and the generation of Abraham to the Christian era?

5. I have already confessed my own adherence to the traditional Christian view that there is no reason to expect any change
50   in unredeemed human nature while human life on Earth goes on. Till this Earth ceases to be physically habitable by man, we may expect that the endowments of individual human beings with original sin and with natural goodness will be about the same, on the average, as they always have been as far as our knowledge
55   goes. The most primitive societies known to us in the life or by report provide examples of as great natural goodness as, and no lesser wickedness than, the highest civilizations or religious societies that have yet come into existence. There has been no perceptible variation in the average sample of human nature in the
60   past; there is no ground, in the evidence afforded by History, to expect any great variation in the future either for better or for worse.

6. The matter in which there might be spiritual progress in time on a time-span extending over many successive generations

of life on Earth is not the unregenerate nature of man, but the 65
opportunity open to souls, by way of the learning that comes
through suffering, for getting into closer communion with God,
and becoming less unlike Him, during their passage through this
world.

7. What Christ, with the Prophets before Him and the Saints 70
after Him, has bequeathed to the Church, and what the Church,
by virtue of having been fashioned into an incomparably effective
institution, succeeds in accumulating, preserving, and communi-
cating to successive generations of Christians, is a growing fund
of illumination and of grace—meaning by "illumination" the dis- 75
covery or revelation or revealed discovery of the true nature of
God and the true end of man here and hereafter, and by "grace,"
the will or inspiration or inspired will to aim at getting into
closer communion with God and becoming less unlike Him. In
this matter of increasing spiritual opportunity for souls in their 80
passages through life on Earth, there is assuredly an inexhaustible
possibility of progress in this world.

�✷✷✷✷✷✷✷✷✷

The general drift of the questions after the preceding selection,
and especially Ques. 14, apply to this piece as well.

1. Look up the following words: *Spartan, Leviathan, paramount, dispensation, secular, mundane, endowment,* and *unregenerate.*

2. What further assumptions (beyond those asked for in Ques.
14, p. 249) are to be found in Toynbee's argument? For example,
examine the word *evident* in line 17. What assumptions does it
carry? What further proof of the *evident* is given in the paragraph?

3. Test the *any,* line 24, in the same way. Look up the fable
of Solomon's Choice and explain the validity of its application
here.

4. What is the force of *if* in line 40? Is the question here
rhetorical? If so, what answer does it assume? The question will

resolve itself, perhaps, into the relation—if any—between individual spiritual progress and social progress.

5.   Put the thesis of Par. 5 to the test of what you think *might* be contrary facts. Where are the most questionable assumptions? What of lines 58–62?

6.   Examine the choice set up between "unregenerate nature of man" and "opportunity open to souls" (65–66). Does it include the only alternatives?

Saint, Warrior, Gentleman

WILLIAM EDWARD HARTPOLE LECKY

1. It had been boldly predicted by some of the early Christians that the conversion of the world would lead to the establishment of perpetual peace. In looking back, with our present experience, we are driven to the melancholy conclusion that, instead of diminishing the num- 5 ber of wars, ecclesiastical influence has actually and very seriously increased it. We may look in vain for any period since Constantine, in which the clergy, as a body, exerted themselves to repress the military spirit, or to prevent or abridge a particular war, with an energy at all comparable to that which they displayed in 10 stimulating the fanaticism of the crusaders, in producing the atrocious massacre of the Albigenses, in embittering the religious contests that followed the Reformation. Private wars were, no doubt, in some degree repressed by their influence; for the institution of the "Truce of God" was for a time of much value, and 15 when, towards the close of the middle ages, the custom of duels arose, it was strenuously condemned by the clergy; but we can hardly place any great value on their exertions in this field, when we remember that duels were almost or altogether unknown to the Pagan world; that, having arisen in a period of great super- 20 stition, the anathemas of the Church were almost impotent to discourage them; and that in our own century they are rapidly disappearing before the simple censure of an industrial society. It is possible—though it would, I imagine, be difficult to prove it —that the mediatorial office, so often exercised by bishops, may 25 sometimes have prevented wars; and it is certain that during the period of the religious wars, so much military spirit existed in

From *History of European Morals*.

Europe that it must necessarily have found a vent, and under no circumstances could the period have been one of perfect peace. But when all these qualifications have been fully admitted, the broad fact will remain, that, with the exception of Mohammedanism, no other religion has done so much to produce war as was done by the religious teachers of Christendom during several centuries. The military fanaticism evoked by the indulgences of the popes, by the exhortations of the pulpit, by the religious importance attached to the relics at Jerusalem, and by the prevailing hatred of misbelievers, has scarcely ever been equalled in its intensity, and it has caused the effusion of oceans of blood, and has been productive of incalculable misery to the world. Religious fanaticism was a main cause of the earlier wars, and an important ingredient in the later ones. The peace principles, that were so common before Constantine, have found scarcely any echo except from Erasmus, the Anabaptists, and the Quakers; and although some very important pacific agencies have arisen out of the industrial progress of modern times, these have been, for the most part, wholly unconnected with, and in some cases been directly opposed to, theological interests.

2. But although theological influences cannot reasonably be said to have diminished the number of wars, they have had a very real and beneficial effect in diminishing their atrocity. On few subjects have the moral opinions of different ages exhibited so marked a variation as in their judgements of what punishment may justly be imposed on a conquered enemy, and these variations have often been cited as an argument against those who believe in the existence of natural moral perceptions. To those, however, who accept that doctrine, with the limitations that have been stated in the first chapter, they can cause no perplexity. In the first dawning of the human intelligence (as I have said) the notion of duty, as distinguished from that of interest, appears, and the mind, in reviewing the various emotions by which it is influenced, recognises the unselfish and benevolent motives as essentially and generically superior to the selfish and the cruel. But it is the general condition of society alone that determines the standard of benevolence—the classes towards which every

good man will exercise it. At first, the range of duty is the family, 65
the tribe, the state, the confederation. Within these limits every
man feels himself under moral obligations to those about him;
but he regards the outer world as we regard wild animals, as
beings upon whom he may justifiably prey. Hence, we may explain the curious fact that the terms brigand or corsair conveyed 70
in the early stages of society no notion of moral guilt. Such men
were looked upon simply as we look upon huntsmen, and if they
displayed courage and skill in their pursuit, they were deemed
fit subjects for admiration. Even in the writings of the most enlightened philosophers of Greece, war with barbarians is repre- 75
sented as a form of chase, and the simple desire of obtaining the
barbarians as slaves was considered a sufficient reason for invad-
ing them. The right of the conqueror to kill his captives was generally recognised, nor was it at first restricted by any considerations of age or sex. Several instances are recorded of Greek and 80
other cities being deliberately destroyed by Greeks or by Romans,
and the entire populations ruthlessly massacred. The whole career
of the early republic of Rome, though much idealised and transfigured by later historians, was probably governed by these principles. The normal fate of the captive, which, among barbarians, 85
had been death, was, in civilised antiquity, slavery; but many
thousands were condemned to the gladiatorial shows, and the
vanquished general was commonly slain in the Mamertine prison,
while his conqueror ascended in triumph to the Capitol.

3. A few traces of a more humane spirit may, it is true, be dis- 90
covered. Plato had advocated the liberation of all Greek prisoners upon payment of a fixed ransom, and the Spartan general
Callicratidas had nobly acted upon this principle; but his example never appears to have been generally followed. In Rome,
the notion of international obligation was very strongly felt. No 95
war was considered just which had not been officially declared;
and even in the case of wars with barbarians, the Roman historians often discuss the sufficiency or insufficiency of the motives,
with a conscientious severity a modern historian could hardly sur-
pass. The later Greek and Latin writings occasionally contain 100
maxims which exhibit a considerable progress in this sphere. The

sole legitimate object of war, both Cicero and Sallust declared
to be an assured peace. That war, according to Tacitus, ends well
which ends with a pardon. Pliny refused to apply the epithet
105 great to Caesar, on account of the torrents of human blood he had
shed. Two Roman conquerors are credited with the saying that it
is better to save the life of one citizen than to destroy a thousand
enemies. Marcus Aurelius mournfully assimilated the career of a
conqueror to that of a simple robber. Nations or armies which
110 voluntarily submitted to Rome were habitually treated with
great leniency, and numerous acts of individual magnanimity are
recorded. The violation of the chastity of conquered women by
soldiers in a siege was denounced as a rare and atrocious crime.
The extreme atrocities of ancient war appear at last to have been
115 practically, though not legally, restricted to two classes. Cities
where Roman ambassadors had been insulted, or where some
special act of ill faith or cruelty had taken place, were razed to
the ground, and their populations massacred or delivered into
slavery. Barbarian prisoners were regarded almost as wild beasts,
120 and sent in thousands to fill the slave market or to combat in the
arena.

4. The changes Christianity effected in the rights of war were
very important, and they may, I think, be comprised under three
heads. In the first place, it suppressed the gladiatorial shows, and
125 thereby saved thousands of captives from a bloody death. In
the next place, it steadily discouraged the practice of enslaving
prisoners, ransomed immense multitudes with charitable con-
tributions, and by slow and insensible gradations proceeded on
its path of mercy till it became a recognised principle of interna-
130 tional law that no Christian prisoners should be reduced to
slavery. In the third place, it had a more indirect but very powerful influence by the creation of a new warlike ideal. The ideal
knight of the Crusades and of chivalry, uniting all the force and
fire of the ancient warrior, with something of the tenderness and
135 humility of the Christian saint, sprang from the conjunction of
the two streams of religious and of military feeling; and although
this ideal, like all others, was a creation of the imagination not
often perfectly realised in life, yet it remained the type and
model of warlike excellence, to which many generations aspired;

and its softening influence may even now be largely traced in 140
the character of the modern gentleman.

✳✳✳✳✳✳✳✳✳✳✳

We can roughly date this passage by its vocabulary and the
length and punctuation of its sentences. After reading it aloud,

1. Look up *ecclesiastical, abridge, anathemas, impotent, censure, mediatorial, vent, fanaticism, indulgences, effusion, theological, atrocity, beneficial, benevolent, generically, corsair, ruth-
less, transfigured, maxim, assimilated, leniency, magnanimity,
raze, comprise,* and *conjunction.* Proper names can be found in
an unabridged dictionary, too.

2. Does the first comma in line 8 set off a non-restrictive modifier? (Does the voice continue to rise on "Constantine"? If so, it
is restrictive.) If the "in which . . ." clause *is* restrictive, the
comma indicates a practice no longer current, for it is there to
control the pauses and cadences in oral reading. Is there another
comma in the sentence that would not appear today?

3. Explain why commas in lines 38, 40, 73, 116, 119, and 124
would *not* appear in formal prose today.

4. Now consider the semicolons in:

> Private wars were, no doubt, in some degree repressed by their
> influence; for the institution of the 'Truce of God' was for a time
> of much value, and when, towards the close of the middle ages, the
> custom of duels arose, it was strenuously condemned by the clergy;
> but we can hardly place any great value on their exertions in this
> field, when we remember that duels were almost or altogether
> unknown to the Pagan world; that, having arisen in a period of
> great superstition, the anathemas of the Church were almost impo-
> tent to discourage them; and that in our own century they are
> rapidly disappearing before the simple censure of an industrial
> society.

Which are strictly structural, and which seem to guide oral reading rather than indicate structural relations?

5. Reread aloud lines 41–47, 55–62, 85–89, and 132–141, stressing as you read how the commas perfectly indicate structure and

so guide both ear and understanding through complex statements. Note, on the other hand, the use of semicolons in these
sentences for oral reading rather than for structure and meaning.

6.   Some of Lecky's diction is formal and dignified to the point
where it is also somewhat indefinite. For example, "mediatorial
office" (25), "effusion" (38), "pacific agencies" (44), "natural
moral perceptions" (55), "general condition of society" (63),
and "assimilated" (108). Try replacing these terms with more
concrete and definite ones, with the least possible alteration of
the tone.

7.   Does "value" (18) indicate that the clergy were less effective than Pagan society in preventing duels—or that Christianity was *responsible* for duelling? With what justice are the
clergy's efforts to be contrasted with "the simple censure of an
industrial society"?

8.   *Superstition* appears (20–21) to make *anathemas impotent*.
But it might be argued that anathemas would be unusually potent
in "a period of great superstition." Write a paragraph or two explaining the *assumptions* under which each of these positions
would be logical; at the same time clarify Lecky's own position.

9.   The selection is plainly organized into four parts, which
correspond to the four paragraphs. Supply a title for each part
and reduce the paragraph to a summary sentence—which may
profitably draw upon the cadenced parallelism of Lecky.

Vainglory in Montenegro

REBECCA WEST

1. "Have the Monte-
negrins not made enormous sacrifices to preserve their independence?" I asked Constantine, and he answered, "Greater than
you can believe. They have sacrificed almost everything except
their heroism. They are nothing but heroes. If they eat or sleep, it 5
is so that they shall wake up heroes. If they marry it is so that they
should beget little heroes, who would not trouble to come out of
their mothers' wombs were they not certain that they would grow
up in heroism. They are as like the people of Homer as any race
now living: they are brave, and beautiful, and vainglorious. A 10
soldier must be vainglorious. He must go into the battle believing
that he is so wonderful a human being that God could not let
it be that the lesser men in front of him should kill him. And since
the men in front of them were Turks who were often really prodigious fighters, there was no end to the fairy-tales that the 15
Montenegrins had to tell to themselves about themselves. You get
it in the two classic stories that are always told about these people. One is really true; it was a thing noticed in the Balkan wars.
You know that when soldiers drill they have to number off—'One
two, one, two.' In the Montenegrin Army it could not be done. 20
No man was willing to be second, so the first man said, 'One,'
and the second said, 'I-am-beside-him,' very quickly. The other
may be true, but perhaps only in the spirit. It is said that a
traveller said to a Montenegrin, "'How many of your people are
there?' and he answered, 'With Russia, one hundred and eighty 25
millions,' and the traveller, knowing there were not two hundred

thousand of them, said, 'Yes, but how many without the Russians?' and the Montenegrin answered, 'We will never desert the Russians.' And it was not a joke, for the vainglory of these people
30 was necessary to them lest they should be conquered in battle.

2. "This vainglory will not permit them to have any other characteristics, except a little cunning that is quite simple, like the cunning of the Homeric heroes, for to be perfectly and absolutely vainglorious you must hold back from all activity, because
35 you dare not ever fail at anything. So the Montenegrins are not really interested in any kind of work, and that makes it very difficult to fit them into the modern state of Yugoslavia. For in earlier centuries they lived by fighting, which always included a lot of looting, and by foreign subsidies, which were freely given,
40 as this state was an important strategic point on the Adriatic coast; and in the late nineteenth and twentieth centuries they lived very much on these subsidies, particularly from Russia. And now all that is over, and they must earn their livings, and they do not want to do anything at all, for even farming used to
45 be done chiefly by their women, since they always were at war or resting between wars, and no work interests them. No child here says, 'I would like to be a builder, or a doctor, or a carpenter,' though some want to be chauffeurs because to them it is still a daring and romantic occupation. So they pester the Government
50 with demands for posts as functionaries and for pensions, which are of a terrible simplicity, for there is no need for so many functionaries, and if there were these people could not perform their functions, and God Himself, if He had a knife at His throat, could not invent a reason why they should all have pensions. This
55 is hard on a poor country like Yugoslavia, and this is not an easy matter to settle by patience and patriotism, as many things can be settled in Bosnia and Old Serbia and Macedonia, because the Montenegrins are empty-headed except for their wild and unthinking heroism, which is to say they are often like madmen.
60 I tell it you, this country is a sacrifice to itself of itself, and there is nothing left."

3. There is no way out of the soul's dilemma. Those displeased by the rite on the Sheep's Field, who would be neither the priest nor the black lamb, who would be neither converted to Islam nor

defeated on Kossovo plain, are forced to fight the priest. Since we 65
must live in the same world as those we fight, this means sharing
this upland bleakness, furnished too simply with its bloodstained
monolith. "Whoso liveth by the sword shall die by the sword"
is only half the damnatory sentence passed on mankind by war;
the other half reads, "Whoso refuseth to die by the sword shall 70
live by the sword." Montenegro was something like a prison.
Though it was airy as Heaven, instead of airless, like other prisons,
it was stony like a cell, and it reeked of heroism as strongly as
institutions reek of disinfectant; and the straitened inhabitants
were sealed up in space with the ideas of slaughter and triumph 75
as convicts are in their confinement with guilt and punishment.
If one shut the eyes and thought of any pleasantness but the
most elemental, any enjoyment that helped the mind further on
its task of exploring the universe, one had to say on opening
them, "It is not here, nothing but the root of it is here." 80

4. So it seemed. Then the road looped round the mountainside
to a steeper mountain, and wound up to yet another pass, so high
that as we rose the noontide sky showed pale above the distant
peaks, though it was deeply blue above us. The country, which
here is highly variable, changed its character again; it was 85
Buckinghamshire on this cool northward slope, so tall the beeches,
so dense the woods they drove to the skyline, so gardenish the
grass. Up and up we drove until we had to stop, to cool the
engine. We none of us regretted it, for there were many gentians
on the banks beside the road, and below us the woods lay like 90
bonfires of green flame on the mild rolling turf, and further the
distant infinity of mountains was blue as wild hyacinths. We sat
there so long that a woman we had passed on a lower curve of the
road overtook us, halted in her trudging, came up to the car, and
laid her arm along the frame of the open window, looking round 95
at us all. Her face had once been perfect but was no longer so,
and was the better for it. "Good morning," she said to Constantine, "who are you?" "I am Constantine," he said. "I am from
Shabats and I am a poet." "And who are you?" she asked my
husband and me. "They are English," said Constantine. "A very 100
fine people," she said. "Why do you think that?" said Constantine.
"Because they are great fighters, and they love nature," she said.

"How do you know they are like that?" asked Constantine. She lifted her arm from the window, took a ball of fine white wool 105 and knitting-needles from her other hand, and set to work again, as if sensing from his question an indication that the conversation might not be of the first order and she might as well get on with her material duties. "Oh, everybody knows that," she answered absently. "And you," said Constantine, "who are you? Are you a 110 native of this place?" "No," she said, "I live here now, but I was born by Durmitor." Durmitor is the great snow mountain, with a black lake at its foot, on the northern side of Montenegro. "Who brought you here?" asked Constantine.

5. She laughed a little, lifted her ball of wool to her mouth, 115 sucked the thin thread between her lips, and stood rocking herself, her eyebrows arching in misery. "It is a long story. I am sixty now," she said. "Before the war I was married over there, by Durmitor. I had a husband whom I liked very much, and I had two children, a son and a daughter. In 1914 my husband was 120 killed by the Austrians. Not in battle. They took him out of our house and shot him. My son went off and was a soldier and was killed, and my daughter and I were sent to a camp. There she died. In the camp it was terrible, many people died. At the end of the war I came out and I was alone. So I married a man twenty 125 years older than myself. I did not like him as I liked my first husband, but he was very kind to me, and I had two children of his. But they both died, as was natural, for he was too old, and I was too old, and also I was weak from the camp. And now my husband is eighty, and he has lost his wits, and he is not kind to 130 me any more. He is angry with everybody; he sits in his house and rages, and I cannot do anything right for him. So I have nothing." "Are you poor?" asked Constantine. "Not at all," she said. "My husband's son by his first wife is a judge in Old Serbia, and he sends me three hundred dinars a month to hire a man to 135 work our land, so we want nothing. Oh, that is all right, but the rest is so wrong." "Oh, sister, sister," said Constantine, "this is very hard." "Yes, it's hard," she said. "And can we do nothing for you," asked Constantine, "for we feel very friendly towards you? Can we not give you a lift to where you are going?" "That you 140 cannot do, though you mean so kindly," she said, "for I am not

going anywhere. I am walking about to try to understand why all this has happened. If I had to live, why should my life have been like this? If I walk about up here where it is very high and grand it seems to me I am nearer to understanding it." She put the ball of wool to her forehead and rubbed it backwards and for- 145 wards, while her eyes filled with painful speculation. "Good-bye," she said, with distracted courtesy, as she moved away, "good-bye."

6. This woman was of no importance. It is doubtful whether, walk as she would on these heights, she would arrive at any con- 150 clusion that was of value even to herself. She was, however, the answer to my doubts. She took her destiny not as the beasts take it, nor as the plants and trees; she not only suffered it, she examined it. As the sword swept down on her through the darkness she threw out her hand and caught the blade as it fell, not caring 155 if she cut her fingers so long as she could question its substance, where it had been forged, and who was the wielder. She wanted to understand . . . the mystery of process. I knew that art and science were the instruments of this desire, and this was their sole justification, though in the Western world where I lived I 160 had seen art debauched to ornament and science prostituted to the multiplication of gadgets. I knew that they were descended from man's primitive necessities, that the cave man who had to hunt the aurochs drew him on the rock-face that he might better understand the aurochs and have fuller fortune in hunting and 165 was the ancestor of all artists, that the nomad who had to watch the length of shadows to know when he should move his herd to the summer pasture was the ancestor of all scientists. But I did not know these things thoroughly with my bowels as well as my mind. I knew them now, when I saw the desire for understanding 170 move this woman. It might have been far otherwise with her, for she had been confined by her people's past and present to a kind of destiny that might have stunned its victims into an inability to examine it. Nevertheless she desired neither peace nor gold, but simply knowledge of what her life might mean. The instru- 175 ment used by the hunter and the nomad was not too blunt to turn to finer uses; it was not dismayed by complexity, and it could regard the more stupendous aurochs that range within the mind

and measure the diffuse shadows cast by history. And what was
180 more, the human will did not forget its appetite for using it.

7. I remembered what Denis Saurat had said about Militsa:
"If there are but twenty people like her scattered between here
and China, civilization will survive." If during the next million
generations there is but one human being born in every generation
185 who will not cease to inquire into the nature of his fate, even
while it strips and bludgeons him, some day we shall read the
riddle of our universe. We shall discover what work we have been
called to do, and why we cannot do it. If a mine fails to profit
by its riches and a church wastes the treasure of its altar, we
190 shall know the cause: we shall find out why we draw the knife
across the throat of the black lamb or take its place on the offensive rock, and why we let the grey falcon nest in our bosom,
though it buries its beak in our veins. We shall put our own
madness in irons. Then, having defeated our own enmity, we shall
195 be able to face the destiny forced on us by nature, and war with
that. And what does that mean? What name is behind nature,
what name but one name? Then there will be the wrestling match
that is worth the prize, then defeat will be eternal glory, then
there can be no issue but magnificence. That contest may endure
200 a million, million years, seeing the might of the combatants. And
after that, what then? Could the mind twitch away the black cur-
tain behind the stars, it might be dazzled by a brightness brighter
than the stars which might be the battle-field for another
splendid conflict as yet not to be conceived. It was towards this
205 splendour that the woman was leading, as we passed her later,
leaving the road and treading a path over the turf among gentians
which she did not see. "Good-bye!" Dragutin cried to her. "Good-
bye, Mother!"

❋❋❋❋❋❋❋❋❋❋❋

This selection is from a very long book on Yugoslavia which
looks at first like a history and a travelogue but turns out to be
much more—a profound inquiry into the human condition. It
deals particularly with the idea of non-violence or passive resistance, which exercised a compelling force on thinking people of
the western world between the first and second World Wars. Why

in terms of Yugoslavia?—Because the Yugoslavs would not submit
when the rest of Europe was collapsing, but waged a hopeless war
against the Nazi forces of Hitler, fighting in their rugged hills
against impossible odds until they were overwhelmed.

When the western world was fascinated—in the full sense of
the word—by ideas of non-violence, Rebecca West wrote of nationalism and the will to fight. Central to her thesis is the conviction that non-violence is guilt-ridden, that it reflects the ideal of
sacrifice, which she deplores. She contends that the idea of sacrifice has its roots in the tormented reasoning of people who say
that because it is bad to inflict pain, it is good to suffer pain. But
this leads to the conclusion that if it is good to suffer pain it may
be good to inflict it, for how can pain be suffered if there is no
one to inflict it?

Returning again and again to the ideal of sacrifice, she develops
the thesis that it involves a hideous pact between the tormenter
and the tormented. It does not matter whether the suffering or the
inflicting of pain was first glorified: the resulting pact is what
matters. Her title indicates her two great symbols. The black
lamb has his throat cut in a Mithraic ritual, and his blood flows
down a stinking clotted rock over which the blood of innumerable
black lambs has flowed for centuries. The Grey Falcon is the
Turkish commander who defeated Tsar Lazar, chief of the Serbs,
at the battle of Kossovo, in 1389. The Tsar was defeated because
he laid down his arms, hoping to gain a heavenly kingdom by
forgoing an earthly one. What followed, in fact, was brutal
Turkish domination of Serbia for 500 years—from which the Slavs
learned that sacrifice is evil and that sometimes one must fight
even against irresistible force and numbers.

The Montenegrins (their country now, like Serbia, Croatia,
Herzegovina, Macedonia, Bosnia, and Dalmatia, a part of Yugoslavia) resisted the Turks and held them at bay, saving western
civilization, but, as you will read in this selection, at a terrible
price to themselves.

A word about the characters. Constantine is a brilliant Serbian
poet, as sensitive as he is knowledgeable. Gerda, his wife, is a
German and a Nazi at heart. Dragutin is their chauffeur on this
trip into the uplands of Montenegro. Rebecca West and her husband complete the party.

1. The theme of Par. 1 is stated in lines 4–5. What is it? Is
the "sacrifice" described a voluntary one?

2. Look up *vainglorious* in a good dictionary. The word itself is so colorful that you may be surprised to discover how unfavorable it is.

3. How does the author, in herself defining the word (10–13), modify its unfavorable connotations? How does the word *must* function in this process? What word in the last sentence of the paragraph echoes it?

4. You have identified the theme of Par. 1. Now mark off the five illustrations of it that follow.

5. We have observed the principle of syllabic increase in the writings of Macaulay and Gibbon. The same principle appears in the numbers of words devoted to these five illustrations. Indicate how they increase in length by numbering and marking them in the margin. Why would it not be effective to have them in the opposite order?

6. Paragraph 1 defines and exemplifies vainglory as a necessity for the Montenegrins. Paragraph 2 illustrates its limitations. List them; there are several.

7. In line 53, the theme of the knife at the throat refers to the symbol of the black lamb. Is the use of it here only whimsical —or does it function in the development of the theme? You will have to refer this question to later questions about "the mystery of process," for the author is ready to question everything in the universe.

8. From Constantine's summary (60–61), we find at Par. 3 a profound shift in tone. We move from his indignant, colorful, and impassioned exposition to an awed speculation on the condition of man. Explain why *those* in line 62 refers to the Montenegrins. The rite (63) is the sacrifice of the black lamb on the rock. The words "priest . . . black lamb" bring it back to our attention. Explain how the pair, "converted to Islam . . . defeated at Kossovo" refer in the same way as "priest . . . lamb" to the other great symbol described in our note preceding the questions.

9. An aphorism or maxim such as "Whoso liveth by the sword shall die by the sword," quoted from the Bible, is a concrete and colorful way of saying that violence begets violence. "Whoso

refuseth to die by the sword shall live by the sword" is the author's invention and states an extreme of the *nationalism* that she is defending—an extreme that seems to be as bad as the alternative of slavery. Write a short paragraph explaining this latter maxim.

10. From the invention of maxims, the author turns in lines 71–80 to the figure of a prison. Words take on special freshness and vigor when they suggest more than they say, or when by some means special attention is called to them. Let us consider *prison*. If you call a tenement a prison you indicate its confinement, darkness, perhaps also its squalor and dirt. This is good writing, unless tenements have been called prisons so often that the comparison has lost its force. When a truly new comparison is made a word suddenly comes to life and glows with meaning. See what happens when Rebecca West calls the spacious airy uplands a prison (72 f). Explain how her use draws special vigor and expressiveness from the word. Can you show where she uses a figurative meaning figuratively? That is, is her use of *prison* more or less figurative than calling a tenement a prison? How do such words as *stony, reeked, straitened,* and *sealed* contribute to the prison image? Which are the more imaginative? Are there others?

11. Now look at *root* (80). On one level, we have a picture of a stony upland with a root but no tree. Why did the writer choose this image to suggest man with his spiritual powers cut down? Why not, for example, the image of a foundation without a house on it?

12. The root becomes the woman of the next two paragraphs, out of whose stricken and blighted life grows the quality of spirit that gives meaning and value to Man. Explain how *seemed,* line 81, effects the transition from the apparent prison to the flowering of the "root." This transition carries the thought across into what may seem at first glance to be a complete change of subject. Exactly what is the linking thought? Can you show that it is the central idea of the whole selection?

13. With Par. 6 we turn, in this search into the plight and destiny of man, from the raw material of Pars. 4 and 5 (the anecdote of the old woman) to the author's speculation on its meaning. *Doubts* (152) refers to the substance of what earlier paragraph? That is, to what thought does the word carry us back—before the "raw material" of Pars. 4 and 5?

14. Just as we saw *prison* used in an extraordinary context, so in Par. 6 we see a two-sentence description of the origin and purpose of art and science (158–168) used to illuminate the quest of the old woman on the lonely heights! What other phrase than "the desire for understanding" might have been used to point to the problem itself, which Miss West indicates somewhat obscurely with the phrase, "the mystery of process"? Does this phrase intentionally contain some of the mystery that it labels? You can find a very simple equivalent to it in lines 141–2. What is it? What is the *instrument* in lines 175–6. How could an instrument be *dismayed?* Comment on the other powers attributed to "it" through to the end of the paragraph.

15. The "desire for understanding" is considered the source of both art and science in Par. 6. Many critics would say that the *imagination* is the power the artist brings to the task of understanding, but to say this is to assume that understanding is a creative process, not merely a static process of knowing what already exists, because the order it makes is a creation of the mind and does not exist apart from the mind of man. If this is so, what further relation does it point to among the old woman, the cave-man, the nomad, the artist, and the scientist?

16. Note that *confined* in line 172 and *stunned* in 173 recall the earlier image of the prison and so compare the old woman with the typical vainglorious Montenegrin. How? A powerful figure or symbol gains force when the reader comes upon it a second or a third time in the development of a theme by a skillful writer. The reader is drawn into a realm of the mind that the artist has created, and the effect is a sense of illumination and excitement. Where in Par. 7 is the same re-use and enrichment of a symbol effected? What is the Biblical reference in *wrestling* (197)?

17. Is the greatest problem of humanity, then, Man or Fate—what we are or what we confront in nature? Vast as this problem is, you can make it the subject of an essay about a situation with which you are familiar, a situation in which external challenges or hazards are mingled with the personal problems of the people involved in them. Some problem in your college, your home, your job, or your social group would be best, even though it may seem anti-climactic after the grandeur of Rebecca West's theme.

How Probable Is Probability?

JOSEPH WOOD KRUTCH

1. Some years ago an ingenious journalist filled his column with speculation about the people who would jump from the Brooklyn Bridge during the twelve months to come. At the moment probably none of them knew that he was going to do anything of the kind. Probably at 5 the moment each would have been appalled by the fate in store for him. But somebody would be compelled to jump because statistics prove that somebody always does.

2. When the time came each would suppose that he had his private reasons. But the real reason would be that the Law must 10 be obeyed. The question is merely: Who will be picked out by the God of Mathematics to demonstrate His infallibility? Will it be, perhaps, you or I? In any event it will be some of us, and the number will be not much larger or much smaller than usual. Figures don't lie and some will have to be sacrificed to prove that 15 they do not.

3. Presumably most of the journalist's readers saw the joke and smiled, but it is less likely that very many realized just why the jest was so good. He was pointing his finger at a paradox which has come, in our day, to have enormous practical importance and 20 philosophical significance. This is the Age of Statistics as well as the Age of Anxiety, and statistics furnish a set of tools without the use of which the theory that men are predictable and controllable machines would be very difficult to maintain. No mechanist claims that he can either foresee or determine what an 25

individual man will do. At most he asserts that he can determine and foresee in terms of an average.

4. But how and to what extent are we bound by such averages? If, for instance, a new bridge is built and more people
30 jump, does that mean that you or I are somehow compelled to do our part toward keeping up the new average? Whether or not God's foreknowledge is incompatible with free will is a very old problem. The statistician has invented a new kind of foreknowledge. He is, indeed, a new kind of god. Does that raise
35 a new problem? Or does it settle the old one once and for all?

5. The very idea of compiling statistics and the very notion that they may mean something are relatively new though both may now seem to us to be inevitable. One Sir William Petty who published in 1691 a book with the engaging title *Political Arithmetic*
40 is said to have been the first Englishman to see the possibilities of the statistical method as applied to the investigation of social phenomena. He compared, for instance, the average mortality rate for patients admitted to hospitals in London and in Paris, and it seems to have occurred to no one before him that this might throw
45 some light on the question of which was the better managed. A good many people, including Samuel Pepys, sensed the originality of his investigations but few can have guessed that we should come in time to live by averages more truly than we can be said to live by anything else.

50 6. In Sir William's time men were already in hot pursuit of the "laws" of nature. The assumption that her phenomena were dependably regular and could be described in mathematic formulae had already taken possession of the mind. Newton was in mid-career. But it was the precise, the dependable, the inevitable
55 which engaged the attention. It was with what *always* happens that science, or the New Learning, seemed destined to concern itself, and it was the idea of the certain, not of the probable, that excited the mind.

7. Mathematically that meant the concept of "function." A
60 equals B, or twice B, or B squared, or perhaps, even, the instantaneous rate of variation of B with respect to C. But whatever A is equal to it is always and precisely equal. One value is tied to the other directly and unchangeably and the description of this re-

lationship constitutes a "law of nature." The idea of a "law" which is only sometimes true, of a relationship which exists and yet can- 65 not be formulated in such a way as to make prediction more than a probability is something quite different. It is less easy to understand metaphysically or to apply for practical purposes. Even the most eminent mathematicians are not in agreement.

8. As a matter of fact—and this is the point which really con- 70 cerns us—in every case where a "law" can be stated only in terms of statistical averages two possible interpretations present themselves. One is that the uncertainty involved is simply the result of partial ignorance. Perhaps the data on which we base our prediction is inaccurate or perhaps we are considering only some of 75 the factors which determine the result. Naturally, therefore, we are sometimes wrong, either because the inaccuracy is gross or because the factor we are not taking into account is, in this instance, of paramount importance.

9. A plant, let us say, usually blooms after the sun has shone 80 on it for a certain number of hours. This year it doesn't. But that is because there has been a very abnormal lack of rainfall, and we were wrong in our prediction simply because we were basing it on the single factor which is usually decisive. But we may, nevertheless, be right in our assumption that definite factors produce 85 definite results. On this interpretation a statistical law is simply one which has not been fully formulated or applied.

10. This is, of course, the interpretation usually given and the one which the present set of our minds predisposes us to accept. It is what the Frazier of *Walden Two* had in mind when he pro- 90 tested: "I didn't say that behavior is always predictable, any more than the weather is always predictable. There are often too many factors to be taken into account. We cannot measure them all accurately, and we couldn't perform the mathematical operations needed to make the prediction if we had the measurements." 95 Frazier was, in other words, sure that everything is determined, even though he does not even hope that everything will someday be predictable. Thus, though he admits a limit to the knowable, he will not consider even the possibility that anything may be indeterminate. 100

11. If you ask him how he can be sure that what is admittedly

forever unpredictable is nevertheless ineluctably determined, he will answer only that it would be very inconvenient to assume anything else. He is committed, as all physical scientists once
105 were, to belief in the fixed order of nature. That means that even the word "chance" is useful only as a way of referring to what happens within an area where the determining factors are unknown to us and that the concept of "freedom" is logically absurd. You cannot, as he protested, have a science if things "hop
110 about," and he has resolved to have a science. The "proof" that this is a universe which never violates a "natural law" is simply that you have assumed that it is.

12. There is, nevertheless, another possible meaning for some part of the margin of error in statistical predictions. It is less easy
115 to grasp, almost impossible to formulate. But in the physical sciences it is today almost universally accepted and it frankly assumes that an element of uncertainty is not necessarily the result of imperfect knowledge or of imperfect method but may be the consequence of the primary fact that the *unpredictable* and
120 the *indeterminate* are part of ultimate reality.

13. Now one might have expected that the observers of human behavior would have been the first to suggest this seemingly desperate conclusion. If they reject it, they are compelled to disregard the whole difficulty of reconciling human experience with
125 the supposed laws of behavior. Yet it was the physicist, who faced no such difficulty, who first came to see that statistics do not really mean what they were taken to mean. It was the physicist who first realized what the sociologist frequently denies, namely that statistical results are *merely* statistical, and that no fully de-
130 termining laws are operating.

❋❋❋❋❋❋❋❋❋❋

1. Look up *infallibility* (12), *paradox* (19), *mechanist,* in its technical, philosophical sense (25), and *ineluctably* (102).

2. This whole exposition moves toward the word *merely* in the last sentence, and if you have read carefully you should be able to write a summary sentence or two in which, by defining this *merely*, you state the central idea of the selection.

3.   Next, explain how two meanings of the word *law* create the confusion which is Krutch's subject here. You can explain the confusion by a discussion of the statement, "the Law must be obeyed" (10–11). What kind of laws must be obeyed? What kind merely describe? What kind deal with ineluctably *acting* properties of the thing described? To what extent does a statistical law resemble a law of physics, to what extent a civil law? Follow the word *law* through the essay.

4.   Indicate—and explain—the sequence of terms in Par. 2 which mounts in absurdity to the final "Figures don't lie . . ."

5.   Trace the development of the essay by formulating a topic phrase or sentence for each paragraph, subordinating the merely illustrative paragraphs. That is, when you have written (or identified) a topic sentence for each paragraph, you will be able to indicate which summarize major steps in the argument and which serve as illustration, explanation, or proof.

6.   Distinguish carefully between *determined* and *predictable* as they are used in Par. 10. That which is indeterminate *must* be unpredictable; but that which is determined *may* be. Why?

7.   Most fiction in one way or another explores the individual's sense of his own freedom and the limitations which heredity, environment, and chance impose upon it. Freedom has been defined as "the recognition of necessity [i.e. law]"; Krutch suggests that it may involve the "concept of the ultimately random . . . or of a causeless cause." If you are of a speculative turn of mind you may want to explore those two definitions of freedom, trying to show precisely where they differ and perhaps following some of their implications. Which definition underlies Emerson's sentence, "Any distrust of the permanence of laws would paralyze the faculties of man"?

The Loss of Confidence

JOSEPH WOOD KRUTCH

1. Not since the Middle Ages has eschatology—or how a world ends—been so popular a subject of discussion. Though some seem convinced that civilization will emerge perfected after a world-wide calamity, at least
5 as many predict that it will soon disappear altogether. On one thing only is there almost universal agreement: things can't go on this way much longer.

2. At the very least, the comfortable conviction, dominant over two centuries, that everything would grow slowly better has dis-
10 appeared almost completely, and we are again believers in catastrophe rather than evolution. Even the most extravagant of Communists insist that chaos must precede Utopia, and they join eagerly with the pessimists to discuss the question of how a world ends.

15 3. Two world wars and more than one third of a century lie between the last days of the Age of Confidence and the present moment. Many of us still living can, nevertheless, remember what a very different world was like; and we are aware, as younger men cannot be, how drastic and all-pervasive the change has
20 been. Had you told us in 1914 what men would be thinking, believing and expecting in 1954, we should have found it harder to believe than the fantastic predictions of George Orwell are now. . . .

4. Shall we say only that the mood of an age, like the mood of
25 an individual, is merely the superficial by-product of its recent

experience; that the early nineteenth century was confident because it had lived for several decades in peace and growing comfort, while the mid-twentieth century is anxious because it has
gone through two wars, a depression and various revolutions? Or
shall we assume that what we *thought* had some sort of direct 30
relation to what happened—that we, with the best intentions in
the world, *guided* ourselves toward a conviction of coming disaster?

5. To some degree this is what we must assume, unless we
embrace in its simplest and most absolute form the conviction 35
that either the dialectic of matter or some other form of Fate determines what will happen to us, while ideas, convictions and
intentions are no more than phosphorescent epiphenomena which
accompany the unfolding of Destiny. And if we do assume that
what the world believed had some influence on what happened 40
to it, then we ought to examine its most significant beliefs, asking
ourselves as we go along what was wrong with them.

6. Very orthodox Communists and very orthodox Christians
think they know already. The latter can sum it up very briefly by
saying simply that we "forgot God." The Communists need a few 45
more words, but not really very many. They tell us that though
Wells, Shaw and most of their declared disciples called themselves
Socialist in a sense which implies an acceptance of Marxian teach-
ings, they did not really "understand Marxism." In the first place,
they often forgot to take literally enough and absolutely enough 50
the Marxian doctrine which asserts the decisive role played by the
dialectic of matter. In the second place, they clung sentimentally
to all sorts of bourgeois ideals and weakly supposed that history
could fulfill herself without requiring that those who wished to
cooperate should sacrifice anachronistic scruples concerning indi- 55
vidual rights, the sense of fair play, and the essential evil of violence. Therefore, even as an attempt to control it, their ideology
was confused and timid. They pretended to announce the future,
but they were not wholeheartedly with it. Those who have implicitly and completely accepted either Rome or Moscow see 60
clearly what is happening and know what to think. Nothing
which occurs surprises them, and they know that in the long run
everything will turn out as it should. Theoretically at least, they

have escaped from the Age of Anxiety and live again in an Age
65 of Confidence.

7. But those who have not undergone either of these two con-
versions are puzzled and apprehensive. Either something *was*
wrong in the thinking, or something *went* wrong in the plans, and
they are sure neither what it was nor even which it was. Still less
70 are they sure to what extent the errors are corrigible, the opera-
tional mistakes susceptible of rectification. And since they are
not, as Wells and Shaw were, on the point of death, they are less
ready merely to exclaim "All is lost" as they prepare to make their
exits.

75   8. Man has, after all, survived up to now. He was "good
enough," and he could learn quickly enough to achieve at least
the minimal degree of success necessary for continued existence.
Though he was neither good enough nor educable enough to create Utopia, many of us never supposed that he was. But if it has
80 at last become evident that he is not even good enough to survive,
that is quite another matter. He was good enough to do so for
many thousands of years. He survived his first struggles with
animate and inanimate nature; he survived his diseases, his wars,
his social systems, his religions, and a series of misconceptions
85 which now seem to have been sometimes almost suicidal. What
has made him in 1952 less fitted to survive than he was in
5000 B.C.?

9. There is, to be sure, one answer to that question currently
familiar in one form or another. Reduced to its simplest terms,
90 that answer is this: Man's ingenuity has outrun his intelligence.
He was good enough to survive in a simple, sparsely populated
world, where he was neither powerful enough nor in sufficiently
close contact with his neighbors to do them or himself fatal harm.
He is not good enough to manage the more complicated and
95 closely integrated world which he is, for the first time, powerful
enough to destroy. He is, perhaps, no more prone to war than
he used to be and no more inclined to commit other evil deeds.
But a given amount of ill will or folly will go further than it
used to. And what is so obviously true in connection with war
100 is equally true in less spectacular affairs. The complexities of
an industrial society make men more dependent on one another

than they used to be, and the whole machinery of government is harder to handle. Wisdom and good will have either not increased at all or, in any event, have not kept pace with the necessity for them. 105

10. If we grant this familiar interpretation, then there are obviously at least a pair of alternatives to extinction. On the one hand we can say with Wells, "Let us get wise as soon as possible." On the other hand we could, of course, say with Thoreau, "Simplify." 110

11. If civilization is too complicated and there is no immediate prospect of our learning enough to manage it, we might suggest a reduction of that complexity. Instead of constantly seeking new sources of power, either in the oil of Arabia or in the interior of the atom, we might dispense with some of the sources we now 115 have, and we might deliberately attempt to return to a political and social order which we would be capable of managing.

12. Our neighbors in different parts of the world were less a threat to us when we could not reach them and they could not reach us as readily as now—when, as a matter of fact, we could 120 not even communicate with them, except after an interval of months. We would not need to be afraid of the Russians and they would not need to be afraid of us if we were as far away from each other as we used to be. In the thirteenth century, man was good enough at least to survive, and he would be good enough to 125 survive now if things were as simple as they were then. We may think that we would hate to give up our "higher standard of living," but is that what we have really got—or is it only a higher standard of dying? What we ride toward at high speed may not be a more abundant life, but only a more spectacular death. 130

13. If you object that it would be as difficult to persuade mankind to simplify as it would be to make it wise, you may get from the enemies of complexity a grim answer. Events will not make man wise, but they may simplify him, willy-nilly. As a witticism current during the Second World War had it: "I don't know what 135 will be the most important weapon in the next war, but I know what will be the most important weapon in the war after that— the bow and arrow." No one fought our most recent war for the purpose of "reducing the standard of living," but in all the coun-

140 tries involved, except the United States, it was reduced. After the
next world war, or at latest by the time the next two or three are
over, the reduction in complexity may be evident enough to the
survivors. These wars might not, as Wells suggested, reduce man
to the status of an extinct species, but they would very likely put
145 him back into a new Dark Age, and he would probably be good
enough to survive again in that environment, just as he was good
enough to survive in it once before. A thousand years later, he
might get another chance to try an industrial as opposed to an
agricultural society. And if there is anything in the belief that
150 he is getting better, no matter how slowly, then he might, by that
time, be capable of making a go of it. If not, time is long. Back
he would go again into something simple enough for him to be
able to manage.

✳✳✳✳✳✳✳✳✳✳

This inquiry into the human condition in mid-twentieth century deals perforce in abstractions because it concerns the rôle of
ideas in history. It is included for study because of the scrupulous,
almost dedicated simplicity that Krutch brings to his subject;
he is attempting to be perfectly clear, with no mystification, no
unnecessary long words, no parading of devious logic or abstruse
references. Yet the passage is difficult enough. G. B. Shaw and
H. G. Wells, who were optimistic socialists in 1900, died some
decades later with the conviction that mankind was heading
rapidly toward self-destruction. They are cited frequently, as
tremendously popular and eloquent "public educators." Before
their deaths, they "formally renounced the human race as a failure."

1. Look up *chaos, Utopia, pervasive, dialectic, epiphenomena,
corrigible, rectification, anachronistic,* and *scruple.*

2. There is a thread from "eschatology" (2), through "calamity" (4), to "catastrophe" (10–11) and "chaos" (12) which
leads to the "question of how a world ends." In the histories
and etymologies of these words, you may be able to discover
how the writer is bringing together (somewhat ironically)

at least two very different worlds and modes of thought about man—the historical religious, the modern political, and perhaps the modern scientific. You can make all this clear, after a bit of research, in an explanatory essay.

3.   How does Krutch *establish* his attitude toward Communism in Par. 2? What is the effect of the repetition of "very orthodox" in line 43? Is he implying that Communism is a religion? What word in Par. 7 answers the question?

4.   How does Krutch indicate, in Par. 6, that he is, in lines 46 to 59, representing the Communist point of view ironically and unsympathetically? In this connection, look carefully at the connotations of *sentimentally, bourgeois, weakly,* and *anachronistic.* What other words in the paragraph participate in the same tone?

5.   The word *theoretically* (63) carries a world of suggestion. Write a paragraph explaining it.

6.   Paragraph 4 is developed around a contrast of two opposing notions of the rôle of *ideas* in history. Show how Krutch's choice between the two is indicated by the tone and value connotations of *mood, superficial, confident,* and *anxious.* Specifically, these terms tend to downgrade the power of ideas over history and hence their importance. Can you tell whether Krutch thinks ideas are by-products of events or the causes of them? Perhaps it will help explain the second notion if we say that it is a parallel, with respect to ideas, of Oscar Wilde's famous remark that "Life copies art." Why?

7.   Has Krutch rejected the two orthodoxies of religion and science because they are too simple, too optimistic—or for some other reason?

8.   The notion (Par. 8 ff.) that man is not "good enough" comes with a richly ambiguous use of the word *good.* Explain it. From which meaning may we turn, properly, to each of the solutions offered in Par. 10? The grim humor of this ambiguity reappears in "willy-nilly" (134). How? If man becomes "better" in a thousand years, will it have been by virtue, necessity, or *what?*

9.   Indicate, by underlining with colored pencils, the elements of parallelism and balance in lines 124–130.

10. Note Krutch's omission of the final comma in a series—as in line 21. Find the other places where this comma is omitted. Standard in journalism, this omission is surprising indeed in a formal treatise. If you look carefully, you will find other situations where Krutch is careless with commas.

The Republic of Silence

JEAN-PAUL SARTRE

1. We were never more free than during the German occupation. We had lost all our rights, beginning with the right to talk. Every day we were insulted to our faces and had to take it in silence. Under one pretext or another, as workers, Jews, or political prisoners, we 5 were deported EN MASSE. Everywhere, on billboards, in the newspapers, on the screen, we encountered the revolting and insipid picture of ourselves that our oppressors wanted us to accept. And, because of all this, we were free. Because the Nazi venom seeped even into our thoughts, every accurate thought 10 was a conquest. Because an all-powerful police tried to force us to hold our tongues, every word took on the value of a declaration of principles. Because we were hunted down, every one of our gestures had the weight of a solemn commitment. The circumstances, atrocious as they often were, finally made it possible for 15 us to live, without pretense or false shame, the hectic and impossible existence that is known as the lot of man. Exile, captivity, and especially death (which we usually shrink from facing at all in happier times) became for us the habitual objects of our concern. We learned that they were neither inevitable accidents, nor 20 even constant and exterior dangers, but that they must be considered as our lot itself, our destiny, the profound source of our reality as men. At every instant we lived up to the full sense of this commonplace little phrase: "Man is mortal!" And the choice that each of us made of his life and of his being was an authentic 25 choice because it was made face to face with death, because it could always have been expressed in these terms: "Rather death

than. . . ." And here I am not speaking of the élite among us who were real Resistants, but of all Frenchmen who, at every hour of
30 the night and day throughout four years, answered NO. But the very cruelty of the enemy drove us to the extremities of this condition by forcing us to ask ourselves questions that one never considers in time of peace. All those among us—and what Frenchman was not at one time or another in this situation—who knew
35 any details concerning the Resistance asked themselves anxiously, "If they torture me, shall I be able to keep silent?" Thus the basic question of liberty itself was posed, and we were brought to the verge of the deepest knowledge that man can have of himself. For the secret of a man is not his Oedipus complex or his in-
40 feriority complex: it is the limit of his own liberty, his capacity for resisting torture and death.

2. To those who were engaged in underground activities, the conditions of their struggle afforded a new kind of experience. They did not fight openly like soldiers. In all circumstances they
45 were alone. They were hunted down in solitude, arrested in solitude. It was completely forlorn and unbefriended that they held out against torture, alone and naked in the presence of torturers, clean-shaven, well-fed, and well-clothed, who laughed at their cringing flesh, and to whom an untroubled conscience and a
50 boundless sense of social strength gave every appearance of being in the right. Alone. Without a friendly hand or a word of encouragement. Yet, in the depth of their solitude, it was the others that they were protecting, all the others, all their comrades in the Resistance. Total responsibility in total solitude—is this
55 not the very definition of our liberty? This being stripped of all, this solitude, this tremendous danger, were the same for all. For the leaders and for their men, for those who conveyed messages without knowing what their content was, as for those who directed the entire Resistance, the punishment was the same—im-
60 prisonment, deportation, death. There is no army in the world where there is such equality of risk for the private and for the commander-in-chief. And this is why the Resistance was a true democracy: for the soldier as for the commander, the same danger, the same forsakenness, the same total responsibility, the same
65 absolute liberty within discipline. Thus, in darkness and in blood,

a Republic was established, the strongest of Republics. Each of
its citizens knew that he owed himself to all and that he could
count only on himself alone. Each of them, in complete isola-
tion, fulfilled his responsibility and his role in history. Each of
them, standing against the oppressors, undertook to be himself, 70
freely and irrevocably. And by choosing for himself in liberty, he
chose the liberty of all. This Republic without institutions, without an army, without police, was something that at each instant
every Frenchman had to win and to affirm against Nazism. No
one failed in this duty, and now we are on the threshold of an- 75
other Republic. May this Republic about to be set up in broad
daylight preserve the austere virtues of that other Republic of
Silence and of Night.

✳✳✳✳✳✳✳✳✳✳

This selection opens with a bold paradox which is the first
step in a sustained definition.

We may investigate here two problems of language so important that to penetrate and understand them is to attain a
linguistic sophistication far beyond that of most people. One of
these two problems is the *way* that words achieve meanings. The
other is the way that language itself affects our sense of what
exists and what it means: in this selection, definition (in this case
the manipulation and reinterpretation of words) shapes our sense
of reality, and so the two problems may be explored in the one
context.

We have said before that the intellect is made of words. Contemporary social scientists have had a great deal to say about
language as a medium of "scientific" communication. They have
generally agreed that the language of common speech, the English
of daily intercourse,—like literary English—is so charged with connotations, overtones, and emotional associations that it cannot be
used for precise scientific communication. And so they attempt
to remedy what they consider a serious defect of common English by creating new terms or redefining old ones to make an
absolutely precise vocabulary—one that approaches the abstract
perfection of number and symbol in mathematics. What is the
result? —Making a devoted effort to approach a problem in
purely general terms, so that the discourse is not tied to any limit-

ing particulars or distracting emotions, a social scientist may set down sentences which are entirely meaningless:

> The organism the biologist studies and the personality the psychologist studies would be the same thing, except that the psychologist would tend to emphasize more complex functions, and more expressly indicate his desire to see all interrelations within the organism at once, as well as the hierarchy of laws governing these interrelations. Psychology of personality would then be that particular kind of general psychology that emphasizes totality and the organic systematic relations which obtain within it.

Phrases such as "complex functions" and "all interrelations within the organism at once" have no meaning whatsoever until they have been explained in—or, rather, replaced by—concrete words that refer to specific objects or situations. If you explore with your classmates or your instructor the notion of *seeing* "all interrelations within the organism at once," you will doubtless begin by discovering that you cannot "see" anything within the organism except maybe the skeleton through an X-ray, certainly not everything at once when most of that "everything" is not things but concepts, that is, presumed states of the mind which nobody really understands, let alone can give you a picture of. Or explore the word "function" or, more entertainingly, the highly charged and emotional term "hierarchy," and you will discover how utterly inaccurate and imprecise is this "scientific" language.

If you were to suggest to a social scientist that literary English is more precise and therefore more accurate than the "scientific" vocabulary he had been laboring to build and perfect, he might look upon you with horror, contempt, despair, or pity—depending perhaps on what he had for breakfast. Yet that is just what we propose to suggest here: colloquial and literary English are far more precise and accurate than this jargon because of the manner in which words actually achieve their meanings.

What the social scientists do not realize is that it is not possible simply to *assign* a meaning to a word. The meaning will not stick because it does not live. Meanings are not "attached" or "assigned" to words. They do not "stick" to them. They grow in them by usage. There is no other way.

For example, consider the difference between "pile" and "stack." Pile is more general; it can be quite a number of sizes and shapes depending on what is piled. Stack contains the ideas of order and symmetry and of human agency. A haystack is carefully *put together*. A smokestack is *built* and *shaped*. A stack of paper is quite different from a pile of paper because it is shaped and ordered, whereas the pile may be disorderly.

Suppose you want to assign these meanings to a brand new pair of words—and you invent "clate" and "potar" so that you will have the exact meanings without any distracting emotional overtones. You discover your first serious problem in trying to define these words so that they take on precisely the meaning you want. You cannot just say that *clate* means *pile* and *potar* means *stack* because doing it this way would probably transfer the connotations of *pile* and *stack* to the new words, and you don't want images of shapely girls to attach to *potar*. So you must work out a carefully limited and abstract definition of *potar* that will leave it quite free of suggestions and overtones. But this will turn out to be just what you cannot do. To get for *potar* the crisp firm concreteness of *stack* you must somehow associate images with it, for if you do not, the word will fail to carry a sharp, immediate meaning for the reader.

Only by using *clate* and *potar* in many sentences could you give them the meanings you want them to have—and even so they will fool and trick you, for no matter how carefully you use them they will develop their own images and associations and you will find that *they* are using *you*. Language has a life and a growth of its own. The wise man finds the word that says what he wants, knowing that its overtones and associations give it substance and form, concreteness and specificity.

The genius of language is that every word that stands for an abstraction or a concept is a metaphor, having as its base some physical appearance or fact. "Right" and "wrong" are derived from Old English forms meaning "straight" and "twisted." It is through attachment to the concrete that a word carries an abstract meaning. We seek new metaphors in poetry and slang because these are the soul of language. A rugged examination, a square guy, a dim bulb, slangy as they are, show language alive and growing.

A purely abstract word is, therefore, as impossible as it is undesirable.

As for the second problem, we shall only say at this point that words are the instruments of thought, and the language available determines the kind of thinking that can be carried on.

1. Before setting to work on this selection, you may prepare for it with a report or a research paper on Esperanto. Esperanto was the creation of an idealistic European philologist who wanted to make a universal language. It was widely studied, especially in Eastern Europe. Its early users found that it needed a body of prose and poetry in order to establish its vocabulary. In creating this literary base, they found themselves creating dialects of Esperanto. You will find the problem both interesting and instructive.

2. Mark the key words in this selection. There are six or eight at least. Then indicate which three or four are most important.

3. Lines 9–20 play around the word "free." Explain how the word is enriched by this process, and try to formulate an explanation of the significant new ideas that are attached to the idea of freedom.

4. The sentence in lines 14–17 says that the atrocious circumstances of the Nazi occupation "finally made it possible for us to live, without pretense or false shame, the hectic and impossible existence that is known as the lot of man." The sentence is ambiguous: startling possibilities of meaning are presented that make you ask basic questions about the "lot of man," for note that Sartre does not say the "lot of man under the Nazi Occupation," but the lot of man universally. Are we, then, blind to our condition if we do not feel that life is as "impossible" as Sartre says it is? Is it better to suffer? How does freedom relate to such suffering? Is it, perhaps, a question of how aware we are of reality?

5. How does line 24 answer the questions raised in Question 4?

6. In lines 40–41 we come to a concrete definition of liberty (here equal to freedom). Phrase a simple statement of what Sartre has said in the paragraph about freedom. The object is to arrive at the central idea.

7. *Silence, solitude, alone*—these terms lead to a further enrichment of the word liberty:

Total responsibility in total solitude—is this not the very definition of our liberty? (54–55.)

Explain what unstated ethical value underlies this idea of liberty.

8. Finally, we move to "democracy" and "Republic." How are these terms conditioned by the uses of the key terms that have led up to them?

9. Explain the crucial statement (70–71) that being free is being oneself. What does this say about the self?

10. You may take a key word from this essay and write a discussion of it, showing how its meaning is enriched through the selection and how this enrichment involves an expansion of the reader's ideas about man and society. Show, in short, how words are the instruments of thought, and the language available determines the kind of thinking that can be accomplished. You may perform the same sort of analysis on some word that is current among your friends or associates.

11. The following passage by a famous historian, François Guillaume Guizot, deals with the thesis of our discussion of language, before the Questions. Compare the two discussions with respect to their *concreteness*. Does one serve to illuminate the other?

For a long period, and in many countries, the word *civilization* has been in use; people have attached to the word ideas more or less clear, more or less comprehensive; but there it is in use, and those who use it attach some meaning or other to it. It is the general, human, popular meaning of this word that we must study. There is almost always in the usual acceptation of the most general terms more accuracy than in the definitions, apparently more strict, more precise, of science. It is common sense which gives to words their ordinary signification, and common sense is the characteristic of humanity. The ordinary signification of a word is formed by gradual progress and in the constant presence of facts; so that when a fact presents itself which seem to come within the meaning of a known term, it is received into it, as it were, naturally; the signification of the term extends itselfs, expands, and by degrees the various facts, the various ideas which from the nature of the things themselves men should include under this word, are included.

When the meaning of a word, on the other hand, is determined by science, this determination, the work of one individual, or of a small number of individuals, takes place under the influence of some particular fact which has struck upon the mind. Thus, scientific definitions are, in general, much more narrow, and, hence, much less accurate, much less true, at bottom, than the popular meanings of the terms.

The Essence of Language

SUSANNE K. LANGER

1. Furness succeeded
in teaching a young orang-utan two words, which it certainly appeared to use intelligently. Unfortunately for science, as well as
for the ape, it died five months after this achievement, so we do
5 not know how much further it might have gone on the road to
Parnassus. But the experimenter had little confidence, despite
his success. His chief obstacle was not the subject's lack of understanding, but of instinctive response, of any tendency to imitate
his mouthings and articulations. Its lips had to be moved by hand
10 instead of by example. Once it learned the trick, it soon had the
words; but *the trick was something it would never in the world
have thought of by itself.*[1] For this reason, if for no other, it is

[1] Furness' own account of this training is worth repeating here. His own
estimate of his success seems to me too modest, considering the difference
in learning-time of the first word and the second. For he says: "It seems
wellnigh incredible that in animals otherwise so close to us physically there
should not be a rudimentary speech-center in the brain which only needed
developing. I have made an earnest endeavor and am still endeavoring, but
I cannot say that I am encouraged.

"In teaching articulate speech I found the first difficulty to be overcome
in both the orang and the chimpanzee is their lack of use of lips or tongue
in making their natural emotional cries.

". . . In the case of the orang-utan it took at least six months to teach
her to say 'Papa.' This word was selected not only because it is a very
primitive sound, but also because it combined two elements of vocalization
to which orang-utans and chimpanzees are . . . unaccustomed, namely: the
use of lips and an expired vowel. . . ." Presumably, this latter fact pre-
cluded the occurrence of the "word" by accident, and the danger of interpreting as a "word" some mere natural sound. The teacher manipulated the

unlikely that the descendants of our great apes, ten thousand years hence, will hold parliaments (the prognosis is better for World Fairs). The apes will not evolve verbal symbolism because they do not instinctively supply themselves with verbal material, interesting little phonetic items that can acquire conventional meanings because they carry no natural messages.

2. The notion that the essence of language is the formulation and expression of conceptions rather than the communication of natural wants (the essence of pantomime) opens a new vista upon the mysterious problem of origins. For its beginnings are not natural adjustments, ways to means; they are purposeless lalling-instincts, primitive aesthetic reactions, and dreamlike associations of ideas that fasten on such material. The preparations for language are much lower in the rational scale than word-uses; they can be found below the evolutionary level of any communication by sounds.

3. Moreover, this originally impractical, or better, *conceptual,* use of speech is borne out by the fact that all attempts to teach

---

ape's lips, and also made the motions and sounds for her with his own mouth.

"At the end of six months, one day of her own accord, out of lesson time, she said 'Papa' quite distinctly and repeated it on command. . . . She never forgot it after that and finally recognized it as my name. When asked 'Where is Papa?' she would at once point to me or pat me on the shoulder."

Once, while being carried into the water, "she was panic-stricken; she clung with her arms about my neck; kissed me again and again and kept saying 'Papa! Papa! Papa!' Of course, I went no further after that pathetic appeal."

Her next word was "cup." The greatest art was needed to teach her the purely physical trick of pronouncing *k* with an open vowel, *ka;* but once this was learned, "after a few lessons when I showed her the cup and asked 'What is this?' she would say 'cup' very plainly. Once when ill at night she leaned out of her hammock and said 'cup, cup, cup,' which I naturally understood to mean that she was thirsty and which proved to be the case. I think this showed fairly conclusively that there was a glimmering idea of the connection of the word with the object of her desire." (Furness, "Observations on the Mentality of Chimpanzees and Orang-Utans," pp. 281–284.)

Once *the idea of the spoken word* was awakened in the ape, which awakening took all of six months, the learning of a second word was chiefly a matter of conquering the unnaturalness of the physical process. Who knows how far this development might have gone if the subject had lived?

apes or the speechless "wild children" to talk, by the method of
making them ask for something, have failed; whereas all cases
where the use of language has dawned on an individual, simian
or human, under such difficult circumstances, have been inde-
35 pendent of the practical use of the word at the moment. Helen
Keller's testimony has already been cited; after all her teacher's
efforts in formal daily lessons to make the child *use* words like
"cup" and "doll" to obtain the denoted objects, the significance of
the word "water" suddenly burst upon her, not when she needed
40 water, but when the stream gushed over her hand! Likewise,
Yerkes' efforts to make Chim use an articulate syllable to ask for
a piece of banana all failed; he articulated no "word" resembling
the speech of man, nor did he seem to establish a relation between the sound and any particular object.[2] Furness, on the other
45 hand, carefully kept all practical interests out of his experiment.
He tried only to associate an impression, a visual experience, with
a word, so that by constant association the two should fuse, not as
sign and result, but as name and image; and he has had the
greatest success on record so far as I know.[3]
50   4. But the most decisive and, at the same time, pathetic evidence that the utilitarian view of language is a mistake, may be
found in the story of Victor, the Savage of Aveyron, written by
the young doctor who undertook to study and educate him. Since
the boy always took notice when anyone exclaimed "Oh!" and
55 even imitated the sound, Dr. Itard undertook to make him use
the word "*eau*" as a *sign* when he wanted water; but this attempt
failed because he used every sign *but* the vocal one, and water
could not be indefinitely withheld to force the issue. So a second

[2] See Yerkes and Learned, *op. cit.*, p. 56: "The experimenter succeeded
in training him to speak for food as a dog may readily be taught to do. This
he did, however, not in imitation of the trainer but to secure the food."
[3] See Furness, *op. cit.*, p. 285: "As to a comprehension of the connection
of spoken words with objects and actions both the orang-utan and the
chimpanzee, I think, exceed any of our domestic animals; both of my
anthropoids have been able to understand what I said to them, more intelligently than any professionally trained animals I have ever seen. In their
education the enticement of food has never been used as an incentive to
action, and praise and petting have been the only rewards. In other words
my object has been to endeavor to make them show signs of thought rather
than a perfunctory performance of tricks."

attempt was made with the word "*lait,*" of which Itard gives the
following account:

5. "The fourth day of this, my second experiment, I succeeded
to the utmost of my wishes; I heard Victor pronounce distinctly,
in a manner, it must be confessed, rather harsh, the word *lait,*
which he repeated almost incessantly; it was the first time that
an articulate sound had escaped his lips, and of course I did not
hear it without the most lively satisfaction. I nevertheless made
afterwards an observation, which deduced [*sic*] very much from
the advantage which it was reasonable to expect from the first instance of success. It was not till the moment, when, despairing
of a happy result, I actually poured the milk into the cup which
he presented to me, the word *lait* escaped him again, with evident
demonstrations of joy; and it was not till after I had poured it
out a second time, by way of reward, that he repeated the expression. It is evident from hence, that the result of the experiment was far from accomplishing my intentions; the word pronounced, instead of being the sign of a want, it appeared, from
the time in which it was articulated, to be merely an exclamation
of joy. If this word had been uttered before the thing that he
desired had been granted, my object would have been nearly accomplished: then the true sense of speech would have been
soon acquired by Victor: a point of communication would have
been established between him and me, and the most rapid progress must necessarily have ensued. Instead of this I had obtained
only an expression of the pleasure which he felt, insignificant as
it related to himself, and useless to us both. . . . It was generally
only during the enjoyment of the thing, that the word *lait* was pronounced. Sometimes he happened to utter it before, and at other
times a little after, but always without having any view in the
use of it. I do not attach any more importance to his spontaneous
repetition of it, when he happens to wake during the course of
the night." [4]

6. Another word which Victor acquired quite spontaneously
was "Li," which Itard identifies as the name of a young girl, Julie,
who stayed at the house for several weeks, to Victor's great delight; but this word he uttered to himself, all the time, and "even

[4] *The Savage of Aveyron,* pp. 93–96.

during the night, at those moments when there is reason to believe that he is in a profound sleep," so no importance was attached to it as a sign of reason.

7. Unfortunately, the young doctor was such a faithful dis-
100 ciple of Locke and Condillac that after his "failure" with the
word "*lait*" he gave up the attempt to teach the Wild Boy spoken
language, and tried to instruct him in the deaf-mutes' alphabet
instead. Victor picked up a few spoken words, subsequently, by
himself; but as he merely said them when he contemplated
105 their objects with joy or sorrow, not when he *lacked* anything, no
one paid much attention to these "mere exclamations" or made
response to them.

8. Young children learn to speak, after the fashion of Victor,
by constantly using words to bring things *into their minds*, not
110 *into their hands*. They learn it fully whether their parents consciously teach them by wrong methods or right or not at all. Why
did Victor not defy the doctor's utilitarian theories and learn
language by the babbling method?

9. Because he was already about twelve years old, and the
115 lalling-impulse of early childhood was all but completely outgrown. The tendency to constant vocalization seems to be a
passing phase of our instinctive life. If language is not developed
during this period, the individual is handicapped—like the apes—
by a lack of *spontaneous phonetic material* to facilitate his
120 speech experiments. The production of sounds is conscious then,
and is used economically instead of prodigally. Victor did not
articulate to amuse himself; his first word had to be stimulated.
Wild Peter, we are told, never babbled to himself, though he sang
a great deal; Kamala, the surviving little "wolf-girl" found at
125 Midnapur, had learned about forty words at the end of six years
in human surroundings, and formed sentences of two or three
words; but even with this vocabulary, which would serve a
three-year-old to carry on incessant conversations, Kamala *never
talked unless she was spoken to*.[5] The impulse to chatter had been

[5] The most trustworthy, because contemporary, accounts of the Midnapur
children are probably the brief notes published in the *American Journal of
Psychology* by Kellogg and Squires. See P. C. Squires, " 'Wolf-Children' of
India," XXXVIII (1927), 313–315; W. N. Kellogg, "More About the 'Wolf-
Children' of India," XLII (1931), 508–509, and "A Further Note on the
'Wolf-Children' of India," XLV (1934), 149–150.

outgrown without being exploited for the acquisition of language. 130

10. In a social environment, the vocalizing and articulating in-stinct of babyhood is fostered by response, and as the sounds become symbols their use becomes a dominant habit. Yet the passing of the *instinctive phase* is marked by the fact that a great many phonemes which do not meet with response are completely 135 lost.[6] Undoubtedly that is why children, who have not entirely lost the impulse to make random sounds which their mother tongue does not require, can so easily learn a foreign language and even master several at once, like many English youngsters born in India, who learn not only one vernacular, but speak with 140 every native servant in whatever happens to be his dialect. A British psychologist, J. W. Tomb, has called attention to this phenomenon and concluded from it that children have a *linguistic intuition* which is lost later in life.[7]

11. But *intuition* is a slippery word, which has to cover, in this 145 case, understanding, reproduction, and use—i.e. independent, analogous application—of words. It is hard to imagine any "intui-tion" that would bestow so many powers. It is better, perhaps, to say that there is an *optimum period of learning*, and this is a stage of mental development in which several impulses and 150 interests happen to coincide: the lalling instinct, the imitative impulse, a natural interest in distinctive sounds, *and a great sensi-tivity to "expressiveness" of any sort*. Where any one of these characteristics is absent or is not synchronized with the others, the "linguistic intuition" miscarries. 155

12. The last requirement here mentioned is really the "higher function" of the mind that shines forth so conspicuously in human intercourse; yet it is the one that linguists and psychologists either overlook entirely, or certainly do not credit to early childhood.

[6] Thus Israel Latif, speaking of the "lalling stage" of babyhood, says: "Many more sounds are produced by the infant during this period than are later used, at least in its own language. . . ." (To this effect he cites many authorities—Stern, Lorimer, K. C. More, Stanley Hall, Preyer, and Conradi.) "Now, out of this astonishingly rich and varied repertoire of sounds, those which are used by the child's elders are reënforced, and become habitual; the others cease to be uttered."—"The Physiological Basis of Linguistic Development and the Ontogeny of Meaning," *Psychological Review*, XLI (1934), 55–85, 153–176, 246–264. See esp. p. 60.

[7] See his article "On the Intuitive Capacity of Children to Understand Spoken Language," *British Journal of Psychology*, XVI (1925–26), 53–55.

160 The peculiar impressionability of childhood is usually treated under the rubric of attention to exact colors, sounds, etc.; but what is much more important, I think, is the child's tendency to read a vague sort of *meaning* into pure visual and auditory forms. Childhood is the great period of synaesthesia; sounds and colors
165 and temperatures, forms and feelings, may have certain characters in common, by which a vowel may "be" of a certain color, a tone may "be" large or small, low or high, bright or dark, etc. There is a strong tendency to form associations among sensa that are not practically fixed in the world, even to confuse such
170 random impressions. Most of all, the over-active feelings fasten upon such flotsam material. Fear lives in pure *Gestalten,* warning or friendliness emanates from objects that have no faces and no voices, no heads or hands; for they all have "expression" for the child, though not—as adults often suppose—anthropomorphic
175 form. One of my earliest recollections is that chairs and tables *always kept the same look,* in a way that people did not, and that I was awed by the sameness of that appearance. They *symbolized* such-and-such a mood; even as a little child I would not have judged that they *felt* it (if any one had raised such a silly ques-
180 tion). There was just such-and-such a look—dignity, indifference, or ominousness—about them. They continued to convey that silent message no matter what you did to them.

13. A mind to which the stern character of an armchair is more immediately apparent than its use or its position in the
185 room, is over-sensitive to expressive forms. It grasps analogies that a riper experience would reject as absurd. It fuses sensa that practical thinking must keep apart. Yet it is just this crazy play of associations, this uncritical fusion of impressions, that exercises the powers of symbolic transformation. To project feelings
190 into outer objects is the first way of symbolizing, and thus of *conceiving* those feelings. This activity belongs to about the earliest period of childhood that memory can recover. The conception of "self," which is usually thought to mark the beginning of actual memory, may possibly depend on this process of
195 symbolically epitomizing our feelings.

✳✳✳✳✳✳✳✳✳✳

This rather difficult passage will give up its exact meaning if we explore it with the assumption that every word in it has been carefully chosen and carefully placed to convey a part of a profoundly speculated theory about language. The key terms are *concept* and *symbol*,—and here the dictionary will not give us all the answers, although if we begin with the dictionary we can stake out the area in which the precise meaning is to be located.

A concept is an idea, something that occurs in the mind along with ("con") an occurrence outside of the mind. It is something that "takes form" in the mind along with an occurrence in the world, but once it has taken form in the mind, in conjunction with a word, it has achieved an independent existence—and this notion of independent existence is essential to the definition of a concept. The word is the symbol that embodies the concept and links it to an aspect of some occurrence in the world. The word "aspect" indicates another step in our definition; words do not merely name; they classify, which is another way of saying that they indicate aspects of things. Thus if we call a man a pedestrian, we have used a word to symbolize an aspect of the whole man-in-the-world in a way that involves or generates a concept. The idea of a pedestrian depends on the word (Latin "ped"—foot) which embodies the aspect of a man that is abstracted from the whole. Abstracting one aspect classifies a man with respect to this activity; the classification itself is a concept and comes to have an independent life in the mind. Using language, we can think "pedestrian." The concept and the word that symbolizes the concept are almost inseparable, although the language itself is ultimately insignificant compared to the concepts it generates.

As our author says elsewhere, "Another recommendation for words [over shrugs or finger language] is that they have no value except as symbols (or signs); in themselves they are completely trivial."

1. Paragraph 2 conveys its key thought by repetition of statement. Two notions of "the essence of language" are presented and enriched with restatements that clarify because they bring out different aspects of the subject. One sequence is natural wants, natural adjustments, ways to means, word-uses, and communication. Could some of these be eliminated without loss of effectiveness? Which two seem nearest to mere duplication? Which is the most comprehensive? Is its position significant?

Now mark or list the terms in the same paragraph that designate the other notion of "the essence of language." Then list the several terms toward the end of Par. 1 that designate the same idea. The writer has, you see, gone from positive statement, to the negative terms like "ways to means," and back to positive in Par. 2. If concepts classify, as we have said, what part do the negative terms play in the process of classification?

2. Underline the words in Par. 3 that restate the concept that speech is originally or essentially aesthetic or conceptual rather than practical. Of the expanded illustrations of this paragraph, which are positive, which negative?

3. With Pars. 4–8, the ground having been prepared, we come to an extended (negative!) demonstration. What data from Pars. 1–3 is used to make the reader participate in the demonstration? Why is the evidence "pathetic"?

4. By the end of this demonstration, is it correct to say that concepts involve or refer to their opposites so essentially that our ideas of positive and negative are meaningless?

5. The [sic] in line 67 means "thus," indicating that the error is in the original. What is the error?

6. You can probably infer something of the theories of Locke and Condillac by the time you come to Par. 7. In the *Encyclopaedia Britannica* (11th Edition), you will find materials for an essay detailing the facts needed for a full understanding. Or you can, with this and Professor Langer's evidence, think about the extraordinary extent to which human observation is controlled by expectation—so that people see only what their theories lead them to expect. "Linguists and psychologists," incidentally, are put in a class with Locke and Condillac. The modern "scientific" desire to acknowledge only what can be easily charted and measured is, after all, a *desire* to view the mind as a collection of "conditioned responses." Explain how the concept "utilitarian" relates to this concept of the mind. Hint: one relates to motives, the other to characteristics.

7. Your editor believes that, on the whole, the straightforward words of standard English are infinitely more accurate and expressive than the supposedly "scientific" jargons developed by social scientists who feel that ordinary language is too encrusted with emotion to be reliable for exact writing. Professor Langer

rigorously eschews such jargon. Her occasional special or technical term is established and useful (*lalling, phoneme, sensa,* etc.). Why does she shy away from *intuition* (Par. 11)?

8. The footnotes to this selection serve a triple purpose: evidence; illustration and enrichment; reference. These are the basic uses of the footnote.

On what principle are some references placed in the text, others in the footnotes? You will find the answer by considering whether the text could stand by itself as exposition—a question that bears very significantly on the proper use of such documentary apparatus in any source paper or treatise.

Thomas Wolfe: The Function of Appetite

1. Periodically, as if
purging ourselves of what we spend our lives making and doing,
the American mind indulges in a hay ride—one climaxed with a
bonfire and love among the haystacks—in order to remind our-
5 selves that there is nobody like us. And indeed there is not. But
we are insecure, as Wolfe was insecure, and never tire of the
convincing reminder. The latest, but certainly not the last, was
Thomas Wolfe. He came from the hills. He was six foot four and
a man in every inch. He believed in doing nothing—as Faulkner
10 reminds us—short of the impossible. The existence of the legend
of Paul Bunyan may have given young Tom Wolfe something to
shoot at, but in many ways he overshot the mark. The word
prodigious—in energy, in scale, in talent, in ambition, and in failure—is the word that most happily characterizes the pilgrimage.
15 For Wolfe made one. He made one for all of us. Although his
song is a song of himself—a choric forest murmur to the lyric
Walt Whitman—his hunger, insatiable as it was, was still too
small. It is the continent itself that seeks to speak in the bellow
of Wolfe. Everything observable, desirable, and, on certain rare
20 occasions, even conceivable is thrown into the hopper of his hunger and—*bolted*. Nothing, absolutely *nothing*, is left on the table.
We see only where his elbows leaned, and the crumbs he dropped.

2. What we observe in Wolfe—if we care to observe him—is
how a man *eats*. As we watch him eat his very appetite grows;
25 he bolts his food, he reaches for more, and in the very act of gorging himself he starves to death. It is a vivid and appalling projec-

From "Thomas Wolfe: The Function of Appetite," © 1958 by Wright
Morris. Reprinted from his volume, *The Territory Ahead*, by permission of
Harcourt, Brace & World, Inc.

tion of our buried life. We want to grasp life whole, grasp it raw
and bleeding, and then gulp it while it's hot. Sometimes we do.
But the results are not what we were led to expect. Our appetite,
rather than being diminished, has increased. In living out this 30
dream of our buried lives—in living it up, as we would now describe it—Wolfe threw himself into the bonfire all of us had built.
His identification with the myth, with its attendant exaltations,
and, as the fire began to die, with the usual premonitions, took
on the nature of a public purge and sacrifice. These premonitions 35
of death are self-induced; an infinite craving finds its resolution
in a craving for the infinite. In his prodigious effort, in his
prodigious failure, was our success. The prevailing tendency to
start well, hewing a path, single-handed, through the wilderness
around him, and then to fail, since to succeed is unheard of, is a 40
credit to everyone. The highest honors, however, to Wolfe, the
highest praise for his thinking that he could do it—but even
higher honors to the unconquerable continent itself, to us, that
is. We are simply too colossal, as Wolfe was too colossal himself.

3. When Thomas Wolfe died, at thirty-seven, it was said that 45
had he lived he might have done it, might have grasped what still
seemed to elude him, might have tamed the untamable, and in
holding out such infinite hope for him, we hold it out for ourselves. It is the sentiment that both sustained and destroyed him
—infinite hope, infinite yearning, infinite love, ambition, and hun- 50
ger, into which the finite world of experience slowly dissolved.
An infinite amount of nonraw material overwhelms a very finite
fragment of craft, and his barbaric yawp drowned out every
voice in the air but his own.

4. The continent too big for one man to tame it, the story too 55
big for one man to tell it, the manuscript too big for one crate to
hold it, one man to shape it—this myth of too-muchness received
its classic affirmation in the figure of Wolfe. In identifying himself, lavishly, with the malady that masquerades as a virtue, he
lived to the hilt the illusion that is fatal to both the man and the 60
artist. The impotence of *material*, raw or otherwise, receives its
widest advertising in his mammoth showcase—almost everything
is there but the imagined thing, and all of it bigger than life.
The sight of all these objects generated in Wolfe sentiments and

65 sensations of a literary nature, and on occasion, unknowingly, he
was moved to something like creative activity. But *that* sensation,
singularly unfamiliar, and smacking unmistakably of self-control,
and self-denial, was the one sensation that he deeply distrusted,
distrusted intuitively one might say. That sort of thing led him
70 away from *himself,* and where, if anywhere, did that lead?

5. He didn't know, and he put off, deliberately, every chance
to find out. His artistic solution was to write the same book over
and over again, each time in the hope that this time the spirit
would inhabit it, each time in the hope that his chronic self-doubt
75 would stop tormenting him. The chorus of praise, world-wide, did
not console or beguile him. After all, he *knew.* He knew better
than those who hailed his failure as success. As a martyr to our
greed, our insatiable lust for life, which makes life itself an anti-
climax, Wolfe is such proof as we need that appetite and raw
80 material are not enough. They are where art begins, but to begin
at all calls for the tools of technique.

6. Loneliness, as a theme of adolescence, rather than aloneness,
a condition of man, is what the reader finds in Wolfe and what
will assure his continued popularity. It is idle to speak of Wolfe's
85 defects as a writer, since it is precisely the defects that we find
immortal. In them, on a cineramic scale, we see ourselves. Wolfe's
impressive powers of description persuaded him, as it does most
of his readers, that imaginative power of an impressive range
was being exercised. On the evidence the contrary is the case,
90 description takes the place of imagination, and an excess of description, a rhetoric of hyperbole, take the place of imaginative
passion.

7. His book—for it is all one book—offers us the extraordinary
spectacle, both haunting and appalling, of the artist as a cannibal.
95 An insatiable hunger, like an insatiable desire, is not the sign of
life, but of impotence. Impotence, indeed, is part of the romantic
agony. If one desires what one cannot have, if one must do what
cannot be done, the agony in the garden is one of self-induced
impotence. It is Wolfe's tragic distinction to have suffered his
100 agony for us all.

※※※※※※※※※※

The critic who writes this passage is a novelist of some distinction, whose books *The Field of Vision*, *The Huge Season*, and *Love Among the Cannibals* have been highly praised. Morris writes here with a novelist's insights, originality, allusiveness, and concreteness as he makes a startling point about American life in terms of American literature.

1. Look up *bonfire* (4); note especially its relation to *purge, myth*, and *sacrifice*, as well as its etymology. Consider whether a humorous reference to its origin is implied. A *hay ride* is not explained or justified. Is it a celebration, a ceremony, an escape, a ritual, or what? *Choric* (16); *Paul Bunyan* (11); "Song of Myself" (16) and "barbaric yawp" (53) are title and passage from the same poem. Is Wolfe singing a Song of Himself?

2. *Insatiable* (17), *bellow* (18), and *bolted* (21) suggest animals: are they suggestive of the same animal? Is a *hopper* involved in the feeding of animals? How does it relate to a *table*? Are both hopper and table used figuratively? Is one used *more* figuratively than the other, since with "table" we are back to the image of a man? How, precisely, do we know "where his elbows leaned"? —Not, surely, from a depression in the table. Look up *chronic, bolt, gorge, premonition, craft, lavish, smack, beguile, cineramic*, and *hyperbole*.

3. Wolfe writes prodigious descriptions of food in *Look Homeward, Angel* and *Of Time and the River*—pages-long enraptured accounts of groaning tables and bulging refrigerators. In Par. 2 we see the eating metaphor, which is undoubtedly mysterious at first reading of Par. 1, given its meaning and application.
"Appalling projection of our buried life" (26–7), which for the moment specifically applies the metaphor, slides right into

> We want to grasp life whole, grasp it raw and bleeding, and then gulp it while it's hot.

Explain exactly the illogical mixture of images between "raw and bleeding" and "gulp it while it's hot." Can this be explained as other than a confusion? If, as is not at all unlikely, the confusion is studied and intentional, what is accomplished by it—and by the more elaborate confusion of lines 30–32—.

> In living out this dream of our buried lives—in living it up, as we would now describe it—Wolfe threw himself into the bonfire all of us had built.

—where it becomes apparent that the confusion of images is indeed wilful? Your answer must deal with the tone that grows with the wild exaggerations of this paragraph.

4. The *myth* (33) is not defined. What other words in lines 33–38 relate to the concept (or, to be more concrete, we should say anthropology) of myth?

5. "In his prodigious effort, in his prodigious failure, was our success" (37–38).

This is perhaps not the theme of the passage but a comment on the theme. In a mythic agony, Morris says, Wolfe enacts a ritual, a pageant, a spectacle which expresses a deep-seated American belief (or is it just a feeling?) about America. Develop, comment on, and illustrate what this belief is by drawing upon and explaining the materials in this passage. Consider why "to succeed is unheard of." Who accords "the highest honors . . . to Wolfe" (not the author!) and why? "We are simply too colossal, as Wolfe was too colossal himself"—for what?

6. *Dissolved* (51) is a difficult metaphor here. What does it literally mean?

7. ". . . finite world of experience" (51)

and

    ". . . finite fragment of craft (52–53)

are firmly parallel in form Now how are

    "infinite yearning . . . love . . . ambition" (50)

and

    "infinite amount of nonraw material" (52)

parallel? Are they perhaps the *same* thing? Or how are they related? Explain in a carefully stated paragraph.

8. By Par. 4 "the myth of too-muchness" has been defined. What other words in the paragraph identify or correspond to *myth*? This paragraph suggests—but does not say, in line 66 that something vital is missing in Wolfe's activity, something that is "fatal to . . . the artist." This something is to be found in "imagined," "sensations of a literary nature," "something like creative activity," "self-control and self-denial," and "away from *himself*"

—all of which missing desiderata are set against the word *show-case*. Define and explain *what* is missing, what is fatal to the artist.

9. Explain how *martyr* (77) relates to the theme of myth-ritual which dominates the selection.

10. *Rhetoric of hyperbole* (91) takes the place of *imaginative passion*. Which phrase corresponds to "the tools of technique" in line 81? We have here a very different notion of *imagination* from its common acceptance. You will perhaps have to go back to Wordsworth or Coleridge or to a modern literary critic like I. A. Richards or Cleanth Brooks or William K. Wimsatt to find the definition of imagination that illuminates this passage. Such an investigation will provide material for an excellent essay in definition.

11. What *garden* is meant in (98)?

12. "The artist as cannibal" (94) is still another metaphor for an idea that has been approached from all sides in this essay. List the phrases and metaphors which in various ways develop or express this idea. Then see whether you can explain in perfectly simple and concrete language what is the American trouble that Morris is expounding. A difficult but rewarding undertaking would be to inquire whether Morris's thesis throws any light on the problem of defining America and deciding what picture of America should be conveyed to Europe, that you have seen in the group of essays, pp. 185–207. Can it be, in brief, that we do not at all know ourselves?

An American in England

THOMAS WOLFE

1. As Eugene looked
at the young college fellows playing in the fields below the house,
their shouts and cries, the boyish roughness of their play, their
strong scurfed knees, and panting breath, evoked the image of
5 a life so familiar to him that he felt all he had to do to enter it
again was to walk across the velvet width of lawn that separated
him from it. But if he passed these same people two hours later
in the High Street, their lives, their words were stranger than a
dream, or they seemed to have an incredible fictitious quality
10 that made everything they did or said seem false, mannered, and
affected, so that when he listened to them he had a feeling of
resentment and contempt for them, as if they spoke and moved
with the palpable falseness of actors.

2. Eugene would see two young fellows before a college gate,
15 and one, fragile of structure, with a small lean head, a sheaf of
straight blonde hair and thin, sensitive features which were yet
sharply and strongly marked, would be talking to another youth,
his hands thrust jauntily into the pockets of his baggy gray trou-
sers as he talked and the worn elegance of his baggy coat falling
20 across his hands in folds of jaunty well-worn smartness. . . .

3. In conversations such as these, in the choice and accent of
the words, the sharp crisp and yet blurred inflections of the speech,
even in the jaunty nonchalance of hands in pockets, the hang
and fold of the coat, in the exultant little laugh and the sharp
25 strong upward movement of the small lean head, there was

something alien, suave, and old. To Eugene it seemed to be the style of a life that was far older, more suavely knowing and mature, than any he had ever known, so that at such a time as this, these young boys who on the playing fields had almost the appearance of tousled overgrown urchins, now seemed far more 30 assured and sophisticated than he could ever be.

4. At the same time, the sound and inflection of their words—their assured exercise of a style of language that knew exactly where to use and how to inflect such words as "very," "quite," "superb," "priceless," "terribly," "marvellous," and so on—this 35 style and use seemed to Eugene almost false, fictional, affected, and theatrical.

5. He felt this way chiefly because he had read about such people all his life in books and for the most part had heard them speak in this manner only in smart plays upon the stage. He was 40 always connecting these young Englishmen with actors in the theatre, and for a moment his mind would resentfully accuse them of being nothing but cheap and affected actors themselves and, bitterly, of "trying to talk with an English accent"—a phrase which obviously had no meaning, since they were only speaking their 45 own language in the way they had been taught to speak it.

6. But then, at tea-time, Eugene would see these youths again in Buol's, flirting, with the clumsy naïveté of a grubby schoolboy, with a leering rawboned hag of a waitress, and obviously getting the thrill of their lives from the spurious grins which this dilapi- 50 dated strumpet flashed at them through her artificial teeth. Or, as he went up the road towards his house at night, he would pass them standing in the dark shadows of the stormy trees, with their arms clumsily clasped around the buttocks of a servant girl, and their lives seemed unbelievably young, naked, and innocent 55 again.

7. Around Eugene was the whole structure of an enchanted life—a life hauntingly familiar and just the way he had always known it would be—and now that he was there, he had no way of getting into it. The inn itself was ancient, legendary, beautiful, 60 elfin, like all the inns he had ever read about, and yet all of the cheer, the warmth, the joy and comfort he had dreamed of finding in an inn was lacking.

8. Upstairs the halls went crazily up and down at different
levels, one mounted steps, went down again, got lost and turned
around in the bewildering design of the ancient added-on-to
structure—and this was the way he had always known it would
be. But the rooms were small, cold, dark, and dreary, the lights
were dim and dismal, you stayed out of your room as much as
possible and when you went to bed at night you crawled in
trembling between clammy sheets, and huddled there until the
bed was warm. When you got up in the morning there was a
small jug of warm water at your door with which to shave, but
the jug was too small, you poured it out into the bowl and shaved
yourself and added cold water from the pitcher then in order
to get enough to wash your face and hands. Then you got out
of the room and went downstairs as quickly as you could.

9. Downstairs it would be fine. There would be a brisk fire
crackling in the hearth, the old smoke-gold of morning and the
smell of fog, the crisp cheerful voices of the people and their
ruddy competent morning look, and the cheerful smells of breakfast, which was always liberal and good, the best meal that they
had: kidneys and ham and eggs and sausages and toast and
marmalade and tea.

10. But at night there would come the huge boiled-flannel
splendor of the dinner, the magnificent and prayerful service of
the waiter, who served you with such reverent grace from heavy
silver platters that you felt the food must be as good as everything
looked. But it never was.

11. Eugene ate at a large table, in the centre of the dining-
room, provided by a thoughtful management for such isolated
waifs and strays as himself. The food looked very good, and was,
according to the genius of the nation, tasteless. How they ever
did it he could never tell: everything was of the highest quality
and you chewed upon it mournfully, wearily, swallowing it with
the dreary patience of a man who has been condemned forever
to an exclusive diet of boiled unseasoned spinach. There was a
kind of evil sorcery, a desolate and fathomless mystery in the
way they could take the choicest meats and vegetables and ex-
tract all the succulence and native flavor from them, and then
serve them up to you magnificently with every atom of their

former life reduced to the general character of stewed hay or well-boiled flannel.

12. There would be a thick heavy soup of dark mahogany, a piece of boiled fish covered with a nameless, tasteless sauce of glutinous white, roast beef that had been done to death in dishwater, and solid, perfect, lovely brussels sprouts for whose taste there was no name whatever. It might have been the taste of boiled wet ashes, or the taste of stewed green leaves, with all the bitterness left out, pressed almost dry of moisture, or simply the taste of boiled clouds and rain and fog. For dessert, there would be a pudding of some quivery yellow substance, beautifully moulded, which was surrounded by a thin sweetish fluid of a sticky pink. And at the end there would be a cup of black, bitter, liquid mud.

13. Eugene felt as if these dreary ghosts of food would also come to life at any moment, if he could only do some single simple thing—make the gesture of an incantation, or say a prayer, or speak a magic word, a word he almost had, but couldn't quite remember.

14. The food plagued his soul with misery, bitter disappointment, and bewilderment. For Eugene liked to eat, and they had written about food better than any one on earth. Since his childhood, there had burned in his mind a memory of the food they wrote about. It was a memory drawn from a thousand books (of which *Quentin Durward*,[1] curiously, was one), but most of all it came from that tremendous scene in *Tom Brown at Rugby*,[2] which described the boy's ride with his father through the frosty darkness, in an English stage-coach, the pause for breakfast at an inn, and the appearance of the host, jolly, red-faced, hospitable, who had rushed out to welcome them.

15. Eugene could remember with a gluttonous delight the breakfast which that hungry boy had devoured. It was a memory so touched with the magic relish of frost and darkness, smoking horses, the thrill, the ecstasy of the journey and a great adventure, the cheer, the warmth, the bustle of the inn and the delicious abundance of the food they gave the boy, that the whole thing

[1] Novel by Walter Scott.
[2] Novel by Thomas Hughes (1850's). Correct title is *Tom Brown's School Days*.

was evoked with blazing vividness, and now it would almost drive Eugene mad with hunger when he thought of it.

140   16. Now it seemed to him that these people had written so magnificently about good food not because they always had it, but because they had it rarely and therefore made great dreams and fantasies about it, and it seemed to him that this same quality —the quality of *lack* rather than of *possession,* of desire rather
145   than fulfilment—had got into everything they did, and made them dream great dreams, and do heroic acts, and had enriched their lives immeasurably.

17. They had been the greatest poets in the world because the love and substance of great poetry were so rare among them.
150   Their poems were so full of the essential quality of sunlight because their lives had known sunlight briefly, and so shot through with the massy substance of essential gold (a matchless triumph of light and color and material, in which they have beaten the whole world by every standard of comparison) because their lives
155   had known so much fog and rain, so little gold. And they had spoken best of April because April was so brief with them.

18. Thus from the grim gray of their skies they had alchemied gold, and from their hunger, glorious food, and from the raw bleakness of their lives and weathers they had drawn magic.
160   And what was good among them had been won sternly, sparely, bitterly, from all that was ugly, dull, and painful in their lives, and, when it came, was more rare and beautiful than anything on earth.

19. But that also was theirs: it was another door Eugene could
165   not enter.

※※※※※※※※※※

This passage from Thomas Wolfe's long novel, *Of Time and the River,* is taken from the section about the hero, Eugene Gant, in England. He does not feel a part of England, although his literary education has prepared him for the closest imaginative reception and identification. The people and the country and the towns continually present him with doors of understanding which he cannot open; the rooms are barred; the door is shut in his face just when he thinks it is beginning to open. Thus Eugene is forever the lonely outsider, by turns sad, angry, desolate. The place described is the university town of Oxford, one of the most "historic" spots in England.

This passage provides a fine testing ground for what Wright Morris says (pp. 300–302) about Wolfe. Morris finds that Wolfe's fierce hunger for experience drives him to gorge on the *fact*, to try to record and re-experience everything—and thus to fall short as an *imaginative* writer. The word imagination, by the way, when used by an artist and critic like Wright Morris, has a special meaning. It indicates the power of mind that selects, orders, and shapes the raw materials of experience in a way that gives them human importance and significance. Life is infinitely various and infinitely disorderly; the imagination brings it under the control of the mind. Thus imagination is a creative power because it provides the form and order that do not exist in raw nature or raw experience.

We may ask whether Morris is completely fair to Wolfe—how much evidence there is in the passage of artistic ordering and discrimination, of, in short, imaginative creation. Let us consider where, between the voracious man gorging on experience and the shaping and discriminating artist, Wolfe is to be found.

1. Make sure you know the meaning of: *evoked* (4), *palpable* (13), *exultant* (14), *alien* (26), *spurious* (50), *elfin* (66), *glutinous* (106) and *alchemied* (157).

2. Once a good writer has command of the rules of punctuation, he can (and often does) break them for special effect. Mark at least four (there are many more, of course) places in this passage where Wolfe "breaks" a punctuation rule and explain what effect is achieved. You might choose the extra commas in line 4, or the "run-on sentences" in Par. 1 or 8.

3. In Pars. 1–6 underline or list all the words and phrases which describe the boyish qualities of the students. Then list the words that indicate their sophistication.

4. What is Eugene's attitude toward the English students he sees in Pars. 1–6? What accounts for his shifting opinions of them —is it something in them, in him, or in both? Explain.

5. To what later idea in the passage does the Englishman as a false-mannered actor relate?

6. Where in Pars. 1–6 does Wolfe describe Eugene as an outsider? Where in the rest of the selection?

7. The great problem in description is to control the reader's imagination. That is to say, a writer must choose details that will evoke the response he wants. Also, he must get the first details right because a wrong first detail can easily produce a total impression entirely different from what he intended. Examine Wolfe's description of the English inn (Pars. 7–8) by these standards. Namely, what details out of the hundreds he might have chosen and the order in which he presents them serve effectively to control the reader's imagination?

8. In Par. 8 Wolfe suddenly shifts from a third-person narrative (*he* had dreamed) to a second person narrative (*you* stayed). What effect does this have? Why do you think Wolfe used the less formal "*you* stayed out" rather than "*one* stayed out"?

9. A key to the understanding of this selection is the word *enchanted* (Par. 7). On the one hand the word describes something charming and lovely, something magically beautiful; on the other hand it suggests something locked in a spell and therefore inaccessible. Wolfe, of course, draws upon these two different meanings of the word.

(a) All enchanted things are not beautiful. What, then, is the relation between the two meanings?

(b) How do the words *chant, cant, incantation, cantabile, cantor* relate etymologically to *enchanted?* Use a good dictionary for this exercise.

(c) Underline all the words in the passage that relate to the word *enchanted.* There are about a dozen.

(d) Just what is enchanted—England, the schoolboys, the food, the poetry, Eugene himself?

(e) How does Wolfe draw on the implications of the word *enchanted* in lines 97–103? In lines 116–120?

(f) The Part in the novel from which this selection is taken is called "Jason's Voyage." With a bit of research you can discover how this title relates to Eugene and to the word *enchanted.*

10. Write a short précis of the ideas in Pars. 16–18.

11. Here is a list of the conditions under which the English live, the "qualities of lack," as Wolfe describes them:

hunger for food
rarity of "the love and substance of great poetry"
brief sunlight
fog, rain
short April
gray skies
raw, bleak lives and weathers
ugly, dull, painful parts of life

Insert beside each of these "qualities of lack" the compensation or substitute with which, according to Wolfe, the English balance it.

12. Is the "hunger" in lines 140–144 and in line 158 literal or figurative? Explain.

13. Does the hunger Wolfe describes as a "quality of lack" account for the way English food (a) tastes? (b) is served? or (c) is written about? Or all of these?
In short, do all these aspects of English food relate to the "quality of lack" category, or are some merely expressions of what Wright Morris calls Wolfe's "impressive powers of description"?

14. Perhaps the main problem in this selection is this: Is Wolfe here the observing artist or the lonely adolescent? Support your view with reference to the text.

15. If you answer Ques. 14 by saying that Wolfe is the lonely adolescent, are you admitting that Eugene *is* Wolfe, that the character *is* the author?
James Joyce in *Portrait of the Artist as a Young Man* says this about the relation between the writer and his work:

The personality of the artist, at first a cry or a cadence or a mood and then a fluid and lambent narrative, finally refines itself out of existence, impersonalizes itself, so to speak. The esthetic image in the dramatic form is life purified in and reprojected from the human imagination. The mystery of esthetic like that of material creation is accomplished. The artist, like the God of the creation, remains within or behind or beyond or above his handiwork, invisible, refined out of existence, indifferent, paring his fingernails.

Has Wolfe fulfilled this requirement? Explain.

Norman Rockwell: The Abuse of the Past

WRIGHT MORRIS

1. In speaking of the
future of the novel James said: "Beginnings, as we all know, are
usually small things, but continuations are not always strikingly
great ones . . ." In the beginning was Norman Rockwell. The
5 continuations have not been strikingly great. From such a fact
there is more to be gleaned than the usual sophisticated despair,
or ironic amusement.

2. We can say, first, last, and always, that Norman Rockwell
has been true to his beginnings, to his trust in his own and Amer-
10 ican sentiment. He is a genre painter; he uses graphic means to
tell a story. His technique may be described as the most perfect
where it dissolves, imperceptibly, into anecdote. This anecdotal
picture that tells a simple story is the father of the story that
gives us the simple picture, the *same* picture, as a rule—an un-
15 adorned, unpretentious, photographically convincing portrayal of
real life.

3. In a period of forty years Rockwell has supplied the *Post*
with more than three hundred of its covers. He has taught a
generation of Americans to see. They look about them and see, al-
20 most everywhere they look, what Norman Rockwell sees—the tomboy with the black eye in the doctor's waiting room; the father
discussing the Facts of Life with his teen-age son; the youth
in the dining car on his first solo flight from home; and the
family in the car, headed for an outing, followed by the same
25 family on the tired ride home.

4. The convincing *realism* of the details, photographic in its accuracy, is all subtly processed through a filter of sentiment. It is this sentiment that heightens the reality, making it, for some, an object of affection, for others—a small minority—an object of ridicule. It all depends on that intangible thing the point of view. 30

5. Countless young men and women at the beginning of careers in art, have tried, and usually failed, to explain *their* point of view to a puzzled mother, a skeptical father. What can be wrong —Father would like to know—with Norman Rockwell, who is so obviously *good?* The answer is his very *goodness*, of course, but 35 this usually ends the argument. Discussion leads nowhere. The two points of view go their different ways.

6. After considerable exposure to "modern" art, in museums, fashion magazines, the world of advertising, and everyday living, that mythic figure, the man in the street, will still go along with 40 Norman Rockwell. And so—whenever they can get him—will the *Saturday Evening Post*. In that respect, the times have not changed. A vote for Norman Rockwell is a vote for the *real* America. It is the nature of his gift that his very technique appears to dissolve into the subject, leaving the deposit of sentiment we like, 45 otherwise no trace. After we have recognized the figures as our neighbors, and the street they live on as our own, we are left precisely where we came in—at the beginning. It is the nature of the genre piece to limit itself to clichés.

7. But if this charge is leveled at Norman Rockwell, it is lev- 50 eled in suspension and will never reach him. Norman Rockwell is not there. In the picture we attack there is only ourselves. This is why such an attack gets us fighting mad. That row of photographs we keep on the piano has been maligned. However, this will help to explain the almost total absence of transitional mate- 55 rial between Grant Wood's "Iowa Gothic"—which is true to the Rockwell tradition—and the sort of painting that most young people are doing today. It was easier to leap directly into the arms of God or the Devil than fight across the no man's land of raw-material clichés. A clean break—on such a battlefield—was 60 the only one possible.

8. The extent to which this gap remains—and will continue to remain, we can feel with assurance—is evident in Rockwell's

painting of Jennifer Jones in *The Song of Bernadette*. When the
65 movie was released, Twentieth Century-Fox turned to Norman
Rockwell, the illustrator, rather than to the resources of the movie
camera, to portray and advertise the star in the leading role.
That the movie industry should choose Norman Rockwell is both
a testimony to his craft and a revealing commentary on the pre-
70 vailing American taste. Our *realistic* front still has its soft, yellow-
filter sky.

9. A more recent example, in the form of a tribute, were Rockwell's portraits of the Presidential candidates. It was left to
Rockwell, in this sense, to reveal what the camera angles con-
75 cealed, and to give the people—insofar as they were self-evident—
the facts. Mr. Rockwell's Stevenson is the most instructive: we
see the wit and intellectual cut down to our size, not cut down
with malice, but, rather, with affection, as the neighbors of a
"famous" man know him to be a simple, regular guy. Mr. Steven-
80 son emerges as the man we usually find behind a drug counter,
shrewd in his way, of independent mind, and willing to both take
and give advice. He is one of us, not at all the sort of egghead
we had heard about.

10. Scrutinized, held under the light that we find the most
85 illuminating—the soft-sharp lens of Rockwell's craft—our raw
material is seldom raw at all. It is hardly material. The clinical
word for it is cliché. In the beginning, this credo reads, was the
cliché. The raw-material effect is like the tinseled snow hung on
the rootless trees at Christmas, stimulating the sensation without
90 the embarrassment of the facts.

11. The paradox of our situation might be put like this: having
either exhausted, or depleted, the raw material that appeals to
us, we needed a technician to create the illusion that it was still
there. Rockwell is that technician. He understands the hunger,
95 and he supplies the nourishment. The hunger is for the Good Old
Days—the black-eyed tomboy, the hopeless, lovable pup, the
freckled-faced young swain on his first date, the kid with white
flannels at his first prom—sensations we no longer have, but still
seem to want, dreams of innocence, as a rule, before they became
100 corrupt.

12. This entire genre world, crowded with the artifacts that

give it pathos and conviction, is generally inhabited by children, friendly animals, loving mothers, and wise old ladies and gentlemen. The beginnings of life come in for sentimental comment—often touching and penetrating—the Huckleberry Finn myth of 105 our lost youth, the territory of dreams that always lay ahead. But what that territory turned out to really *be,* neither Mark Twain nor Rockwell will tell us. It is a world of onsets, maiden speeches, first blushes, first impressions, and new departures; a universe of firsts: first dog, first kiss, first heartbreak, and first love. At the 110 end of this journey, somehow sweetened by a life that has evaded both realization and comment, we find the very old engaged in prayer, dozing with kittens, tolerating youngsters, or humorously caught in one of the innocent traps of life: a barber chair, a rumble seat, a train coach shared by a pair of young lovers, or a 115 bench where the squirrels rifle our pockets while we sleep.

13. Between our first love, which is implicitly our last, and our last nap, which is implicitly forever, there is very little. What there is can be summed up in a word. *It's a joke, son.* In what is perhaps his most revealing work—one in which he portrays his 120 full range of types—Rockwell illustrates the joke in question making its round. Here is *la ronde,* the permissible *ronde* American. It is clear that a good joke is something that good Americans can exchange. The democratic process can be seen at work as this joke makes its rounds from man to man, woman to woman, level 125 to level, until it finally comes full circle—back, that is, to the man on whom the joke was played. They are all, needless to say, *good* American types. The democratic process is also at work, since we see no black men, no yellow men, no obvious Jews, Italians, or roughnecks—just plain folks, one of us. What the joke is we can 130 almost guess. It is one that is funny to all these people. And it goes without saying that it is not *dirty,* though it might have an edge. It is basically goodhearted, basically good clean fun.

14. This interlude between first love and last breath is an illustrated version of Old Macdonald, forever down on his farm, 135 where funny things are forever happening. Sex raises its adolescent murmur, not its ugly head. In this panel of profiles, this great family portrait, Rockwell gives us the long span of a lifetime between the first and the last joke we have heard. In this report,

140 consciously or otherwise, a note of comment can be detected
that is usually conpicuously absent from his work. His people
are always, we might say, *comfortably* real. But in this portrait
they verge on the uncomfortable. The raw material is so raw it
almost speaks for itself. The effect—the cumulative effect, since
145 we deal here with a group portrait—is something more than the
sum of its parts. If the eye remains on the page, and slowly follows the joke through all of its phases, a disquieting, nonhumor-
out impression builds up. How does it happen? It is clear that
they are all just goodhearted folks. But it is also clear, increas-
150 ingly, that they have nothing else on their minds, that until the
joke came along they had nothing else to *exchange*. It is the joke
that binds them together in brotherhood. Missing from this tab-
leau is the dirty-minded lowbrow who would have spoiled all the
fun, and the egghead who might have used it for his own ends.
155 The joke comes full circle pretty much as it was told. . . .

15. We might say that Mr. Rockwell's special triumph is in the
conviction his countrymen share that this mythic world he evokes
actually exists. This cloudland of nostalgia seems to loom higher
on the horizon, as the horizon itself, the world of actual experi-
160 ence, disappears from view. The mind *soars off*—in the manner
that highways, with new model cars, soar off into the future—
leaving the drab world of commonplace facts and sensations behind. In soaring into the past, rather than the future, Mr. Rockwell is true to himself and his public, since that is where the true
165 territory ahead actually lies. In knowing this he illustrates, with
admirable fidelity, the American Land of Heart's Desire.

✳✳✳✳✳✳✳✳✳✳

The lesson to be learned from studying this essay is how, in an
entirely different set of terms, it deals with the same materials
and ideas as the previous essay by the same author, on Thomas
Wolfe.

1.   Look up *cliché, genre, credo, artifact, graphic.*

2.   The central idea appears, disguised, ambiguous, and ironic,
in the word *real* (16) and in its related forms like *realism.* How

does the topic sentence of Par. 3 ("He has taught a generation of Americans to see.") bear on the idea of *real*—ironically, ambiguously, or directly? You will of course have to read the whole essay to answer this question, marking later sentences that develop specifically the implications of *real*. Such a word as *heightens* (28) bears on the question, raising the doubt as to whether it is ironic or straightforward. Which is it?

3. The same topic sentence (19–20) implies another idea that you may trace through the essay or indeed may investigate in your library and develop into a research paper in literary theory. That is that "Life copies art,"—a notion originated by Oscar Wilde—with its corollary that the original artist must educate a public to appreciate his work. You may investigate the early reception of Beethoven, Brahms, T. S. Eliot, James Joyce, Picasso, or Cezanne to learn whether they had to educate their publics.

4. The contest between Morris's idea of art and his idea of what interests America appears in the next emphasized use of *real*:

> A vote for Norman Rockwell is a vote for the *real* America. It is the nature of his gift that his very technique appears to dissolve into the subject, leaving the deposit of sentiment we like, otherwise no trace. (43–46)

This picks up and slightly alters the *filter* metaphor of line 27. When technique *dissolves*, it must, if the figure is accurate, vanish. Why does the disappearance of technique produce an effect of *reality*, and why is this effect defined by the "deposit" of sentiment? In short, examine the terms of this sustained metaphor and see whether they add up to an effective statement.

5. Exposition of an idea through Par. 6 culminates in Par. 7. To understand it you must first identify the *us* of line 53; it is by no means all of *us*, and it certainly does not include the author of the essay. What is the antecedent of *this* in line 54? "Raw-material clichés" (60) is another version of the key-idea in *real*. Write a paragraph explaining why there can be no transition between the two sorts of painting mentioned in the paragraph.

6. After the developed illustrations of his point in Pars. 8 and 9, Morris produces an arresting paradox in Pars. 10 and 11, which turns upon the word *hunger* (94, 95). Explain how this term links this essay to the preceding one on Thomas Wolfe.

7. How does the stress on *ends* and *beginnings* (Par. 13) play on the idea of *real* and modify it? What, as they are described by Morris, do old age and extreme youth have in common? What is, in Rockwell's world, "unreal" about the years between? Morris does not tell us, and he says that Rockwell and Twain will not. What is his apparent purpose in leaving us to infer it? Since it is really very obvious, you may have to conclude that Morris was concerned to ridicule the notion of avoiding this unavoidable middle by playing at life rather than living it seriously.

8. The *joke* introduced in Par. 3 becomes the core of a figure sustained all the way to line 155. How does it alter the ideas associated with *real*, which extend through the whole essay? *Note:* "La Ronde" is the title of a French motion picture that was banned in some cities of the United States, depicting a chain of love affairs that finally brings the two original lovers back together.

9. Discuss the two uses of *dissolves* in lines 12 and 45. Are they the same, or does the context alter their meanings somewhat? You will have to explain the two passages before you can answer, giving particular thought to the fact that in both uses *dissolves* is a metaphor. You may also compare the use of the same word in line 51 of the essay on Wolfe (p. 301).

10. Explain "The territory ahead lies in the past" as an allusion to and comment on the idea of *real*. The phrase, "the territory ahead," is used throughout the volume in which these essays appear as a symbol of the American Dream or ideal, the traditional goal of American democracy.

11. A difficult but rewarding task would be to explain how the metaphor of hunger and appetite, in the essay on Thomas Wolfe, conveys a meaning similar to that conveyed by the cluster of metaphors and images that we have seen associated with the idea of *real* in this essay. You may perhaps find it helpful to proceed with a major division of your material into 1) *values*, 2) notions of the *good life*, and 3) the nature of *art*. Note where the figurative language of the two pieces coincides.

12. Write an essay exploring the thesis that Rockwell's America is the America of Russell Lynes's lower middlebrow (see p. 112).